The publisher gratefully acknowledges the generous
contribution to this book provided by Sally Lilienthal
as a member of the Literati Circle of the University
of California Press Foundation.

After the Massacre

ASIA: LOCAL STUDIES/GLOBAL THEMES

Jeffrey N. Wasserstrom, Kären Wigen, and Hue-Tam Ho Tai, Editors

After the Massacre

*Commemoration and Consolation
in Ha My and My Lai*

Heonik Kwon

With a Foreword by Drew Faust

UNIVERSITY OF CALIFORNIA PRESS
Berkeley · Los Angeles · London

University of California Press, one of the most
distinguished university presses in the United States,
enriches lives around the world by advancing scholarship in the humanities, social sciences, and natural
sciences. Its activities are supported by the UC Press
Foundation and by philanthropic contributions from
individuals and institutions. For more information,
visit www.ucpress.edu.

University of California Press
Berkeley and Los Angeles, California

University of California Press, Ltd.
London, England

Library of Congress Cataloging-in-Publication Data

Kwon, Heonik, 1962–
   After the massacre : commemoration and consolation
in Ha My and My Lai / Heonik Kwon ; with a foreword
by Drew Faust.
      p.   cm. — (Asia—local studies/global themes ; 14)
   Includes bibliographical references and index.
   ISBN-13: 978-0-520-24796-3 (cloth : alk. paper)
   ISBN-10: 0-520-24796-5 (cloth : alk. paper)
   ISBN-13: 978-0-520-24797-0 (pbk. : alk. paper)
   ISBN-10: 0-520-24797-3 (pbk. : alk. paper)
1. My Lai Massacre, Vietnam, 1968.   2. My Lai 4
(Vietnam)—Historiography.   3. Vietnamese Conflict,
1961–1975—Atrocities.   I. Title. II. Series.
   DS557.8.M9K96   2006
   959.704'342—dc22   2005037445

Manufactured in the United States of America
15   14   13   12   11   10   09   08   07   06
10   9   8   7   6   5   4   3   2   1

This book is printed on New Leaf EcoBook 50, a 100%
recycled fiber of which 50% is de-inked post-consumer
waste, processed chlorine-free. EcoBook 50 is acid-free
and meets the minimum requirements of ANSI/ASTM
D5634–01 (Permanence of Paper).

Contents

Preface and Acknowledgments

This book grew out of my general interest in the social and intellectual histories of the Vietnam War, which I have been slowly exploring since 1993, when I completed my doctoral work on an indigenous hunting society in eastern Siberia and began teaching. Initially, I was primarily interested in how the experience of a large-scale human conflict can affect the development of ideas and paradigms in human sciences. I was interested in theories of human evolution and the hunting hypothesis of the human origin in particular, and in how the hypothesis metaphorically collapsed human predatory activity into war against nature and how this scientific imagining was popularized during violent world events, including the Vietnam War.[1] However, as I started reading the large collection on the history of the Vietnam War in the library of the University of Manchester, it became increasingly difficult to contain my interests within the specific intellectual historical parameter that I set for myself. The reading experience pried open a set of critical issues related to those that Marshall Sahlins introduces under the rubric of "culture in practice" as a way of bringing together cultural analysis and moral engagement with historical events as an anthropological project.[2] The experience also made me aware that my life was somehow intertwined with the historical events that I was reading about.

My curiosity about Vietnam began, in hindsight, around the time of the events described in this book. At the end of the 1960s, children in my primary school in a suburb of a South Korean town liked reciting the songs composed for the Korean troops in the Vietnam War. Boys of our neighborhood used to walk to the school along the barb-wired walls of Camp Henry of the Eighth U.S. Army, singing "The Fierce Tigers March [to Vietnam]." We looked forward to the regular visits to the local Monument against Communism, where pictures and caricatures of the Vietcong were on permanent display. The display and song were both about the virtue of helping other nations to fight communism as if the fate of that nation were ours. I relished the stories from Vietnam told by my maternal uncle and other veterans of the war in the neighborhood. This playfully militant environment probably helped me later win my prize in the national children's contest for best anticommunist slogans. Meanwhile, the general material conditions of life were improving in my former, poor neighborhood. Only recently I learned that this improvement and the onset of export-economic development in South Korea were intimately linked to assistance from the United States (and from Japan under U.S. influence) made in exchange for Korea's extending its role in the global struggle against communism to the Vietnamese theater of war.

Over the years since I set out to learn about modern Vietnamese history and the international history of the Vietnam War, the orientation of my research has changed from a focus on the history of ideas to one on social history. As a result, this book is less about how the destruction of human lives in Vietnam has influenced theories of culture than about what cultural analysis can do in exploring the global origins and local experience of the destruction, although some of my earlier interests materialize in the discussion of the impact of mass war death on cultural transformation. I came to know about the massacres in Ha My and elsewhere in the Quang Nam province during my first visit to central Vietnam in the summer of 1994, and this resulted in my fact-finding work in the national and provincial archives. The Evans Fellowship of Cambridge University allowed me the opportunity in 1997 to study the history of the Vietnam War civilian massacres ethnographically at the village level, and a fellowship grant in 2000 from the British Academy enabled a further study in Ha My and several research visits to My Lai. A three-year grant and fellowship from the Economic and Social Research Council (2003–2006) gave me the opportunity to develop my findings presented in this book into a key element within a broader framework of comparative Cold War history and culture. I thank these institutions for their generous assistance. The preparation of the manuscript has benefited from dialogues with friends, my colleagues in

Edinburgh, from the inquisitive students in my "War and Culture" course, and from talks in London, Durham, Cambridge, Seoul, Tokyo, and New York. Comments from Hue-Tam Ho Tai, Mark Bradley, and anonymous reviewers were immensely helpful for clarifying my thoughts. The decision to write this particular book was driven partly by my personal sense of moral predicament, relating to the experience of growing up in an economically prosperous Cold War society whose prosperity is inseparable from the destruction of another society seized under the same geopolitical bipolarity. Yet, the book also has the prospect of bringing bipolar history to a more appropriate subject of anthropological research.

Foreword

To whom do the dead belong? And how must they be claimed? War produces unnatural death, deaths that occur out of place—away from home and kin—and deaths that occur out of time, to the young and strong. Modern war kills more noncombatants than soldiers; death strikes outside the rules meant to contain and rationalize the violence of war. The nations that are war's agents claim the dead for political purposes and ideologies, wrenching them away from family and leaving deep wounds, turning them into instruments rather than agents of history. Religious tradition is subordinated or expropriated by state imperatives as well as by war's exigencies. A massacre of civilians represents an extreme case of all these unsettling conditions; it is the most unnatural and disruptive death of all.

The death tolls of contemporary wars are often of a scale that renders the individual, the known death, almost unimaginable. Yet it becomes the work of culture to retrieve and honor the war dead, to name them as a way to restore them to the continuum of life and death that constitutes the social order. Identity arises from this continuity, from the knowledge that one lives in death as well as in life. The "grievous death" in Vietnam is a death with grief, but without the mourning that reintegrates the soul and the memory with kin and community. The dead must be incorporated vertically into society and horizontally into history.

To claim the dead for the state, to use them as heroes, can mean removing them from the web of relationships with their communities and lineage groups; the national and the local can work at cross purposes. As political power shifts, so too do bodies. To change the actual location of a body through reburial is actually to shift its place in understanding, to reinterpret as well as to reinter. Corpses in postwar Vietnam are moved from place to place, reflecting changing and conflicting political identities and economic forms, the assertion of ties of family against those of the state, the new legitimacy of the private sector, or simply the opportunities peace offers to attend to the dead. An altered political economy yields a different moral economy, with new ways of defining and expressing obligation. The insistent presence of ghosts helps to define these duties and necessities, rendering the cultural implications of war's meaning unavoidable.

My Lai and Ha My, catastrophes in themselves, began a wider social and cultural catastrophe for the living confronted with remembering these deaths. The massacres produced a ritual crisis that persisted for decades and became an important legacy of the war. In Vietnam and in many other societies across the world, the dead of modern war live on as ghosts, challenging war's survivors to mend the ruptures of belief and meaning that accompany the unnatural destruction of lives and reminding us all of war's terrible and lingering cost.

Yet the process of recovery in the aftermath of any war requires attention to these "bad deaths." Commemoration is a social and cultural process of healing and reclaiming, through thought and memory, through action and ritual. Often this reclaiming involves reburial, either metaphorical or real or both. The ghosts must be resettled.

Drew Faust

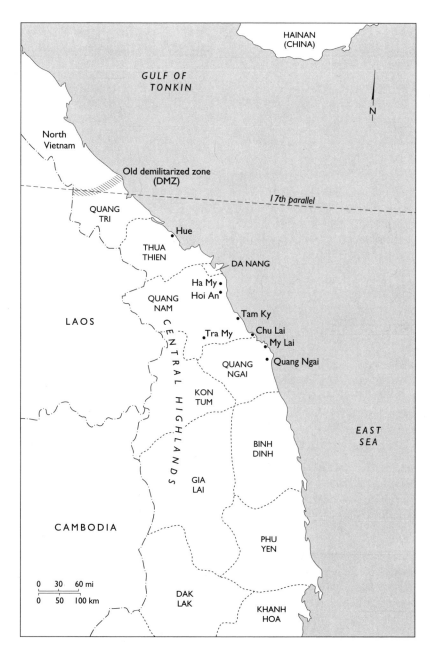

Central Vietnam

Introduction

On the twenty-fourth day of the first lunar month of 1968, the Year of the Monkey, Ha My suffered the shattering tragedy of surrendering an entire village population to a crime of war. On this fateful day, three platoons of foreign soldiers closed in on the small coastal settlement south of Da Nang from three directions and assembled the villagers at three different locations. The killing began with a hand gesture from the officer, which triggered the automatic rifles and grenade launchers. One hundred and thirty-five elders, women, and children from the village's thirty households were massacred within two hours. After the killing, the army bulldozers buried the bodies en masse and desecrated the shallow graves of the victims that had been hastily prepared by the few survivors. This was the time of the Tet Offensive, when practically the entire countryside in southern and central Vietnam became a "free-fire zone," meaning that any objects within it were legitimate targets of destruction, in response to the nationwide assaults by the communist forces against the urban areas controlled by South Vietnam and its allies. A month after this incident, a similar tragedy happened in the neighboring province of Quang Ngai, later known to the international community as the My Lai Massacre.

These two incidents were only a small part of the gigantic human catastrophe that devastated Vietnam in the second half of the 1960s. A systematic mass killing of civilians by ground troops was sweeping across a vast area of the central region, and the indiscriminate bombing of populated areas had become routine. The massacres in Ha My and My Lai were closely connected too, and their connectedness was at once regional and global in scope. Two key military allies to the former South Vietnam, the United States and the Republic of Korea, were responsible for the atrocities. The massacre in Ha My was one among the numerous incidents of mass killing in central Vietnam perpetrated by the South Korean expeditionary forces from 1966 to 1969, and it took place on February 25, 1968, according to the Western calendar, shortly after the Fifth U.S. Marine regiment had handed the responsibility for security in the village area to their Korean colleagues.[1] My Lai also suffered devastation related to a changeover of troops. On March 16, 1968, three platoons of Task Force Barker closed in on the area of My Lai from three directions and forced the villagers to assemble at three locations. Just before this operation, which resulted in hundreds of civilian deaths, "the area circled in red ink under the special duty of Brigade 2, South Korean Marine from January 1967 to December 31, 1967, was handed over to Task Force Barker, Brigade 11, Americal Division from the above mentioned time."[2]

The connectedness of these incidents was not limited to the dynamic theater of a territorial war but also had a global dimension. This was not merely because the guilty were international actors coming from across the East and the West. The crimes were inseparable from the bipolar geopolitical structure and the interstate network dominant at the time, which we call the Cold War. This structure brought the two (and other) international actors together in the name of a crusade against communism, and this network ultimately drove the minor actor, which some earlier observers called "America's rented troops," to be more active in violent village pacification operations than the dominant one without attracting attention from the international community.[3]

It took only a few hours to annihilate each village; it has taken more than thirty years to revive the ruins. After the war was over in 1975, the survivors were not able to commemorate the tragic death publicly and in ways they considered appropriate. The postwar state hierarchy of Vietnam promoted the worship of the heroic war dead to a civic religion and, in doing so, demoted the traditional culture of death commemoration.[4] The bodies of the fallen revolutionary soldiers and the monuments that celebrate their regenerative spirits were prime symbols for the nation's unity and for its prosperous and enlightened future. The unmarked graves that held the entangled bodies of village women and children were not a desirable object in this postwar construction of national memory. These mass graves were evacuated as village land was prepared for agricultural production; the individual tombs of fallen soldiers took their place at the center of the village to bless the nation's posterity.

A generation after the end of the war, the political economy of memory is changing in Vietnam. Since the beginning of the 1990s, the people of Ha My and My Lai have been busy renovating the places of the dead. This intense activity is part of "the commemorative fever" and the popularity of *viec ho,* or "the work of family ancestral worship," which has been rising since the late 1980s, when the global structure of the Cold War began to disintegrate and general economic and social reform was initiated in Vietnam.[5] Ancestral rites, according to Shaun Malarney, became a critical locus for state action in revolutionary Vietnam and, after 1989, a principal site for a contest of power between the state and the family.[6] Hy Van Luong argues that the demise of the centrally planned socialist economy resulted in the revival of ancestral rituals as a way of strengthening the moral basis of the family—a principal unit in the new economic environment.[7] The marginalized, informal memory of war dead under the dominant cult of heroic war death benefited from the economic vitality and political liberalization in the 1990s.[8]

As in other places in Vietnam, the privatization of agriculture promptly promoted family ritual activities in Ha My and My Lai.[9] Today, massive numbers of old bones have been moved to new places, and renovated places of the dead have mushroomed across villages. Relatives assemble to rebury the long-neglected remains of the war dead, and individual families are saving their resources in the hope of holding an appropriate ritual to console the spirits of the tragic dead. New private graveyards and renovated ancestral shrines are among the most demonstrative symbols of a new Vietnamese modernity after the reform. The situation indeed indicates that the commemoration of war in Vietnam, like the nation's economy, is shifting from the state monopoly to the private and communal sectors—although there are limitations to the use of a framework of political economy in interpreting the developmental process at community level (see chapter 3).[10] In the midst of this great exodus of the dead, placing the memory of mass village death in the fabric of social life became a critical issue in Ha My and My Lai, and the villagers began to explore ways to bring the memory of the tragic dead closer to their everyday lives.

This book is about the Vietnam War's legacy of civilian massacre. Part of it deals with the historical circumstances of the atrocity, but its main focus is on what people do now with the physical and spiritual remains of the tragic incidents. The book engages with the enduring wounds in social life caused by the mass violence, but its primary objective is to describe the social practices emerging to attend to these wounds. I discuss the changing moral identity of mass civilian death in the domestic politics of Vietnam and its changing international environment. However, my main aim in this book is much more modest: to explore the legacy of the massacres in the everyday life of Vietnamese villagers, their domestic life in particular.

The moral and political identities of mass death discussed in this book primarily concern the everyday actions taken to assimilate the tragic dead to the full spectrum of village ritual life. This process of assimilation is not set in stone, and it faces a number of formidable challenges. Some of these challenges come from revolutionary politics, and some from traditional cultural concepts, although it is certainly debatable whether recent revolutionary experience or prerevolutionary cultural tradition is more "traditional" to contemporary Vietnamese life. Sometimes, the challenges rise from a powerful alliance between revolutionary ideals and dominant traditional norms.

The apparatus of the unified Vietnamese state put great emphasis on centralizing and controlling commemorative practices.[11] The new elites "sought to shift the focus of festivals and commemorations away from the village and the family and toward the state," according to Patricia Pelley, and propagated a genealogy of heroic resistance wars against foreign powers, or "selective redemption of the past," in the words of David Marr, situating the heroic dead of the revolutionary war in a line of descent reaching to the mythical heroes of ancient victories.[12] Ancestor worship, according to Le Van Dinh, "is welcomed with enthusiasm [by people in central Vietnam], like a regulating agent of family customs, a high and noble principle of life, which works to put family life in good order, . . . exalting moral virtues and the principles of duty, obliging the living to keep their eyes always fixed on the actions of the dead."[13] As such, ancestor worship celebrates an ordered continuity of generations and the wealth of honor and merit preserved and augmented in genealogical progression.[14] This system of values sits uneasily with radical social ruptures and does not easily tolerate death that disrupts the genealogical order. Moreover, the system, based on the continuity of the family, has no space for death that means the termination of a family line. Mass civilian war death is characterized by many negative, ignoble, unproductive values in terms of both tradition and revolution.

Placing the tragic mass death in the organization of social life, therefore, involves paradigmatic conflicts with dominant ideologies, although it is possible to counter them by letting one work against another. The revived tradition of ancestor worship can help to bring the memory of the victims to private or communal places of worship, especially a generation after the tragedy when the victims, the young ones included, become ancestors. If the tradition happens to exclude those who died a tragic death from the venerable site of ancestor worship, however, the revolutionary morality of antihierarchy and antitradition can moderate this idiosyncratic tendency. If revolutionary doctrine preaches against all superstitious practices, including unauthorized attention to the fate of the dead, the traditional religious ideals, when revived, may counter it by adopting some elements from the politically dominant hero worship. Part of this book is devoted to describing this bricolage of popular political consciousness and moral sensibilities.[15] Between tradition and revolution, or between ancestor worship and hero worship in a more restricted sense, the space for the remembrance of mass death nevertheless remains restricted, and carving out this space requires continuous symbolic struggles.

The principal site of the conflicts and struggles that I discuss in this book is the domestic ritual space, broadly defined, in which the Vietnamese interact with gods, ancestors, and ghosts on a daily basis. The fact that I choose domestic space as the center of my investigation does not, however, mean I ignore the wider historical and ethical issues of the massacres. On the contrary, I acknowledge that domestic ritual space is an arena as relevant as any public, more secular, domain for thinking about crimes of war and the wounds they inflict on human society. The hidden forces of modern body politics, according to Hannah Arendt, may be unraveled in the very realm of life that the political forces strive to reduce to privacy, that is, within the "rich and manifold" conditions of intimate domestic interaction.[16]

There are certain ideas about human rights and justice embedded in Vietnamese domestic ritual practices, and it is necessary to understand these ideas as culturally grounded concepts before we can think of bridging the gap between how international justice is defined in a universal, predominantly legal language and what it means in a lived, local reality.[17] Likewise, it is within the structure of Vietnamese commemorative ritual, and in the context of everyday cultural practices, that I discuss the significance of the massacres for the history of the Cold War and the politics of nationalism in the era of transition from the bipolar order. Bipolar politics not only constituted the background of the mass killing but also remains integral to the reality of mass burial. The materiality of mass village death embodies the political history of the Cold War. The killing took place partly according to the zero-sum geopolitical logic that regarded people as having taken the enemy's side if they didn't take one's own side. After the war was over, public commemoration of the victims was difficult partly because of the extension of this logic. Within the schema of heroic war death, the mass graves not only lacked regenerative value but also were ambiguous objects in which the remains of "our side" and those of "their side" were enmeshed inseparably. As we shall see, the bipolar body politics of purity has made it especially difficult for the communal initiatives to acknowledge the mass death publicly. Doing justice to their memory, therefore, involves unmaking the bipolar political worldview and creating an alternative vision of the world, and this is what I believe is manifested in Vietnamese domestic ritual practice.

Domestic ritual organization in central and southern Vietnam is two-sided, and commemorative ritual practice consists of shifting between the two sides and between the two different milieus of memory they represent. The organization follows a principle of concentric dualism and consists of an architectural complex that demonstrates this principle in a form of horizontal duality. The two sides of the complex are identified as "house" and "street" *(nha* and *duong),* or inside and outside. The "house" can be an ordinary village house in which an ancestral altar is kept, or a lineage and village ancestral temple, or any other built place of worship. The "street" refers to the external environment of the "house" in the scheme of concentric dualism, and this is often represented by a small independent shrine for ghosts, popularly called *khom* in the language of central Vietnam, which is usually erected at the edge of the fenced domestic garden. Most communal places of ancestral worship also feature an external shrine on the opposite side of the house of worship. Such shrines may be nominally dedicated to the Spirit of the Land *(tho than),* but today people use them primarily to make ritual offerings to wandering ghosts.[18]

The shrine for ghosts is where people believe spirits visit temporarily, and this distinguishes the place from the house of worship, such as the lineage ancestral temple or the domestic shrine for family ancestors in a private home, where people assume spirits dwell permanently. Whereas people worship in the house because they believe the spirits placed there are related to them in a line of descent, in the external shrine no such genealogical ideology or lineage paradigms are necessary to justify the act of making ritualized associations with the past. "Dwelling," Caroline Humphrey writes, is "both process and artifact."[19] We may say that each of the two built places corresponds to "dwelling-as-residing" or "dwelling-as-wandering," which the philosopher Edward Casey, drawing upon Greek mythology and Renaissance architecture, describes as "the fundamental twofoldness of dwelling" or "two ways of being bodily in the world."[20] The memory of the past in the "dwelling-as-wandering" is unbound in time and space, and global in outlook. The place can accommodate all walks of death—ancient or modern, and Vietnamese or foreign—and, therefore, it is also open to the spirits that are believed to be on the loose because of their failure to enter the house of worship. As for the last point, the dual structure of worship relates to a moral hierarchy of death—the classification of "good death" versus "bad death"—which the Vietnamese express in a derivative way as "death at home" versus "death in the street" (chet nha and chet duong).

This book explores the legacy of mass death in Ha My and My Lai in the light of the conceptual polarity of death and within the related spatial organization of death commemoration consisting of two sides: the side for ancestral memory and the opposite side for displaced ghosts. Death in a civilian massacre is neither exactly "death at home" nor exactly "death in the street." In such a case, the magnitude of violence has turned the traditional spatial structure inside out. Chapter 1 examines the implications of the conceptual polarity for the memory of mass death and discusses relevant sociological theories about death symbolism for that purpose. It highlights the two-sided commemorative ritual practice, relates it to the idea of "symbolic ambidexterity" proposed by Robert Hertz, and considers its practical implications and theoretical significance against the background of the moral symbolic hierarchy of death.

Chapter 2 introduces a brief history of Ha My and My Lai, with a focus on the historical situation of the village being turned inside out by the violent forces of the Cold War. I discuss the history of the village's ancestral temples and their fluctuation between being positive and negative moral symbols as a way of situating the political history within the spectrum of local norms. Chapters 3 and 4 give general accounts of contemporary domestic death remembrance activities and discuss the dual structure of ghosts and ancestors within which these activities take place. I show how the memory of mass death does not fit within the traditional classification of death. Chapters 5 and 6 discuss how the identity of the victims of mass death goes beyond the conceptual boundaries drawn between war heroes, ancestors, and ghosts, and how their memory is distributed across the sites dedicated to these different categories. Chapter 6 also introduces the idea of "liberation from grievance"—a concept central to understanding popular Vietnamese war commemoration practices. Chapter 7 continues the discussion of the dispersion of memory across boundaries and deals specifically with the problems between the dispersed memory and the forms of commemoration that aim to concentrate the legacy of the tragic past. The final chapter explores some aspects of global bipolar conflict from within the spectrum of local social development and process of conflict resolution. This chapter shows that certain democratic and cosmopolitan values are expressed in the everyday practices of the Vietnamese villagers and illustrates how this cultural phenomenon helps undo the historical legacy of the Cold War. The book's conclusion returns to the idea of "liberation from grievous history" and examines its wider political and ethical implications.

I conducted research in Ha My and My Lai on a number of occasions since 1994, mostly during summer breaks from teaching and for longer periods in 1997–1998 and 2000–2001. In order to do the research in Ha My, I lived in the town of Hoi An and near the municipal library of Da Nang and traveled daily to the village. In My Lai, I regularly moved between the city of Quang Ngai and the village. Residence in a bustling urban setting made my presence more tolerable to officials, and it offered the added advantage of enabling me to meet diverse groups of informants on the wartime situation. I often found it as instructive to talk to a former low-ranking liaison officer to the allied forces as to listen to a former regional partisan leader when trying to reconstruct the local situations of 1968. To gather material for a local history of war, I also found conversations with former covert civilian activists most engaging. These actors had diverse social backgrounds and could discuss both the past reality of death and violence and the contemporary themes of religious morality and financial anxiety. In their accounts, they could easily shift between the politics of everyday life during wartime and everyday life in today's political and economic transformation, without giving the impression that they were changing the subject. Their immense knowledge is not explicitly represented in the chapters of this book, and I can't even acknowledge their contributions, believing that their identities are best left anonymous for the moment, but I have no doubt that I would not have been able to write a history of the Vietnam-American War without their often-gripping stories of daily struggle at the marketplace, at school, in the family home, and in the noodle bar near the army base.

I cherished their "history from below," in the sense in which E. P. Thompson used the expression,[21] and I tried to situate the legacy of the massacres within this milieu of everyday actions and popular norms.

In the villages affected by large-scale civilian killings, including My Lai and Ha My, I also spoke to people with various historical and social backgrounds: survivors, close relatives of the victims, government officials, veterans of the guerilla war, former employees of the South Vietnamese administration, lineage elders and keepers of the ancestral temples, cemetery keepers and village undertakers, and ritual specialists. This was partly to obtain a multiperspectival, multivocal account of the relevant historical events and the contemporary ritual reality. Among the survivors, my informants consisted of two groups: the adult survivors and those who were children at the time of the massacres. For an oral history of the massacres, I tried to put together the somewhat divergent recollections from these two groups. I also became close to some of the younger group, who not only sympathized with my research aims but also allowed me the privileged intimacy of an identical age group, and who sometimes protested against the unfriendly attitudes of state officials who disapproved of contact between the villagers and a foreign investigator. It is to this younger group that I owe my deepest gratitude. Within a tightly controlled village political environment, it was not always easy to freely meet up and talk with the villagers. The household death-day anniversaries, funerals, and other ritual occasions, however, proved to offer excellent opportunities to do so. I gradually built and expanded a network of trust with the locals by regularly participating in these ancestral rites, through which I was later introduced to the ritual milieu for the ghosts of tragic death.

This book is a result of long-term fieldwork conducted in combination with a review of historical literature, and, as such, it engages with a historical event of global significance by means of research tools familiar to anthropologists. The year 1968, according to Immanuel Wallerstein, who calls it the year of systemic "world revolution," was a threshold of modern history, when forceful civil protests erupted simultaneously across the West against the governing power structure.[22] Civilian massacre in the Vietnam War was at the heart of the moral and political awakening that provoked the critical historical turn. The massacre in My Lai, in particular, has since been a subject of intense scrutiny in the scholarship of American history, international history, and international criminal and humanitarian law, and this book contributes to the ongoing

debates and vast corpus of literature on the subject. It adds to the literature a review of the incident and other related events from within the life-
world of the victims, drawing upon their own conceptions of justice.

I also submit this book as a form of commemorative offering. To this
end, I have structured the book to create something akin to a progressive
symbolic transformation. Within the book, I sought to move the discussion progressively closer to the esthetics and morality of Vietnamese
death commemorative practices in the hope that, if I did this, the memory
of the tragic deaths would perhaps move closer and more easily to the
realm of these cultural practices to be consoled by them. Hence, this
book begins with an account of domestic death commemoration, then
moves outward to more public domains of war remembrance, and then
back to the domestic sphere. This descriptive strategy relates to the way
in which the social life of tragic death, in popular Vietnamese thought, is
characterized by forced displacement from the security and comfort of
domestic life and an arduous struggle away from this forced mobility. It
also relates to how the villagers practice their death commemoration—
by turning their bodies between the two opposite orientations of inside
out and outside in, and between the place for ancestors and the space for
ghosts.[23] (Robert Hertz describes this concentric spatial structure of
moral hierarchy with the metaphor of the right and the left hand, and
describes his vision of overcoming the hierarchy with the metaphor of an
ambidextrous human body.) I wrote this book in the belief that a simple
movement of the body—to face opposite directions in turn—within an
asymmetrical binary structure is instructive for understanding wider
political and historical issues. I also wrote it in the hope that the
ambidextrous action might really be a positive instrument for human liberty, as Hertz believed.

CHAPTER I

The Bipolarity of Death

Dead people, in popular Vietnamese culture, can be powerfully sentient and salient beings who entertain emotions, intentions, and historical awareness. The ethnological literature about their mortuary customs and religious imaginations confirms this. Remembering ancestors means, in Vietnam, according to Le Van Dinh, relating to them "as if they were alive."[1] A French Jesuit missionary to Vietnam and author of classical studies on Vietnamese popular religions, Léopold Cadière, wrote that the Vietnamese perception of the world incorporates the awareness that the life of the dead is intertwined with that of the living, and that the Vietnamese idealize a harmonious relationship between the two forms of life.[2] Their social life consists in both relations among the living and interactions with the dead, according to Nguyen Van Huyen, and it follows that the history of war, for the Vietnamese, can be as much about what to do with the dead here and now as about how to interpret the past events of destruction.[3] In Vietnamese mortuary knowledge, the souls of the dead may refuse to depart from the living world, and their unwillingness is expressed when, for instance, the coffin suddenly crushes the shoulders of the pallbearers with unbearable weight.

In a funeral that I saw in a suburb of Da Nang, the pallbearers complained of the excessive weight of the coffin of an unmarried man when they were passing by a particular house in the community. People speculated that the problem was caused by the young man's affection for the daughter of the family in the house. The man's family persuaded the reluctant young woman to come out to the street and console the deceased so the journey could continue. She was instructed to speak to the coffin, to say she regretted having stolen the man's heart, and her parents supplemented this gesture of apology with gifts of votive objects. Whether the woman knew about or had anything to do with the man's feelings was not an issue. It was the feeling of the dead man, with or without her knowledge, that made the woman culpable for the complication in his fateful journey. The drama about a spirit of the dead with unfulfilled wishes may take on an explicitly political meaning. At the funeral of a young schoolteacher in the city of Quang Ngai, the family was alarmed by the state of the corpse. They believed that the man's corpse refused to close its eyes for an unknown reason. The crisis continued until the school principal arrived at the scene. The principal approached the corpse of his junior colleague and acknowledged publicly that he had bullied the hardworking man for years. Apparently the principal had conspired against the wishes of the schoolteacher, who had wanted to join the Communist Party.

If personal anguish and unfulfilled desires complicate a funeral, death without a funeral complicates even further the deceased's afterlife. The dead who do not benefit from an appropriate burial continue to inhabit the space between *am,* the world of the dead, and *duong,* the world of the living—expressing the Vietnamese concept of the duality of life.[4] The dead whose final moments were violent also have problems in making the mortal transition, and a violent, "unjust" death whose fate is not ritually recognized presents particularly critical problems. Such a tragic death means the deceased does not really leave *duong* nor really move to *am,* a condition that Arnold van Gennep conceptualizes as perpetual liminality.[5] In popular Vietnamese knowledge, the souls of those who died a tragic death roam between the margins of this world and the periphery of the opposite world, and being unsettled in either world, they can be unsettling to the inhabitants of both. The Vietnamese address these unattached and undetached mobile spirits of the dead with the kinship and interpersonal referential term *co bac* ("aunt" and "uncle"; more precisely "[paternal] junior aunt" and "senior aunt/uncle") in distinction to *ong ba* ("grandfather" and "grandmother").[6]

The distinction between *co bac* and *ong ba,* or between displaced wandering ghosts and ritually appropriated ancestors and deities located in designated places, relates to the contrast between "bad death" and "good death." The Vietnamese mortuary culture shares with other agrarian traditions a house-centered morality of death. Dying a good death is "to die in the house and home," writes James Fox about an Indonesian society, and "in his hut, lying on his bed, with his brothers and sons around him to hear his last words," according to John Middleton's description of the Lugbara in northwestern Uganda.[7] This is called *chet nha* in Vietnamese and contrasts with *chet duong,* which literally means "dying in the street and outside" but has the connotation of "dying accidentally" or "dying in violent circumstances."[8]

The "house," which is central to the moral classification of death for the Vietnamese, refers to two separate but interrelated forms of dwelling. The tomb is a house for the dead that shelters the body and demonstrates the deceased's social identity, and this is made explicit in Vietnamese mortuary art, in which the place of the dead is built in the form of a house. Ideally, people should exhale their last breath under the roof of the living house and move to the roofed tomb to live their life after death. In both places, the dead are not alone but surrounded by relatives, and hence the transition from one to another place is supposed to have elements of continuity. Janet Carsten and Stephen Hugh-Jones argue that the house and the body form a unity in Southeast Asia, and I add that this is particularly the case with the dead body.[9] A dead body without a house of its own is the body of a nonperson, and a physical condition such as this is associated with the imagined state of tragic afterlife. The shallow burial of an unknown soldier in an alien place is one of such tragic conditions of afterlife—as Shaun Malarney points out, "Death on the battlefield was the quintessential bad death"[10]—but so is the burial in a mass grave of people unrelated in kinship, even if it is in their home village.

Tragic death has many specific forms, and the classical literature and the traditional ritual knowledge of Vietnam list at least seventy-two such categories.[11] All these categories, which constitute a vast spectrum of human destiny stretching from death on the battlefield to death by a mad buffalo, fall under the general notion of tragic or bad death. If a man suffers a violent death while away from home, according to this conceptual scheme, his soul will remember the pain of death and the sorrow of solitude, and it will yearn for opportunities to ease this "physical" pain and spiritual sorrow.

The Vietnamese express this undesirable state of afterlife as "grievous death" *(chet oan),* in which the agony of a violent death and the memory of the terror entrap the soul.[12] The human soul in this condition of self-imprisonment does not remember the terror as we the living normally would, but relives the violent experience repeatedly. Memory of death for the tragically dead, in other words, is a living memory in its most brutally literal sense. This perpetual reexperiencing is conveyed by the idea of "incarceration" *(nguc)* within the mortal historical drama. The grievance of *oan* and the self-imprisonment of *nguc* describe the same phenomenon, but from opposite sides. Grievance creates the imaginary prison, but once established, the prison arrests the grievance and augments its intensity. Acts of liberating the suffering souls of tragic death are called *giai oan* (to disentangle the grievance) or *giai nguc* (to break the prison). These expressions are used interchangeably, but this does not mean they are identical. Breaking the prison by force and helping the captive free itself from the grievous memory (although the two acts have a common objective of emancipation) can take on different meanings and forms. In Vietnamese ritual tradition, a genuine liberation from the incarceration of grievous memory should be a collaborative work. It ought to involve not only the appropriate intervention of sympathetic outsiders but also the inmate's strong will for freedom from history. The growth of self-consciousness and self-determination on the part of the prisoners of history is in fact fundamental to a successful process of liberation from grievance.

Tragic death that falls out of the established mortuary order is unwelcome to the commemorative order. In Debbora Battaglia's account, the Sabarl Islanders of Melanesia conceptualize the spirits of violent death they call *piwapiwa* as "an unintegrated, untamed existence in the bush," in contrast to those of good death, *baloma,* "which have legitimately severed ties with the living."[13] For the Merina of Madagascar, Maurice Bloch observes, "there is no worse nightmare than that one's body will be lost. . . . 'Bad' death occurs at the wrong place, away from the ancestral shrines to which the deceased's soul cannot therefore easily return; and at the wrong time so that the orderly succession of [obituary] speech cannot occur."[14] In the conventional sociology of death, the presence of fertility symbols marks "good death" as opposed to "bad death." Good death is a socially constructive and regenerative death: it reinforces corporate solidarity, revitalizes historical continuity, and can renew symbolically the ecological resources. The burial of particular ancestral bodies in the ancestral land is believed to "fertilize" the land in some cultures.[15] The body that experiences a bad death—the untimely death of a child, for instance—takes on the opposite meaning in these cultures and is believed to adversely affect the productivity of the land.[16] Given this background, it is argued that "bad death" signifies not only an absence of regenerative potential but also a threat to social continuity.[17] About the aftermath of a socially negative death, Middleton writes, "Deaths that are considered as bad lead to a condition of confusion and disorder but without the means for removing and resolving them."[18] In the words of Robert Hertz, "Death will be eternal [in the sphere of bad death], because society will always maintain towards these accursed individuals the attitude of exclusion."[19]

What happens to the moral and symbolic order of death, however, if "bad death" becomes a generalized phenomenon rather than an isolated event? Can society still exclude the "accursed individuals" eternally even if virtually everyone in the society is related to their memory? The dual symbolism of death derives from an investigation of social conditions that we may call stable. What happens to the ideal of "good death" and the related principle of "social triumph over death" if the social practice of grieving has to come to terms with a historical reality in which the ideal has become an almost unattainable goal?[20] If the scale and magnitude of tragic death is such that it becomes a universally shared legacy, this historical background may affect the conceptual moral hierarchy of death.[21] Otherwise, what kind of social order can we possibly conceive of?

The war in Vietnam that formally ended in 1975 increased the numbers of displaced, troubled, and ritually "uncontrolled death[s]."[22] The violent mechanical destruction, on the one hand, and a mass-mobilized mobile guerrilla war, on the other, created countless instances of "death in the street," death with memory of extreme violence, hastily and improperly buried bodies, death without funerary atonement, and dead denied even the possibility of a ritual transformation. In this historical landscape of generalized violence, as a number of observers have noted, people perceive that ghosts of war proliferate. According to Derek Summerfield, "In Vietnam, the 300,000 still missing twenty years after the war ended are considered wandering souls. . . . They have lost their place in the order of things, in the social and historical fabric. There are personal memories of them but no external evidence or sign to embody these memories. Who can show that these people once lived, had values and causes, and thus what their deaths mean?"[23] Malarney states, "The deaths of young soldiers on the battlefield posed serious dangers [to the families and communities] as their prematurely terminated lives created an army of wandering souls."[24] Lady Borton writes of her experience of meeting war widows in southern Vietnam:

> She leaned forward. "If I knew the location of my husband's grave," she said, "I would visit it before Tet and invite his spirit to join us. I'd offer food and fruit to nourish his spirit. But where do I go?" She paused, examining

her fingers. "And if I knew the day he died, I would invite neighbors and family to honor my husband's spirit on the anniversary of his death. But what day should I choose?" She ran her hand across her face, a common Vietnamese gesture. "All that's left," she said, "is the Fifteenth Day of the Seventh Lunar Month."[25]

The idea of "good" regenerative death, as Jonathan Parry and Maurice Bloch correctly point out, "can only be constructed in antithesis to an image of 'bad' death, which it therefore implies. It requires and must even emphasize what it denies, and cannot obliterate that on which it feeds."[26] In the expression of Louis Dumont, "If uniting through differences is at the same time the aim of anthropology and the characteristic of hierarchy, they are doomed to keep company."[27] It follows that there is no inherently negative death as such and, as Parry and Bloch mention, that the moral hierarchy of death and the fear of bad death are meaningful only within the specific ideological orientation of a society.[28] This is an important point, and it is unfortunate that Bloch forgets it in his later work, where he launches an ambitious, generalizing argument that the empowerment of collective fertility symbols is necessary because a social order is created through it, and that this is done through the *conquest* of the uncertain, ambiguous vitality.[29]

I find this idea of "symbolic conquest" problematic and the attempt to generalize it as a human religious universal untenable (see chapter 5). Bloch argues that the symbolism of conquest is inherent in the structure of religious ritual, whose purpose, across cultures, is to construct a transcendental ideal in sacrifice of impure vitality. This reduction of ritual to an instrument of social control is empirically unsustainable,[30] and it misrepresents the very idea of symbolic conquest, which means, in its original formulation by Robert Hertz, strictly an ideological phenomenon and hence is itself a subject for analytical scrutiny, not to be confused with the nature of society.

MASS DEATH

Robert Hertz, a student of Durkheim and a formidable independent thinker, opened a way to rethink moral symbolic dualism. Whereas Durkheim was mainly concerned with how social solidarity was created and maintained, Hertz "took upon himself the task of studying the responses of society to breaches in that solidarity."[31] His promising life was cut short in Marchéville, in 1915, in circumstances that would bring about a sea change in the way mass death was viewed—the mass slaughter of European trench warfare. One of Hertz's central concerns was semantic opposition between two apparently identical objects—such as the right hand and left hand. He questioned why the right side represented, in the French language and beyond, positive values of strength, dexterity, faith, law and purity, whereas the left stood for all the opposite values and meanings—including "bad death," which is closely associated with the left hand in the ethnographic material Hertz drew upon.[32] Right and left, for Hertz, was often expressed in terms of inside versus outside and, as such, this was both a complementary bipolarity and an asymmetrical relationship, which Dumont later called "hierarchical opposition."[33] Furthermore, he inferred from ethnological literature that right and left was "reversible dualism" in archaic or egalitarian societies. Based on this observation, Hertz proceeded to argue that the polarity was universal but not the asymmetry. He wrote, "The evolution of society replaces this reversible dualism with a rigid hierarchical structure."[34] In the spirit of the time, however, Hertz was fundamentally optimistic about social evolution:

> The tendency to level the value of the two hands is not, in our culture, an isolated or abnormal fact. The ancient religious ideas which put unbridgeable distance between things and beings, and which in particular founded the exclusive preponderance of the right hand, are today in full retreat. Neither aesthetics nor morality would suffer from the revolution of supposing that there were weighty physical and technical advantages to mankind in permitting the left hand to reach at least its full development. The distinction of good and evil, which for long was solidary with the antithesis of right and left, will not vanish from our conscience. . . . If the constraint of a mystical ideal has for centuries been able to make man into a unilateral being, physiologically mutilated, [nevertheless,] a liberated and foresighted society will strive to develop the energies dormant in our left side and in our right cerebral hemisphere, and to assure by an appropriate training a more harmonious development of the organism.[35]

As it turned out, Hertz's biopolitical vision partly came true, but not through a peaceful, civilizing progression as he envisaged. The First World War, which claimed Hertz's own young life shortly after he published his works on moral symbolism, killed some ten million men and made bereavement a universal, simultaneous, "democratic" experience in much of western Europe and beyond.[36] The encounter with catastrophic mass death was disseminated far beyond the trenches by means of new communication technologies. It invigorated the traditional belief in martyrdom and resurrection, and it developed the process in which this belief was projected onto the nation as "an all-encompassing civic religion."[37] The mechanical mass production of death on the Western Front, however, provoked a contrary awareness and countermovements that questioned the dominant traditional belief and commemorative forms.[38] These movements refused to glorify violent war death, to relegate bereavement to the political-religious symbols of resurrection, or to falsely bless the nation-state that caused the mass violence in the first place.[39]

The meaning of mass war death, in this turbulent and dynamic environment, became decentered and contestable, shifting and uncertain. After the outbreak of what Stephen Kern calls "the Cubist War," any previously solid forms—and this includes the permanent structure of the memorial tower or the cenotaph—became flexible and had to be looked at from shifting perspectives to grasp their true shapes.[40] Rilke wrote in 1920 on the mass death of the Great War: "With no figure to draw all this around itself and expand it away from itself—this way tensions and counter-tensions are set up without a central point that first makes them into constellations, into orders, at least orders of destruction."[41] The moral identity of death was no longer in the right or left hand alone. The correlative categories did not vanish from consciousness or from the landscape, but the moral symbolism of death, mass death in particular, began to pass between two moving hands, like juggling balls.

Since the Great War, a panoramic change of a novel dimension has taken place in the identity of mass war death. Eighty percent of those who died in the First World War were enlisted soldiers; 50 percent in the Second World War. Since 1945, 90 percent of war casualties have been civilian noncombatants.[42] The increasing demilitarization of mass war death has been a product of technological advancement in the weapons of mass destruction, and a product of the globalization of the "total war" theory, which has broken the traditional division of labor and distinction between armed combatants and unarmed civilians within the paradigm of total mobilization of human and material resources for a war of liberation (see chapter 2). The war in Vietnam was a culmination of technologically progressive warfare and philosophical total war, and it was a theater in which these two quintessential aspects of modern war contested each other's strength. It was a war that imagined the unimaginable ideal of "each inhabitant [is] a soldier, each village a fortress."[43] It was also a war whose great machinery of destruction was not yet so advanced as to be able to identify mechanically the lawful targets for destruction as opposed to the unlawful varieties.[44]

The ideal of a combat village was meant to be a strictly ethnocentric concept. It was intended to be relevant to the Vietnamese villagers but not to the foreign combatants. The term *inhabitant-soldier* did not necessarily mean a total fusion of the two identities, but rather the hyphenated identity was expected to be seen differently from two opposite angles. From the perspective of *ben ta,* "this side," or the revolutionary side, the hyphenated person ideally was a soldier. *Ben ta* anticipated that the same person would appear to be a mere inhabitant in the eyes of *ben kia,* "that side." Sometimes, "that side" betrayed this anticipation, assimilated the view of "this side," distorted this view and magnified the distortion, and defined all living persons and all material objects in the village as justifiable military targets for destruction.[45] If this happened, "this side" took on the view that it had originally projected onto the opposite side. The destroyed target then turned into ordinary villagers and civilian victims in the view of "this side," and the act of wanton destruction of unlawful targets triggered indignation and denunciation. Each side of the war defined the status of civilians from a perspective borrowed from the opposite side, and the mass killing of innocent village inhabitants completed this lethal transaction.

A total political unity was impossible in the violent Cold War and remained pure fiction in the wartime villages of southern and central Vietnam.[46] Moreover, victims of a village massacre, even if the massacre happened in a village that seemed fairly close to the ideal in which "each inhabitant [is] a soldier," never came close to being identified as war martyrs. A dead revolutionary villager and "inhabitant-soldier" became a mere villager, even if she was killed while fulfilling her active political and military duty "to defend the village" *(tru bam).* The death of an armed soldier and the deaths of his village supporters were clearly differentiated in the official commemoration of the war, and the latter were rarely marked by any of the rich fertility symbols that surround the former.[47] Mass civilian death was *tham sat* (tragic mass death), which offered no generative meanings or positive commemorative possibilities. The official approach to war death in contemporary Vietnam is to preserve heroic death and to transcend tragic death in the nation's modified march toward a prosperous future. My Lai is an exception, however, as the state hierarchy has intervened to manage this particular site of civilian massacre as a historic monument. (In chapter 7, I compare My Lai and Ha My in terms of politics of monument.)

It has been argued that the appropriation of war death is central to the construction of modern national memory.[48] In Jean Baudrillard's emphatic words: "The power of the State is based on the management of life as the objective afterlife."[49] The equivalent process in Vietnam consisted of conquering the tragic meaning of war death by means of culturally adopted heroic symbols of modern nationalism,[50] and, in southern regions, it also involved ignoring the material traces of civilian sacrifices. The systematic oblivion partly resulted from the imposition of a particular North Vietnamese view of the war (national liberation) on the differential realities of war (civil war/cold war, as well as liberation war) experienced in the southern half. This regional variation in the memory of war ultimately relates to the complexity of parallax visions inherent in the geopolitics of the Cold War.[51] The absence of civilian mass death in the national memory of Vietnam, and the related difficulty in commemorating it, is intelligible only in the context of the Cold War's global history (see chapter 8).

AMBIDEXTERITY

Unlike modern hero worship, traditional ancestor worship in Vietnam is not preoccupied with the military trope of "All Forward!," and it encompasses opposite symbolic movements. In Vietnamese death ritual, the mourners may wail, roll around on the dusty red soil, grab the legs of the pallbearers, and block the advance of the funeral party. The close relatives of the deceased may prostate themselves on the ground in front of the funeral procession until they are gently pulled away by distant relatives to make way for the must-be-departed. Some close female relatives choose instead to stand against the funeral car with their arms wide open, reminding the spectators of the painted images of wartime village women defying the advancing enemy's tanks. Part of this funeral fight is voluntary and genuine, and part of it is theatrical and customary. The idea is to demonstrate publicly the conflict between the fateful separation and the desire to deny it.

To point out this difference, however, is not to deny the similarities and mutually constitutive elements of ancestor and hero worship. Pham Van Bich notes, "Marxism and Confucianism are opposite to each other in many ways. Nonetheless, Confucianism and communism also have something in common. A leading communist intellectual even emphasized the similarities between Confucianism and Marxism."[52] Vietnamese hero worship places the martyrs of the revolutionary war in a lengthy genealogy of patriotic heroes from ancient times;[53] traditional ancestor worship assigns a high value to the meritorious ancestral heritage of contribution to the feudal state in terms of military duty and courtly service.

The highest form of filial piety in this convention is considered to be the act of honoring family ancestors by the election of a descendant to the imperial bureaucracy.[54] It is understood that the ancestors, who did meritorious service of *cong duc* to the country, bless the descendants with the wealth of *phuc duc*—the genealogically conceptualized idea of consecration specific to ancestral cult. Nevertheless, there are notable differences between ancestor worship and hero worship practices, and some of these differences may be crucial to thinking about the representational crisis in social memory caused by extreme historical events such as the civilian massacres.

War memorials in Vietnam, like their equivalents in the American and European "invented tradition" of war commemoration, follow an egalitarian principle—the commissars and the foot soldiers, or the regular soldiers and the peasant guerillas, lie in humble, identical graves.[55] This internal egalitarianism, or what Thomas Laqueur calls "democracy of death," is based on a systematic exclusion externally.[56] The fallen soldiers who also fought for national independence, but who happened to have done so on the wrong side of "the puppet regime," have absolutely no right to the space of the virtuous war dead. In a very suggestive note to her recent work on Vietnamese commemorative practices, the eminent historian Hue-Tam Ho Tai writes, "To be truly comprehensive[,] . . . the study of commemoration would need to include the dead of the South [Vietnam]. To do otherwise risks turning them into the scholarly equivalents of the wandering ghosts of those who, dying unmourned, constantly haunt the living in an attempt to force their way into the consciousness of the community, to be acknowledged as worthy of being remembered if only because they once walked the earth."[57] Popular ancestor worship, by contrast, follows a fairly hierarchical principle internally based on genealogical order, but, in its broad structure, it demonstrates a growing tendency of social inclusiveness externally. From the domestic ancestral altar, where one worships the immediately preceding generations, to the communal temple that shelters the virtuous founding ancestors of the community, the revived popular ritual practices in central Vietnam strengthen simultaneously a genealogy-based social solidarity and the opposite generalized social relatedness.

The genealogical model of society, according to Tim Ingold, consists of "a dendritic geometry of points and lines," as in the image of the tree of generations, and "collapses the life of each person into a single point, which is connected to other such points by lines of descent."[58] What Ingold calls "a relational model" presents an opposite picture. Here, there are no such points or lines and every "being is instantiated in the world as the line of its own movement and activity: not a movement from point to point, as though the life-course were already laid out as the route between them, but a continual 'moving around,' or coming and going."[59] These modalities of life, according to Ingold, generate different conceptions of the person: in the genealogical model, the person receives the specifications of identity from the preceding generations, whereas the relational model "situates the person in the lifeworld from the very start, as a locus of self-organizing activity." Thus he concludes, "Whereas in the genealogical model life is encompassed within generations, in the relational model generation is encompassed within the process of life."[60]

Hy Van Luong argues that patrilineal descent and a broad bilateral model of relatedness constitute "the fundamental parameters" of Vietnamese kinship and worldview.[61] These two structural opposites concern gender relationship primarily, but they do so in "isomorphic relation to other conceptual dichotomies such as center/periphery and spatially bound/spatially unbound."[62] In support of this idea, which is also raised by other specialists in Southeast Asian cultures, Luong discusses the principle of patrilocal residence in North Vietnam and what happens to the principle of patrilineal descent when the household residential pattern extends to multiple sites.[63] The large landholding families in one North Vietnamese village, according to him, observed a strict patrilineal descent in the main house, where the household head and his first wife resided, whereas this genealogical modality was weak in the peripheral houses of his second and third wives. Luong describes how the dominant rule of descent had to be negotiated with the reality of strong matrilateral ties in the peripheral houses, and he emphasizes the interplay between the two opposite structural principles of genealogical exclusiveness and bilateral inclusiveness for understanding the traditional Vietnamese social organization.[64]

Maurice Halbwachs insists that collective memory can exist only on the basis of a socially specific spatial framework.[65] The ritual actor in the old battlefields of central Vietnam, when engaged in an act of commemoration in the domestic ritual, faces the past in two distinctive ways and according to opposite orientations. One is the enclosed world of genealogical relationship. The other is the unbound world in which being-in-the-world indeed means what Ingold calls "continual 'moving around,' or coming and going," and in which relationships are made proactively rather than retroactively according to a predetermined order. The body of the ritual actor is in motion, and his view shifts between the two worlds of relationship in coordination with the movement. In the simplest setting, the movement consists of making kowtows and offering incense to one side and then turning to the opposite direction in order to repeat the act. Each of these paired actions may be accompanied by a single beat of the gong followed by three or four strikes of the drum. In a more complex arrangement, the participant may divide the two acts of a single ritual complex and hold them on separate occasions.

Ritual revival in central Vietnam empowers two opposite expressions of relationship simultaneously, and this is done by means of the technique of the body that keeps oscillating between the two points of polarity. The *viec ho* effort gathers the scattered remains of war dead and places them in a common burial ground, promotes a traditional culture of commemoration, and stimulates ritual activities. It contributes to rebuilding the infrastructure of traditional social solidarity and demonstrates this in the form of renovated domestic and communal sites of worship. The ancestral cult—both that of place ancestors and that of lineage ancestors—occupies a prominent place in this general process of renovation, although the details vary from place to place and across regions. These new sites of kinship and place identities rise in parallel with the semantically opposite side of anonymous ghosts, and the two sides are increasingly becoming equal in moral prominence, religious power, and cultural significance. Ritual in this context is "an arena of contradictory and contestable perspectives," and the ritual actors who work in such a dynamic environment advance the art of decentering the spatial structure of worship and demonstrate the agility of shifting perspectives.[66]

Paul Connerton writes, "[If] there is such a thing as social memory, we are likely to find it in commemorative ceremonies. Commemorative ceremonies prove to be commemorative in so far as they are performative. . . . Performative memory is bodily."[67] Ritual remembrance, in the revived tradition of central Vietnam, situates the actor within the spatial duality of "house" and "street" and in between the polar identities of *ong ba* (ancestors and gods) and *co bac* (ghosts). It encourages the actor's body to move between the opposite expressions of relationship and to create intimacy with both modalities of life. In the prerevolutionary tradition, it may be that this bodily movement was mainly a symbolic gesture to draw the territorial boundary of genealogical social order and, following Bloch, to signify its moral dominance over the anonymous exterior world. Gerald Hickey argues that the ritual conducted on behalf of ghosts, in a prewar Vietnamese village, was intended mainly "to pla-

cate the errant spirits" and "to avoid their wrath."[68] I am not able to
judge this statement as I never had an opportunity to study a prewar
Vietnamese village, although it should be noted that the negativity of
ghosts is a matter of perspective and an aspect of how one is positioned
in the structure of worship. Victor Turner states, "The term 'anti-
structure' is only negative in its connotations when seen from the vantage
point or perspective of 'structure.'"[69] The moral identity of the dead
changes, depending on where and how the living interact with them.

What I can say with confidence, however, is that the identity of ghosts
in a contemporary Vietnamese village does not always carry such negative associations, and this is partly demonstrated by the fact that the
gifts for ghosts and the gifts for ancestors are becoming increasingly
indistinguishable. In central Vietnam, people often worship their ancestors who died tragic deaths at the shrine for ghosts, believing that the
ancestors prefer this place for their memory. The magical reality that the
dead are conscious that they do not merit worship in a pure ancestral
place because they experienced a tragic death is an expression of the
social reality that the living are actively remembering them and that the
tragic dead are undergoing a transformation. As I noted earlier about the
notion of grievous death, the symbolic transformation of the dead,
according to popular belief, is partly expressed by their becoming self-
conscious. Moreover, it is the ritual act that enables this symbolic transformation. The ritual actor's shifting perspective between the "house"
and the "street" is a practical action partly intended to help the dead to
cross or move beyond the conceptual boundary. There is no such mysterious drive for symbolic conquest in this practical action of "liberation
from grievance."

The house of worship, as a place for honoring the ordered "death at
home," excludes the violent "death in the street" in a selective redemption of the past. To be an ancestor and to be commemorated as such in
this system requires not only an appropriate genealogical background
but also a historical background of dying in socially acceptable circumstances. For this reason, death in a mass killing does not fit the criteria
for the "house"—the magnitude of the violence alienates the memory of
the dead from the place of ancestors. It does not easily meet the criteria
for the "street" either. The victims of massacres died violently but did so
"at home," and most of the victims, including the small children, became
"ancestors" a generation after the end of the war. Remembering these
known and related identities, and so many of them, at the place of
anonymous ghosts is a problematic option. Being unsuitable for both

places, remembrance of the village massacre could become associated with either side of the commemorative structure. Indeed, recent social development in Ha My and My Lai points to a growing movement of the memory of the mass death across the entire spatial spectrum of commemoration, and this was certainly related to the process of ritual revival that empowered the "house" and the "street" coactively. In other words, the conceptual polarity of death, against the historical background of mass death, parts company with the moral hierarchy of values and becomes meaningful as an indicator of mobility rather than as a boundary marker.

In my view, this coactive vitalization of the opposite moral symbols, and the bodily movement of the social actor that enables it, relates to what Hertz intended to convey with his idea of ambidexterity—the condition in which the human body, upon which are marked "the opposition of values and the violent contrasts of the world of morality," reaches its full potential, free from the constraints of mystical ideals.[70] The parallel social development—identity and anonymity, order and disorder, fertility and futility, purity and impurity, and good death and bad death—cannot be properly understood if one assumes social transcendence is a given and unproblematic. Tragic death, as the stories in the following chapters illustrate, is not a disciplined, docile being. The idea that a social order emerges through a symbolic conquest over impure death may not apply at all to a society in which a decent future for the victims of tragic death is everyone's concern. The history of mass death can change the social order, and this change, as in the European social history, takes place mainly in how people relate to the symbolic structure of the social order, rather than necessarily in the outlook of the structure.

The morality of death, in modern history, cannot be considered independently from the history of mass death, nor can we investigate their interconnectedness while ignoring the arena of social life in which the weight of this history is felt most intimately. In Ha My and My Lai, mass death was a central episode in family and village history. However, its place in village social life has been marginalized, and it is unlikely to become central in the future. What is likely to happen in the future, judging from the present circumstances and trends, is that the political relationship between center and periphery will be reconfigured. "Centrality is movable," writes Henri Lefebvre. The "centre of the Greek city was forever being moved: from the semicircular area where chiefs and warriors conferred about their expeditions and divided up their booty to the city temple, and from the temple to the agora, a place of political assembly."[71] This geographical truism is manifested, in contemporary Vietnam, by the shift of attention from the state-administered sites of hero worship to the communal sites of ancestor worship. This great shift, as I mentioned earlier and as other observers have noted, indicates a change in the management of war memories, from the state's command economy to the family and community,[72] but this describes only the surface of the great migration of memories. Shelly Errington writes, "The center and the periphery . . . structure the shape of 'space' and movement in [Southeast Asia]. A center is still; its periphery is active."[73] The centrality in ancestor worship, unlike the exemplary centrality in hero worship, cannot obliterate the peripheral existence of unassimilated deaths, for the social center in this system of values requires the vitality of the periphery in order to manifest its own vitality. When centrality moves elsewhere, the very relationship between center and periphery also moves.

Clifford Geertz argues that, against certain historical backgrounds, the revival of a religious order simultaneously raises moral concerns about the problems in the order and creates practical measures to counter the problems. He calls this process "religious modernization."[74] This human creativity for cultural invention, according to Turner, "flowed from the margins to the centers more often than the reverse."[75] The "little tradition" of the troubled, marginal death of village women and children is not the same as the "great tradition" of the ordered, assimilated death of war heroes or prominent ancestors. A place for the former cannot share the same geography with the places for the latter. Finding a place for the memory of tragic death is not the same as giving it a place where good deaths are memorialized. For the latter often means giving it no place at all.

Salvation for the grievous dead, in Vietnamese worldview, means not only rescuing them from the undifferentiated space they are imagined to inhabit but also from the most placelike of all places—the prison—where they are incarcerated. The Vietnamese history of tragic mass death carries with it the radically opposite imagery of disturbing liberty and painful captivity. Therefore, to do justice to this history—the emancipating act of *giai oan*—involves both giving freedom and removing coerced freedom. It is a challenge to understand these two logically opposite acts as a unitary deed, but this is probably a small challenge compared to the challenge of actually creating a place that can promote belonging and freedom at once—that is, a "place of openness" and a "place movement is intrinsic to."[76] If memory requires cultural vehicles and concrete places in order to be expressed, remembering tragic mass death, in Ha My and

My Lai, happens to require giving it a place but also the freedom to move between places.[77]

If there is no place at all to locate the memory of tragic death in the ideological world, the memory can rest in the movement of the remembering body before this work of the body can change the world. The rest of this book focuses on showing how a simple movement of the human body—in facing opposite directions in turn—can militate against the politics of symbolic conquest and rescue the massive history of "bad death" from the state of coerced oblivion. And the "ambidextrous" human body has far-reaching implications for undoing the Cold War's bifurcation of left and right, which is in fact the origin of the tragedy in Ha My and My Lai.

CHAPTER 2

Massacres in the Year of the Monkey, 1968

"Pump out the water and catch the fish" was one of the informal instructions to some foreign combat troops deployed to Vietnam. The instruction was a clever, cynical distortion of a slogan used for the Vietnamese resistance wars: "People are the water, and our army the fish."[1]

Truong Chinh, one of the founders of the Indochinese Communist Party and the party's radical theoretician, employed the fishpond metaphor to explain the meaning of the "people's war" to the masses in a language that was graphically familiar to them.[2] The paradigm of the people's war was a marriage between two conventional doctrines of warfare: the doctrine of "just war" and the idea of "total war."[3] It was based on a radically relativist view of warfare that envisaged two substantively different kinds of war on the same battlefield—the "revolutionary, popular and just" war versus the "counter-revolutionary, anti-popular and unjust" war.[4] The people's wars are justified, Truong Chinh argued, for they are "wars against oppressors and conquerors to safeguard the freedom and independence of the peoples."[5] The legitimacy of people's war is derived also from the war's total nature. A people's war is a war of the people as a whole, not of the army alone, and it is conducted by the people and for the people. In this popular, mobile, guerrilla warfare, Truong Chinh asserted, the people are the eyes and ears of the army, and they should feed and keep the soldiers and help the army in sabotage and battle.[6] This integration of civilians with the army is supposed to reach an ideal state when "each inhabitant [is] a soldier, each village a fortress."[7]

This idealistic model of a morally just, methodically total, generalized people's political and military struggle contributed to the image that this was a "war without fronts" fought by an "invisible enemy."[8] The model might have turned to reality in some places of armed conflict, yet, in most places under crossfire, it remained an abstraction or a partial reality throughout the war's duration. A great number of people in central and southern Vietnam supported the people's war, and a greater number of people were sympathetic to the war's heritage of anticolonial struggles against France and Japan.[9] What preoccupied most people in central Vietnam during the war, however, were day-to-day survival and subsistence. The abstraction of total war had to be weighed against concrete needs for survival, and this painful negotiation was indeed a genuine people's struggle in the streets during the violent Cold War.

This paradigm of the people's war also became a reality, with tragic consequences, to some of those who fought against the paradigm. The U.S.-Saigon administration's village pacification strategy imposed on civilians the often impossible choice of displacement or persecution. This strategy was intended precisely to pump out "the water" (the people) to find "the fish" (the enemy combatants). It separated people from the basis of their subsistence and the locale of their religious and moral attachment. It was still rare to find the real enemy. The Saigon military bureaucracy continued to encourage its soldiers to produce tangible statistical results—demonstrating the number of enemy combatants they killed among the elusive guerrilla enemy—and thereby opened the possibility of inventing enemies within the more accessible, stagnant pool of civilians.[10] The already precarious distinction between combatants and civilian noncombatants became dangerously and tragically irrelevant to some operations in hazardous or confused areas. Thus rose additional idioms among the soldiers assigned to the pacification of villages: "Kill clean, burn clean, destroy clean," "Anything you see is all Vietcong," "Children also spy," "Better to make mistakes than to miss."

From 1966 to 1969, the ideal of a people's war—"each inhabitant [is] a soldier, each village a fortress"—was brought across the unbridgeable theoretical gap between the two different kinds of war. Atrocious war crimes resulted from the lethal translation of a pond metaphor from a culturally familiar abstraction to an imagined alien reality.[11]

The civilian massacres during the Vietnam War may be divided into two distinct, though related, patterns. In one type of killing that was more prevalent, the scale of violence was relatively limited and the victims

were predominantly elders and small children. The massacre of Ha Gia
falls into this category, as do numerous other incidents that occurred in
Quang Nam in 1968 and Quang Ngai (also in Binh Dinh and Phu Yen)
in 1966. The circumstances of these killings, although they vary, demonstrate one commonality. In Ha Gia and Ha Quang, by the time the mass
killings took place most villagers had been relocated to the refugee camps
called "strategic hamlets" or had moved to urban slums. Those who
remained in the village were mainly elders who maintained the rice paddies and vegetable plots in the absence of their families.

In 1966, in the Binh Son district of Quang Ngai province, the local
militiamen were consolidated with expeditionary units of the regular
North Vietnamese forces. This large fighting force relied partly on the
scattered, barely populated villages for food and information. In a number of cases that I investigated in the area, the remaining elders had either
children or close relatives working in the local partisan force, and thus
they stayed on to keep in touch with them as well as supply them with
food. After a successful action against the enemy, the militiamen in
Quang Ngai temporarily evacuated the area and encouraged the villagers
to do likewise. They knew that postambush retaliatory acts against civilians had become a routine phenomenon by the summer of 1966. However, village elders were unable to evacuate the village even temporarily,
according to the locals, either because they had nowhere else to go or
they had never gone beyond the boundary of their village before and
were reluctant. In the case of Ha Gia, a neighbor of Ha My, some of the
elderly victims were old Viet Minh activists and longtime supporters of
the nationalist movement against the French colonial occupation. Their
children and grandchildren were moving back and forth between the village and the refugee camp, whenever the situation allowed, to help on
the family farm. In most cases of what Noam Chomsky calls "the 43-
plus My Lais," the search-and-destroy missions conducted by America's
closest allied troops from South Korea attacked these relatively small
groups of villagers.[12]

The other type of civilian massacre is related to the first but nevertheless remains different in one crucial aspect. In 1972, the American
Quaker aid workers Diane Jones and Michael Jones collected information on mass killing of civilians, particularly the incidents committed by
the ROK (Republic of Korea) forces, in the Quang Ngai and Quang
Nam provinces. They reported that more than a hundred civilians were
reported killed in thirteen of more than forty-five incidents in which
ROK soldiers were said to have killed groups of more than twenty un-

armed civilians.[13] The massacres in Ha My and My Lai belong to the category of the thirteen large-scale killings, and so do the incidents in Thuy Bo, Phong Nhat, and Phong Nhi of Quang Nam; Vinh Hoa of Quang Ngai; five villages in the Binh Dinh province; and many more.[14] If the situation in a village remained stable, the villagers in the refugee camps usually began to visit their homes more frequently and to extend the duration of their visits. The Ha My villagers did this, and so did the people of My Lai toward the end of 1967. Their returns were often facilitated by the presence of strong South Vietnamese or other allied forces in the surrounding area. The U.S. military installation in My Khe, south of My Lai, and the ROK Marines in the Con Ninh base in Ha My contributed to the improvement of security in each area. When they thought their villages were secure, the refugees petitioned the South Vietnamese administration, or went directly to the foreign military authority, in the hope of obtaining permission for a more extensive visit to or temporary resettlement in their homeland. If these appeals were unsuccessful, the villagers could mobilize their resources to bribe the camp authority and other Vietnamese officials to allow them to leave the camp, according to what I was told by elders in Ha My and its environs, as well as by former employees of the South Vietnamese war administration in Da Nang and Hoi An. When some villagers escaped the refugee camp in this way, their escape stirred other villagers. When two or three families successfully returned to their natal village, others watched for and analyzed carefully any information from the village. When the family elders and community leaders came to the conclusion that their village was safe, this triggered a mass return to the village. This happened in Ha My in December 1967 and in My Lai shortly before then. The returning villagers assessed the situation carefully; some of them used a fortune-teller or other magical means to help them estimate the risk of their return.

When the villagers began to resettle, the local allied troops often assisted their resettlement with food and building materials. The Ha My villagers received assistance from the ROK Marines in this way, and the returnees to My Lai considered the U.S. soldiers in My Khe to be friends. This relationship explains why some Ha My villagers believed that the roundup on the day of the massacre was for food distribution. In Phong Nhi of Quang Nam, the villagers and the locally based U.S. Marines maintained a close relationship throughout 1966–1967. Thirty-six families from this village had members who were soldiers in the South Vietnamese army, and ten of these men, according to a surviving veteran still living in the village, were working under the Combined Action program to protect the local area jointly with a group of U.S. Marines. This did not prevent the village from being completely ransacked by a separate, mobile action of pacification in March 1968.

Inside the refugee camps, there were South Vietnamese police informers as well as covert civilian agitprop activists loyal to the communist side. The former disseminated information about violent situations in the rural area and instigated fear; the Vietcong (VC) activists fought this psychological war with counterinformation.[15] Both forms of information were often exaggerated and unreliable. The VC encouraged the refugees to return to their village and to stop, according to a widely disseminated wartime adage, "eating the enemy's food and grabbing America's leg." A covertly delivered communiqué asserted that the villagers should join other safe villages, if they were not able to return to their own village, to help the partisan forces and also to demonstrate their will against forced displacement. When this failed to persuade the anxious villagers, the message became more blunt—"My Lai has many shelters and plenty of food. Move your family to this good place"—as a former covert civilian activist at Quang Ngai recalled.

This war of false information instigated confusion and insecurity among the displaced villagers. In the highly unstable military situation after the Tet, or Lunar New Year, offensive in the first quarter of 1968, the safety of a rural village was a fantasy. The pattern of war-making was evolving to take an unprecedented shape on both sides and at great velocity. The machinery of war was becoming increasingly centralized on both sides of the frontier, and the fate of locality was increasingly unpredictable in a strategic shift "to direct the brunt of the revolutionary war onto the cities, towns, market places, and the leading departments of the enemy."[16] At the same time, countermeasures urged, "We must win the race to the countryside, go on the offensive, re-establish security in the rural areas, and restore the [Saigon] government's presence in the villages."[17] In the midst of this generalized uncertainty, some places were considered to be relatively safe, and these places attracted temporary settlers from other villages. People of "return villages" were proud of their privilege and often provoked envy in people from other, less fortunate villages. This luck, however, could turn into devastating misfortune. The apparent relative safety of a village frequently led to tragedy of a higher proportion. The "safe village" and the "return village" could turn into a site of mass death when the identity of the village suddenly shifted and it became a "VC village" circled in red on the battle map. This shift in identity was abrupt, unknown to the village inhabitants, outside their control, and often, in fact, outside the control of the armed combatants on both sides.

A BRIEF HISTORY

Ha My and My Lai are fairly isolated from Route 1, Vietnam's main transportation artery, but they are close enough to an urban center that one can cycle from these villages to the city's central marketplace.[18] My Lai is fourteen kilometers northeast of Quang Ngai, the capital of the province by the same name, whereas Ha My is hidden on the sandy coastal strip twenty-five kilometers south of Da Nang, the commercial center of central Vietnam. Ha My is also five kilometers north of Hoi An, the ancient port of international commerce and the wartime provincial capital of Quang Nam. This physical proximity to the urban environment had a profound effect on the communities. Ha My and My Lai both played an important role in each region during anticolonial movements at the turn of the century. The revolutionary Viet Minh had strong roots in each place in the 1930s.[19] During the American War—which is what the Vietnamese call the war, partly to distinguish it from the preceding "French War"—each village found itself in a precarious buffer zone between two militarily strategic areas. Ha My was right in the middle of the expansive pacification zone between Hoi An and Da Nang, and My Lai was similarly placed in the military security zone between the provincial capital of Quang Ngai and the important military installation of Chu Lai.[20] For the communist side, too, the two places provided crucial routes for the traffic of goods, personnel, and information—between the sea and their mountain bases, and between the occupied urban center and the liberated inland rural areas.[21] In 1968, the combination of strong anticolonial resistance activity and the area's military-strategic importance left each village vulnerable.

Both communities were predominantly agricultural, but their cultures were not enclosed, isolated, or solely agrarian. Young people of Ha My and My Lai were educated at town schools and were open to new ideas. The portrait of a young villager reading modern literature at the edge of a paddy appears frequently in Ha My village relics, which trace the proud tradition of the scholar-farmer back to the founding ancestors of the community.[22] My Lai history is relatively less explicit about this legendary heritage but equal to Ha My history in its emphasis on the rise of revolutionary literati and peasantry against colonial exploitation.[23] Scholars of modern Vietnamese history emphasize the inception of urban

ideas in rural villages when explaining the origin of revolution in northern Vietnam. It is argued that the "prodigal children" of the landed elite
were introduced to challenging ideas through their experience of modern
education, and that they then disseminated this knowledge to the children of the peasantry and so planted the seeds of a radical movement.[24]
In the villages of central Vietnam, the class distinction between the
landed elite and the landless peasants was less clear than in the fertile
northeast delta regions. The proximity to a township, however, gave
rural youth constant access to modern ideas and critical discourse. Thus
rose another prominent image in the historical poetry of Ha My—the
village youth discussing literature and politics underneath the sacred
banyan tree of the village's ancestral temple.[25]

It is known that the early revolutionaries in Ha My and its environs
rose from the local Confucian schools.[26] The scholar Le Tan Toan passed
the court examination in 1861 and subsequently opened a pedagogical
institute to teach Confucian ethics and ritual knowledge. Widely known
in the Quang Nam and Quang Ngai provinces, the school attracted talented children from many villages. One of them was Nguyen Duy Hieu,
a native of Cam Ha, immediately south of Ha My, who, having taught
Prince Ung Dang, became a leader in the popular insurrection against the
French colonists in the 1880s.[27]

According to legend, Nguyen Duy Hieu's teacher, Le Tan Toan, was
summoned by the commander of the imperial forces, which had been dispatched from the court to suppress the insurrection. The general confronted Le Tan Toan: "People respected your scholarship and pedagogy.
The court had faith in you, trusting you to raise good scholars. But how
did you respond to their expectations? You taught and trained rebels and
enemies. A true enemy like Nguyen Duy Hieu!" Hearing this, Master
Toan stood up in a rage, threw his rice wine cup to the floor, and warned
the general, "In a time like this, it may not be clear to you who is our true
enemy."[28] Master Toan was subsequently convicted of "teaching students wrong ideas" and sentenced to death. Honoring his scholarship,
however, the court gave him the privilege of choosing from three different means of execution: beheading by sword, hanging by silk rope, or
poisoning. Master Toan chose the poison. After his death, this anniversary became an important event for the region's anticolonial resistance.
At the turn of the century, the Le Tan Toan–Nguyen Duy Hieu movement evolved into a powerful local force and, like the better-known
Dong Du (Go East) and Duy Tan (Renovation) movements of Phan Boi

Chau—an anticolonial patriot and national hero—influenced the course of the subsequent political development.[29] It is known that Ha My, together with the neighboring Cam An, Ha Quang, and Ha Gia hamlets, remained a strong base of the Nguyen Duy Hieu patriotic anticolonial resistance throughout the turbulent years at the turn of the century. This movement contributed to the uprising of 1908, when several hundred villagers from the Dai Loc district, urged on by the patriotic literati, held a protest march against the augmentation of corvée, the French colonial labor tax. The incident ended in violent suppression by the French army.[30]

From 1931 to 1934, the villagers of Ha My faced a particularly severe famine, a result of the Great Depression and the falling price of rice.[31] The personal head tax increased in quantity—to 150 kilograms of rice for every man between the ages of eighteen and sixty—in order to make up for the fall in revenue caused by the low rice price. Men were required to pay a tax in labor as well, which amounted to 120 working days per annum. The village men were sent to the construction sites in the Tien Phuoc–Tra My region of the Central Highlands. Poor families were obliged to borrow money from the rich at increasingly higher interest rates in order to free some hands from the forced labor to continue their own farming.[32] "Nothing about the colonial order seemed to infuriate the peasantry more than its taxes," writes James Scott.[33] During this period of extreme hardship, the song below was popular among the Ha My women:

> The blue birds are looking for prey.
> Wife pays husband's tax with strings and strings of coins.
> Husband, please come back and take a look.
> We part with food and clothing
> To save money for their tax.
> Each time I hear the tax collector's wooden gong
> I'm frightened and my body shrinks.
> While you're working on the poisoned land of Tra My
> Each green, each sweet potato is pulled out from our ancestral land
> To satisfy the Frenchman who laid tax on your Vietnamese head.[34]

Ha My's connection to Tien Phuoc–Tra My, which had been forced upon them by the colonial policy, later developed into an enduring relationship of exchange. In the 1960s, each place provided shelter and food to the other when the situation became unbearable, and partisan fighters moved between the two places, sometimes working jointly. The highland

and the lowland had different cycles and developmental patterns of violence, and moving between these two places allowed small, though crucial, spaces of relative safety.

The first Communist Party organization was established in Quang Nam in April 1930 at the regional level, followed by prolific organizational activity at the village level, particularly among the young and the women.[35] The underground communist cell of Ha My openly took over the village administration during the political vacuum following the surrender of Japan and the end of the Pacific War. On August 28, 1945, the Ha My villagers gathered at the village's communal house *(dinh)* and participated in the inauguration of the village's Revolutionary People's Committee.[36] Soon, more meetings were held in the ancestral temple to institute the local Viet Minh Front, as well as various offshoot associations such as Patriotic Peasants, Patriotic Women, Patriotic Youth, and Patriotic Village Elders. The new village administration carried out land reform, dividing the rice fields equally for all villagers above the age of eighteen, and also initiated pro-literacy, antisuperstition campaigns.[37] When the Democratic Republic of Vietnam was formally proclaimed on September 2, 1945, in Hanoi, the revolutionary committees of Quang Nam promptly affirmed their loyalty.

The French expeditionary forces landed at Da Nang on March 17, 1946, in the hope of reclaiming their old colony. This event triggered, at the request of the Communist Party, the consolidation of the various village associations as the unified Soldier-Villager Committee, which was responsible for preparing the village for the imminent resistance war.[38] The committee organized the destruction of the roads in the hope of delaying the advance of the French troops, and undertook the dismantling of village temples, pagodas, and school buildings in order to prevent the troops from using them for shelter. Afterward, the committee carried out the so-called patriotic evacuation, in which villagers were encouraged to hide food supplies, destroy their houses, and evacuate to the town. The personnel of the village resistance war committee prepared a defense line along the village river, Cam Le.

On the morning of March 13, 1947, the French launched an all-out offensive against the Cam Le and other local defense lines.[39] The assault came from their air force, navy, and armored infantry simultaneously. The chief of the village security force, Le Van Sy, was killed on the village defense line, and the village soldier Nguyen Chien jumped out of his underground shelter and wounded a French infantryman with his sickle. Despite these heroic attempts, the village defense forces were helpless against the technologically superior invaders and were swiftly overrun. The French occupied the area by noon. The defeat resulted in a critical change of strategy on the Viet Minh side. When the initial shock of the defeat subsided, the provincial resistance war committee launched an agitprop activity among the evacuated villagers. Propaganda encouraged the villagers to return to their homeland, rebuild the village economy, support the cadre leaders, and prepare for a protracted guerilla war. The political leaders of the Viet Minh quickly realized the futility of confronting the advanced European military forces with imitative, inferior conventional armed forces. The solution had to be found in a creative rethinking of the art of war. In this way, the thirty-year-long village guerilla war began among the ruins of the village temples and houses. Returning villagers repaired the irrigation canal, rebuilt the houses, and reopened the communal house. This was the first of several resurrections in the modern history of Ha My's temple for its founding ancestors.

The Ha My communal house, like other Vietnamese *dinh,* honors the village's founding ancestors as well as local deities. According to the legend inscribed in the *gia pha,* the family historical records, the village is part of a network of places established by the original settlers, the five brothers who traveled southward in the fifteenth century in search of land.[40] The eldest brother set foot in Cam Thanh and marveled at the beauty of the lush tropical forests and the river shaped like a mature dragon preparing its ascent to heaven. He declared this fertile land along the river mouth to be his own. His younger brothers then began to move northward along the coast, retracing their southward migration route. The second brother stopped at the peninsula of Cam An, the long stretch of sandy land facing the East Sea on one side and the lagoon of Tra Que on the other. The other brothers went on further and settled in what is now Ha My, Ha Gia, and Ha Quang. These three younger brothers took smaller, less fertile lands compared to those of their two elder brothers, but they were happy, according to the legend, to show modesty to their elders. Each brother dug a well, found a beautiful tree and built a house beneath it, and planted the seeds they had brought from the north. In this way, the history of the villages began. Their first descendants built a temple in honor of each brother, installed the founder's gong and drum within, and instituted a magnificent rite. Thus, the village's culture flourished. According to the legend, the founder of Ha My, the third brother, was in possession of the best drum among the five brothers, a drum believed to tremble more powerfully than any of the famous drums kept in the most prominent villages in the north of Vietnam.

Among these original communal houses and the many offshoots built in the process of further migration and population growth, the most architecturally sophisticated one was in Cam An, in the community of An Bang. This ancestral temple was destroyed by explosives in 1966. A year later, the troops at the Con Cho military base assembled the two hundred villagers in the base. There, in the late morning, the villagers were lined up for mass execution. The village chief of An Bang, who was also the administrator of one of the strategic hamlets, or what people remember as concentration camps, intervened just in time. In a dramatic confrontation, as the An Bang villagers now eagerly recount, the village chief argued with the Korean marines in the Con Cho base that he could guarantee with his own life that none of his two hundred villagers was a Vietcong supporter. Shortly after the incident, the village chief faced a series of death threats and was soon dismissed from his position. He considers it something akin to a miracle that he was not assassinated after the intervention, which could easily have been interpreted as an act of sabotage.

Other ancestral temples in the area were also destroyed but in a more cruel and dramatic way. These sacred places where villagers worshiped the memory of founding ancestors were used to execute their descendents. During the forced mass evacuation of the rural population in the 1960s, the military planners believed that some villagers were reluctant to join the fortified strategic hamlets because of the existence of the village ancestral temples. They also believed the temples had become subversive places where radical politics were discussed.[41] The communal house in Ha Quang escaped destruction when the temple in An Bang was blown up, only to suffer it in a more bitterly remembered way a few months later. Soldiers assembled twenty-six villagers, mostly elders left behind by families who had moved to the strategic hamlet or the urban slums, inside this ancestral temple, closed the shutters, took up positions outside to ensure that anyone who dared to escape would be shot, and set fire to the building. One elder hurriedly lit incense sticks and prayed to the ancestors for protection. However, the ancestors of Ha Quang could do nothing to help their desperate descendants. In the hamlet of Ha Gia, the ARVN (Army of the Republic of Vietnam [South Vietnam]), U.S., and ROK forces conducted joint surveillance operations. In the spring of 1968, Ha Gia elders and children were rounded up by the ROK forces and escorted to the ancestral temple of the Dinh family in the neighboring Ha Quang village. The few Ha Gia villagers who had escaped climbed the coconut palm trees to see what was happening to their relatives. None of the thirty-five villagers survived the day's massacre, and after the killing, a flamethrower turned the Dinh family temple to ashes.

The Con Ninh base, one of the three military installations in the vicinity of Ha My, changed hands several times. Before it was temporarily abandoned in 1954, a French battalion camped inside its tall barb-wired wall, hidden from view by a wide stretch of pine trees. When it prospered, Con Ninh was a fairly cosmopolitan place where the French ate French food, Algerians cooked their spicy meals, Moroccans baked their tasty bread, and the local Vietnamese conscripts prepared fish-sauce meals, baked French bread, and fried flying fish for the French officers. Catholics, Muslims, and ancestor worshippers conducted their worship ceremonies separately, and some local conscripts debated the strength of the gods and deities in each belief according to the proportional number of casualties in each culturally distinctive group of combatants. This French battalion conducted mopping-up operations in the surrounding villages, and it murdered several groups of civilians during the final phase, in rhetoric a defense against communist expansion but in reality a colonial reconquest (see chapter 8).[42] In 1937–1938, the French authorities conscripted a large number of laborers from Quang Nam and shipped them to the great Mediterranean city of Marseilles. There, the two thousand Vietnamese laborer-soldiers manufactured gunpowder in the notorious *poudrerie*—the powdery of Marseilles. After contributing to France's vital economy and sharing the humiliating experience of German occupation with its citizens, many of these foreign conscripts of the French army perished in the chaos of a war between their colonial compatriots and the village militia soon after their return in 1948. In some cases, according to my interviews with three surviving veterans in Da Nang and Hoi An, these soldiers discovered on their return that the gunpowder they had manufactured had been used against their own families.

In March 1965, the first U.S. expeditionary force, the Third Marine Amphibious Force, landed at Da Nang. The marine battalions quickly began to pacify surrounding villages. This activity typically consisted of surrounding a village in the early morning; dropping leaflets from the air that instructed the villagers to assemble and go through a screening procedure; and advancing into the village to locate any underground tunnels, hidden arms, or food caches. The identification of Vietcong militia was a primary objective of this pacification activity. The activity may have appeared rational and workable to military planners, but, on the ground, it was unrealistic, and the screening procedure was generally based on hunches. Jonathan Schell, reporting from central Vietnam, described this work. He quotes an experienced foreign interrogator who stated, "The V.C. organizes an association for everyone—the Farmers' Association, the Fishers' Association, the Old Grandmothers' Association. They've got one for everybody. It's so mixed up with the population you can't tell who's a V.C. Our job is to separate the V.C. from the people."[43] Beginning in the dry season of 1965–1966, the U.S. Marines began to move southward to occupy the Hoa Vang and Dien Ban districts and to transform this area into a "white buffer zone," clear of the Vietcong influence. They took hold of the old French Con Ninh base on the seashore of Ha My in the spring of 1966.[44]

By this time, all the villages founded by the five brothers had developed complex resistance networks. When a North Vietnamese regular army unit assaulted the province's capital, Hoi An, with artillery fire in early 1965, the local guerilla units, formed mainly by the men and women of the five-brother villages, launched an offense against the South Vietnamese positions and the suburban residence and offices of government officials.[45] Two years before, the villagers of Cam An and Ha My had been at the forefront of the synchronized mass protests against the development of strategic hamlets. If a communal decision in favor of political action was made at that time in a meeting at the village's communal house, it was very difficult to reverse. People aware of this irreversibility then started to focus on how to minimize risk. If the stakes were high, in the sense that the pressure on the village's honor was strong, influential people in the village were sometimes obliged to volunteer for more risky activities. The village men discussed with their relatives the survival of their families after their hypothetical arrest or death, and the village women formed their own anxious circles, sharing the grim prospect and discussing their own strategies for survival without their men.

The situation in each village was swiftly conveyed to other communes and villages. The party activists were informed via a complex chain of *co so cach mang*, or "the infrastructure of revolution," which refers to the covert civilian activists in the occupied zones. The collected information was relayed to the provincial revolutionary committee through an equivalent organizational network at the interdistrict level. Based on their historical affinity, however, the villages of the five brothers had a strong network of their own, and they continued to share information and resources. The work of this cross-village network remained largely independent of the political authorities. Administratively, Ha My, Ha Quang, and Ha Gia belonged to a territory separate from that of the other two five-brother villages, Cam An and Cam Thanh. This was the case not only for the South Vietnam–U.S. war bureaucracy but also for the region's communist war administration. In the political organization of the latter, the southern partisan group in the Cam An and Cam Thanh area (the South Group), and their northern counterpart in Ha Gia and Ha My (the North Group), operated independently, unless their activities were coordinated by the higher party organizations. Underneath this formal military-strategic separation, however, the North Group and the South Group collaborated and communicated with one another through kinship and marriage connections, and these connections changed in strength and importance depending on fluctuations in war activity.

This intervillage network, *giao hieu*, was originally a type of ritual network and a web of relationships that had developed among the community temples.[46] A lineage group in a particular village was related to other lineage groups in adjacent villages through a common historical, legendary background. These related lineage groups held joint ancestral rites and took turn holding these important rites among themselves. These interlocal rites have been vigorously revived since the late 1990s. The opening speech by a Cam An lineage elder on the occasion of an intervillage ancestral rite traced the history of the rite in three distinctive stages—the prewar ritual prosperity, the destruction of family and village temples during the French and American Wars, and the contemporary restoration of intervillage solidarity. As for the second period, he said:

> Rooted out of our ancestral land, the people of Ha Gia and the people of Cam An were herded into a miserable life in the concentration camps. Across the barbed wire and the minefields, our ancestors were left unattended, their places bombed and burned down, their tombs bulldozed, their dignity humiliated. Remember our life in the camp. In that inhumane condition, we could not even contemplate holding a rite such as the one we are holding today. We did not have enough food to feed our children, we had to cross the minefield week after week to collect wild vegetables, and we could not offer the miserable rationed bread to our ancestors. We were displaced and deprived of our rights to worship. Our people did not give in. Patriotic villagers joined their hands to fight the oppressors, and I dare say that our family was always ahead of other families in this struggle. Men of your village and men of our village shared the same underground tunnels and endured humility and hunger together. Women of your village and women of our village shared the little food they had and provided shelter for each other. Our ancestors, although once humiliated and unattended, must be proud of this history of harmony and mutual support among their

descendants. We may rebuild the temples if they are broken; we cannot do so with family feelings. Once broken, they cannot be mended. Today, we gather here to remember and renew our family feelings.[47]

In July 1964, the communist cadres in the area of Ha My held a general meeting at the communal house of Ha Gia. The meeting inaugurated the village-level structure of the National Front for the Liberation of South Vietnam, and leaders urged the construction of "fortress villages" and "combat villages."[48] A prolific exchange and movement of political cadres and combat units took place during this period between districts and provinces, and the seafront area of Ha My became an important location for shipping combat personnel to the regrouping areas in the province of Quang Ngai. Several hundred men were transferred to Quang Ngai via this route, and they fought in the fierce battles of 1966 in the districts of Binh Son and Tu Nghia, as well as Son Tinh, where My Lai is located. Those who remained in their homeland received guidelines: "Obtain higher efficiency in hiding combat forces. Combine legal and illegal struggles. Employ legal actions to mobilize the village mass."[49]

When a directive for a legal political struggle, such as the mass action during the Buddhist crisis (1963–1966), was relayed to the village revolutionary committee, the news circulated along family lines as well as among the village seniors.[50] The impatient activists urged the villagers to act more promptly and more decisively. Opposing voices also existed, and arguments rose between close friends, relatives, and lifetime neighbors. Police informants lived in the village alongside the people they were spying on. In the second half of the 1950s, the Cao Dai sect in Ha Gia and Ha My made a tacit alliance with the South Vietnamese Nationalist Party and fought the VC networks from within the village. By this time, the South Vietnamese administration had classified the village population according to three categories: Group A (illegal people: old resistance fighters and supporters of the Geneva Agreement); Group B (semi-illegal people: relatives and friends of Group A); and Group C (legal and faithful people: supporters of the government programs).[51]

Within the village reality, this classification system was hard to maintain. A single family often had both "legal" and "illegal" people, making Group B a phantom category. Moreover, if an individual wished to remain on his ancestral land and survive the war, he had to be in both Group A and C (see below). "Defend the village," or "Tru bam," was one of the main slogans of the resistance war from 1960 to 1965, and it was intended as a protest against the relocation to, and concentration of villagers in, the fortified strategic hamlets. The ABC classification, which did not reflect the village reality, could work only in the refugee camps. In the strategic hamlets, the refugees had to sit through daily evening classes such as "Essential Lessons in How to Catch the Communists," and people classified as members of Group B were closely watched.

By the time the U.S. Marines took up a position at the Con Ninh base in 1966, partly to prevent the use of Ha My Beach for subversive activities and traffic, fierce battles were taking place in the Bo Bo Hills, Duy Xuyen, Phi Phu, and elsewhere in the inland region on the western side of Route 1. On the road's eastern side, where Ha My and other five-brother villages were located, tensions were still low, and civilian casualties reflected that. One early morning in June 1967, the U.S. troops at Con Ninh ambushed twelve fishermen, which was reported by the news media of the National Liberation Front,[52] and there were other small-scale incidents in various communities. However, systematic mass civilian killing was as yet unfamiliar to lowland Quang Nam in 1966–1967.

The situation was very different in the province of Quang Ngai. As early as 1966, the ROK Marines were sweeping through the rural area to the east and north of the provincial capital, Quang Ngai. The Republic of Korea sent three divisions of troops to the combat zones in central Vietnam: a total of 312,853 men over an eleven-year period beginning on September 22, 1964, and primarily during the period 1965 to 1972.[53] In the provinces of Quang Ngai and Binh Dinh, the ROK troops were met by well-prepared local partisan forces mixed with regular North Vietnamese soldiers and partisans transferred from other provinces, and the troops suffered high casualties. In response to their losses, the marines cleared village after village in what turned out to be a nearly complete destruction of civilian life in most of the Quang Ngai region, including the districts of Son Tinh, Tinh Hoa, and Binh Son.[54] Miraculously, My Lai escaped this round of violence, partly because of its relative proximity to Quang Ngai City, but mostly because a small U.S. military installation was located in the immediate vicinity. This pattern of violence in Quang Ngai in 1966 was repeated in Quang Nam two years later.[55]

In December 1967, U.S. forces handed over their Con Ninh base to the ROK marine brigade with the totemic name of the "Blue Dragons," as part of a general changeover of troops south of Da Nang. Two battalions of the ROK Second Marine Division set up bases along the road from Cam An to Dien Hai on December 4, 1967, establishing their armored unit in Ben Kien. Apart from the towns of Da Nang and Hoi An, the rural area was by this time largely VC-controlled, in the view of the Saigon-U.S. war administration. The new troop deployment south of Da Nang had the strategic objective of pacifying a long corridor of villages from Ha My Beach in the east to the Bo Bo Hills in the west. The objective was to disconnect the VC fighting forces between Da Nang and Hoi An and block their supply lines. By this time, communist authorities were preparing a general uprising and military offense, which would be known as the Tet Offensive. Villagers were encouraged to contribute food, cash, and medicine in preparation for the coming battles. Several hundred "volunteers" carried food and weapons from the coastal area to VC mountain bases across the Ky Lam Bridge. Insurrection units were secretly brought into Da Nang and Hoi An.

At 2:40 P.M. on the Lunar New Year's Day (January 31, 1968, the Year of the Monkey), the combined forces of the regular army and local guerilla units launched a coordinated assault on the town of Hoi An from four directions and subsequently occupied the town's peripheries and two military bases.[56] The National Liberation Front honored the commune of Dien Duong, which includes the village of Ha My, for taking part in the Tet Offensive. In response, the other side swiftly began clearing out villages located in this military corridor. Thus, at least six large-scale civilian massacres took place during the first three months of 1968, beginning at Truong Giang (in Dien Trung commune) and Duy Xuyen in the west, and including An Truong (in Dien Phong commune) and Phong Nhi and Phong Nhat (in Dien An commune) in the middle, and ending at Ha My (in Dien Duong commune) and Cam Ha on the eastern coast.[57] Two secret reports made by the district communist cells to the provincial authority recorded nineteen incidents of mass killing during this short period.[58] The tragedy of mass killing had already been witnessed in Quang Ngai in 1966.[59]

On the twenty-fourth day of the first lunar month in 1968, the ROK Marines had left their tanks and armored vehicles outside the boundary of Xom Tay, Ha My's subhamlet number two, at 9:30 A.M. and started marching into the village from three directions. By 10:00 A.M. the villagers were assembled at three different sites, including the Nguyen family home and the open space between two subhamlets. At the open space, the commanding officer ordered a desk to be placed facing the crowd. Standing behind the desk, he made what felt like, according to the survivors, an unusually long and passionate speech of instruction; the Vietnamese interpreter summarized it for the villagers. There were no heavy arms in sight; soldiers were running around busily. A survivor, Nguyen Thi Bon, said she thought the soldiers were going to give out food and sweets; she had seen this routine before. She was trying to imagine what the day's gift would be. Another survivor, Ba Hoa, heard someone whispering, "What if they kill us?" "Don't be ridiculous. Don't say that. You're calling bad luck," she heard from someone else. "They came to give us food. Believe me. Believe it."

It happened just past 10:00 A.M. The officer finished his speech, turned his back to the crowd and began to walk away. Several steps away from the villagers, he made a swift hand gesture. This gesture triggered the M60 machine guns and the M79 grenade launchers, which were hidden in the bushes. Soldiers began firing at the villagers, and fragmentation grenades exploded on anyone who tried to escape from this living hell. Bon felt village mothers falling on her and her little sister. Ba Hoa saw a grenade coming toward her and she fell on her children. Then she felt nothing and saw nothing, except the distant green sweet potato field she began crawling toward. Bon remembers that it was quiet and pitch dark, and hard to breathe underneath the bodies. She tried to move and, hearing her baby sister cry, stopped. Her sister kept crying, and she feared the soldiers might hear her. Bon heard a rapidly speaking foreign voice, then quiet again, and then the detonation of a hand grenade. The assault went on for two hours. At the other killing site, seventy villagers were squeezed into the main altar room of the Nguyen family's residence. Some villagers thought the soldiers were going to hand out food. The owner of the house was not convinced, and he hid behind the ancestral altar with three of his grandchildren. The killing began as soon as machine gun fire was heard from the open site. By noon, 135 villagers were dead: only three were males of combat age; three were unborn children; and four were unidentified. The rest were village women, elders, teenage girls, toddlers, and infants.

In the My Lai area of Quang Ngai, there had also been a changeover of troops, in December 1967. In the early morning of the seventeenth day of the second lunar month of 1968, the helicopters carrying the Charlie Company of Task Force Barker landed near the perimeter of the Khe Thuan subhamlet of Tu Cung—the area marked as "My Lai 4" on the military map. This was the first major military action to take place after the South Korean expeditionary forces handed over the area. The village had experienced search missions before by different troops, including South Vietnamese and Nung (an ethnic minority) troops.[60] This time, however, some of the villagers sensed a difference in the atmosphere and asked the women and children to hide in underground shelters. The few village guerilla fighters in Khe Thuan dashed toward the village hill in order to better assess the situation. The house-to-house search began, and pigs and buffaloes were killed first.[61] By the time the Charlie Company left, 135 Tu Cung villagers were left dead at three different sites, including the open field between the subhamlets Khe Thuan and Khe Dong.

The night after the massacre, a few local partisan fighters came back to My Lai and helped the survivors to bury the victims. The survivors used bamboo baskets to collect the fragments of the broken bodies of their relatives. They were terrified, and the atmosphere was heightened and unreal. The burial process was slow and the bodies quickly began to decompose. Untouchable, most of them had to be buried where they were and en masse. When U.S. Army investigators reached the deserted village in November 1969, they would find mass graves at three different sites, as well as a ditch full of decomposed bodies.[62]

At Ha My, survivors and their relatives from neighboring villages brought straw mats to wrap the bodies of the dead. They lay the bodies in the shallow holes dug around the killing site and marked each grave with a small piece of stone or a stick. Later in the afternoon, the soldiers returned and the survivors ran away in panic. The troops brought two D-7 bulldozers, which they used to flatten the houses, destroy the shallow graves, and obliterate the unburied bodies. This assault against the corpses and graves is remembered as the most inhumane aspect of the incident,[63] and it has complicated the process of family commemoration.

The wounded villagers of My Lai were brought to the village market-place on Route 521 by people who had been in the marketplace, and from there they were taken by horsedrawn cart to the General Hospital of Quang Ngai. The sole survivor of the Do family remembers this journey more vividly than any other event of that time. He remembers especially how the owner of the horse refused to carry him for anything less than five hundred dong (Vietnamese currency). The wounded survivors of Ha My were brought to a German medical ship in the port of Da Nang. On his desperate run for help to the Lepers' Clinic in Hoa Hai, Bon's father came across an American convoy. The American officer immediately radioed for a rescue helicopter to help the wounded children. He was notified that on Sunday no helicopter was going to fly for civilian passengers. The members of the American convoy were furious; they turned their armored carrier around and set out for Da Nang with the wounded. Ba Hoa of Ha My, who had survived the bullets and shrapnel, was taken to the German medical ship, where her leg was amputated. She had lost a child at the massacre, and arrived at the hospital with her surviving child. Later, whenever she recalled the Year of Monkey, she would speak of the horror she experienced in the floating hospital as being more terrifying than her experience in the village. In the ship, Ba Hoa heard a rumor that the hospital staff was dumping dead Vietnamese bodies into the sea. Her daughter was dying in the intensive care unit, and Ba Hoa became hysterical at the thought of losing her in such a way. She crawled along the hospital corridors, dragging her mutilated body, and grabbed at the leg of anyone she could find. She begged for mercy and protested what was, to her, the most heinous crime against human dignity—the abandonment of a human body to the voracious flying fish. Eventually, a Vietnamese nurse escorted her back to her bed and informed her that her child had died, reassuring her that the rumor was false and she would be given the child's body.

After the massacre, Ha My and My Lai remained largely unoccupied until the end of the war, in 1975. One of the orphan boys of Ha My went to Da Nang to bake French bread for the GIs; a few adults tried to get into the refugee camps in Cam An, only to be refused entry on the grounds that they were allegedly from a VC-controlled area. Thus their many years of life as living wandering ghosts began. Having lost their base as well as their families, the few remaining village guerilla fighters moved to Cam An and joined the southern partisan group. Their southern comrades welcomed them. The survivors of the Phong Nhi and Phong Nhat massacre brought the corpses of their children to the military checkpoint on Route 1 in protest. They might have been encouraged to do so by the VC activists, for their action followed the familiar pattern of postmassacre public protests.[64] The decomposed bodies of the children had to be buried there, where they were lying. The Phong Nhat survivors are reluctant to recall this part of the tragedy; instead, what they remember vividly is the simple fact that, each time they pass the crossroad, they know their children are buried on the roadside. No official inquiry followed their angry protest. Instead, two civilian officials handed out a small amount of cash and a large quantity of white cotton.

After these incidents, a rumor spread across the refugee camps, "A dead Dai Han [Korean] kills dozens of Vietnamese." At the same time, a new slogan rose among the guerilla fighters: "Xe xac Rong Xanh phong thay Bach Ho," or "Eliminate the Green [Blue] Dragon, make many corpses of the White [Fierce] Tiger." The local South Vietnamese soldiers were disturbed by the rumor that a number of the Phong Nhi and Phong Nhat victims were families of active ARVN soldiers. The army kept the incidents a secret on their side, and there was no war correspondent in the area who could have taken an interest in the activities of non-American forces. The crimes committed by America's close ally attracted no investigative journalists like Seymour Hersh, either. The refugees carried the rumors with them, however, and some reached the ears of American aid workers. Meanwhile, Vietnamese police officers and their covert agents disseminated the rumor widely in the rural population. According to a former police officer of the Republic of Vietnam, whom I interviewed, she had supplied ROK marine officers with information about how VC forces had reacted to civilian massacres. She recalled in 1997 that she had informed the officer, who had taken her as his lover, that massive civilian killing was indeed breaking the nerve of the civilian population. The local partisan forces were rapidly losing popular support, according to her, and becoming hesitant to operate in the occupied zones, and the panic-struck villagers were moving back to the city's slums. The local guerrilla forces avoided skirmishes with the Blue Dragon for a while, and in the following months the latter saw a definite drop in the number of their casualties.[65] In 1969–1970, as partisan forces gathered strength and began to launch daring assaults against enemy fortifications, making them increasingly defensive and vulnerable, civilian killings diminished and became a smaller feature of the war's landscape. Then, the war in the region became a more "normal" war, what military historians call conventional war, fought between two parties of combatants.

In 1972–1973, the vicinity of Ha My became a fierce battlefield for four battalions of the South Vietnamese army and the combined force of a regular North Vietnamese army and local guerilla units. The Saigon forces built an air base on the ruins of Ha My, and this made the place a prime target. The communist forces took over the area on March 28, 1975. Pham Van Thuong, an eminent American War veteran of Ha My and Ha Gia, notes in his handwritten essay on the village history:

> This was a victory of the thirty-year resistance against the aggressors. Our village bred the strongest guerilla force in the region, and it played an important role in connecting the town of Hoi An, the revolutionary base of Vinh Dien, and the city of Da Nang. Our village was a strong base for our revolutionary Communist Party cells and an important support base for our armed forces. The people of our village contributed to the revolutionary campaigns in material and human resources. . . . In the anti-French war, our people fought the enemy fiercely and successfully. Thanks to their heroic efforts, the revolutionary rule in the village developed steadily and controlled the whole area, thereby enabling revolutionary organizations to mushroom across villages despite the enemy's systematic terror and destruction. Rice cultivation,

education, the tax system, cultural production—all developed at the highest speed during this period. The early years of the anti-American struggle were a testing time for us. The village revolutionary movement was devastated, and, at times, it seemed that the struggle was at an end. However, people's hatred of oppression rose even higher. Undergoing the difficult stages of historical development, the villagers fought heroically. We defeated the forces of aggression assembled from all over the world. Their modern weapons failed to break us, although we had only bare hands. Our strong will and belief finally overcame the test and obtained great merit. Our commune [Dien Duong] honors 1,240 martyrs and 332 war invalids. One in every four family units has war martyrs, three in four entertain revolutionary merit. Our commune has been awarded the following honors by the government:

The Title of "Hero of the People's Armed Forces"
The Flag of "Bravely killing the U.S. aggressors"
The Flag of "Destroying the enemy tanks"
The Flag of "Attracting the youth to join the resistance"
5 First-Class Liberation Medals
7 Second-Class Liberation Medals
8 Third-Class Liberation Medals
152 Heroic Fighter [titles]
135 Heroic Mother of Vietnam [titles]
191 Gold Certificate of Honor and 377 Glorious Families with
    Gold Certificates
[The list continues.][66]

Of the massacre survivors displaced from the village, some failed to survive the war. Of those who survived the war, some did not survive its aftermath. When surviving villagers returned to their homeland in 1975–1976, the place was unrecognizable. They were shocked to find that they could now see the ocean, as the pine forest that had divided their land from the sea had been destroyed. Moreover, the land was littered with the remains of weaponry. Before the village would become a relatively safe place in the mid-1980s, the stray ammunition and hidden antipersonnel mines would claim more lives; the mines occasionally still claim victims today. And a number of villagers, young and old, continue to suffer the enduring effects of the defoliants and dioxin that were heavily applied in and around the village by the U.S. war administration in the hope of eliminating potential niches for VC agents and generally exposing the area for surveillance.

Those who returned had to rebuild their homes and farms. The state administration of unified Vietnam encouraged an all-out mobilization for economic reconstruction and, equally, an all-out struggle against backward cultural practices. The family ancestral burial grounds were in ruins, and the remains of war dead had to be cleared from the farmland where they had been hastily buried. The unidentified remains were simply moved elsewhere; the village administration organized the removal of the Monkey Year massacre victims. The many, hopelessly entangled skeletons were taken to the sand dunes or to the distant bamboo forest and buried there. This hasty, collective reburial precluded any accompanying traditional rituals. The reburial of the victims was improper, in the view of many ordinary Ha My villagers, and it has been a source of great shame and pain for the survivors.

MAN AND MACHINE

Ideally, the question of why massacres occurred in certain places and not in others would be put to the military strategy planners. Fierce local resistance created the impression that the inhabitants of the entire area were the enemy. Sniper fire, land mines, and ambushes provoked anger, and the failure to locate the real enemy frustrated the soldiers and administration. For the local peasant militiamen, sniper fire and booby traps "worked," since the enemy convoys usually withdrew if they suffered one or two casualties. Without these interventions, the foreign troops simply kept marching forward. To conduct an ambush near a settlement was a dangerous task, however, for it could provoke retaliatory acts against the villagers. It was unclear to most local peasant militiamen how and when their small attacks, which normally made the enemy retreat, could make them react differently. The massacre in Ha My, however, was not an act of rage but a premeditated act of violence that resulted from rational military planning that had been conducted with a concrete objective. Nor was the massacre an isolated incident caused by a breakdown in the command structure, as the general inquiry concluded about the My Lai incident.[67] The incident was coordinated, planned, and conducted as part of an effective military strategy. Seymour Hersh concludes from his investigation of the My Lai massacre and its aftermath that "My Lai 4 was out of the ordinary, but it was not isolated."[68] The same is true of the massacre in Ha My. Given the many similar and simultaneous incidents of mass death that occurred along the corridor, it is very difficult to explain them away as coincidences.

The historian Marilyn Young writes that, for the American public, My Lai was all the more terrifying because the event seemed inexplicable. James Olson and Randy Roberts have concluded that, in proportion to the brutal simplicity of what happened in My Lai, why it happened is complex and remains a mystery.[69] For the survivors of Ha My, the sudden metamorphosis of young foreign lads into a group of red-eyed monsters on that fateful day in 1968 is still a dark, unintelligible mystery. It is like a knot on the rope of history that becomes tighter the more you pull.

In 1967, the Ha My villagers were evacuated to the refugee camps of Hoi An and the town slums of Da Nang. Life in the refugee camps, where there was simply not enough food or space for them, was unbearable. A family of seven to nine would squeeze into a shack with a cement floor measuring three meters square under an unshaded tin roof. Amid the miserable and unsanitary living conditions, as widespread dysentery and other epidemics killed children and the weak, the village elders petitioned the Vietnamese authorities and the ROK combat authority to permit their return home. The petition letter argued that none of the displaced villagers supported the VC, and it put forward the villagers' love of their native land as the main reason for their desire to return.

It is not clear whether the villagers were granted permission to return to Ha My, but they returned there at the end of December 1967. For the next three weeks, foreign soldiers from the fortification on the sand dune between the village and the sea assisted the resettling villagers with food and building materials. In return, village women offered the soldiers baskets of green chillies and other local produce. When a search-and-destroy mission set fire to a thatched roof, some soldiers from the base came around to help put out the fire. The image of two foreign soldiers, one with a cigarette lighter and the other with a bucket of water, arguing with each other in their foreign tongue, remains one of the most cherished war memories in Ha My. When the bucket-holding man accidentally threw the water onto the Zippo-holding man and the bucket onto the burning house, people remember that everyone laughed, even the desperate home-owner. These fragmented memories of small gifts being exchanged and the help in extinguishing the fire have made some villagers unable to accept the hypothesis that the troops who carried out the atrocity were the same troops who had helped them before the massacre. They believe there was a change in troops at the base immediately before the massacre, or that the soldiers from the base did not participate in ransacking the village on that day. There is no hard evidence to support this belief, apart from the survivors' testimony that the killers were complete strangers. But their belief is resolute.

The petition's statement that there were no VC supporters in the Ha My village was probably not true. Likely, a network of relationships connected the villagers across the visible "normal" village life and the hidden, underground revolutionary activities. However, this was a network of bone and flesh; and wartime kinship, no matter how unconventional it might have been forced to become during wartime, does not collapse to the political-military classification of un-uniformed combatants and the fantastical definition of the generic, faceless enemy.[70] Civilians can assist and harbor combatants as civilians. They can do so out of coercion or out of sympathy or out of family and communal obligation. That does not validate the idealized image of a people's war—"People are the water, and our army the fish"—nor does it justify the slogan of village pacification, "Pump out the water and catch the fish." The presence of a lawful target within a defined space does not justify the definition of the entire space as an extension of that specific target. The act of wantonly destroying the space on the basis of that unlawful definition is criminal. It is against nature as well as law to pump out the water in order to catch the fish.

The victims of the massacre were clearly and categorically unarmed civilian noncombatants. First, they tolerated the Vietcong in their village, if there really were any, because these VC activists belonged to their community. Second, if in fact they hid and supported these activists, they did so out of respect for the values and customs of communal life and not necessarily in following the fantastical doctrine of the people's war. Even in the Cold War's arid environment of total destruction, there dwelt moral realities of human kinship. At the heart of the crime against humanity, if it has a heart, lurks the insanity of taking the enemy's fantastical propaganda as reality and making war on the basis of a profoundly superstitious belief in that fantasy. As Olson and Roberts write, "As in all wars, soldiers learned from other soldiers, and myths, rumours, oft-repeated tales, and superstitions became firmly held and scientifically proven axioms. The most common belief was that any Vietnamese man, woman, or child might be a Vietcong operative."[71]

The Ha My survivors believe that the killers were strangers. This belief does not explain why the crime took place, but it does explain at least how the crime could have been prevented. The belief assumes that, even in an extreme condition of total war, you can distinguish the face of a killer from the face of a foreign soldier. If the Vietnamese could do it, why not the foreigners? Why couldn't they distinguish the face of their foe from the face of a toddler? When a soldier from Charlie Company describes his so-called mental process of turning civilians into the enemy—"Who is the enemy? How can you distinguish between the civilians and the non-civilians? . . . The good or the bad? All of them look the same"—what does he mean? If an armed, educated professional soldier cannot distinguish the same from the different in the way that a village schoolgirl can, what can we say about the modern army?[72]

Evidence suggests that locally based troops did harm the local civilians. Evidence indicates that locally based troops refrained from harming the local civilians.[73] There was a coordinated movement of troops across villages and districts during and after the 1968 Tet Offensive.[74] A locally based troop relegated the task of clearing the immediate area to a collateral unit in a neighbouring commune or district. In this system of exchange, the same soldier could set fire to a house in one place and help rescue a similar-looking house on fire in another place. I believe that many soldiers of the Vietnam War suffered from being the pendulum in the war's cold clockwork, and that they struggled with the memory of that cruel oscillation in their postwar lives.[75] From a mechanical point of view, the pendulum—that is, the soldier—was only a functional piece of a much more complex machine. It had its own dynamics, but it could not control its movement, and it had to keep swinging between two extreme points until the machine ran out of power. The survivors of Ha My seem to refuse to see this mechanistic truism. "Yes, they were the same people," the old partisan leader said; "we knew that." "No, they were not the same people," a village elder protested; "you were not there. You didn't see them. I saw them." The elder refused to efface the memory of the soldier with the water bucket, to let this positive memory be corrupted by the bright shining movement of a faceless robotic soldier's single oscillating identity. If this is a state of denial, it is not a denial of truth but a refusal to reduce humanity to truth.[76]

EIGHTY OR TWENTY PERCENT?

In 1974 James Trullinger, a former employee of the U.S. Agency for International Development in Vietnam, conducted a unique project of empirical research on wartime village life, in My Thuy Phuong, seven miles southwest of Hue. He stayed in this village until the very end of the war, in March 1975. Among the many valuable facts he gathered about the war on the village level were those concerning the 1968 Tet Offensive: "For the estimated 5 percent of the people who were Government supporters, Tet of 1968 intensified hatred of the [National Liberation] Front, and for some planted seeds of doubt concerning American dependability as an ally. The 10 to 15 percent who were politically uncommitted remained so, but were deeply impressed by the Front's strength. And My Thuy Phuong's Front supporters, an estimated 80 to 85 percent of the people, were left with proud memories of the boldest strikes yet against the Government and its ally."[77]

"Eighty percent VC" is indeed how some Vietnamese villagers, even today, present the wartime reality of their village. I heard this from two old resistance war veterans in Ha My in 1995, and then heard it again from two survivors in Khe Thuan subhamlet (in My Lai) a few years later. "The village was strong at that time. Eighty percent VC, at least," said the man in My Lai. If 80 percent of the village population was VC, and 80 percent of the village population was massacred in the same year, this makes at least 60 percent of the victims VC. In both instances, however, my informants were invoking the idea of "80 percent VC" without reference to their own community. The informant in Khe Thuan was describing what he knew about Khe Thuan's neighboring communities, Khe Dong and Khe Thuong. The aged veteran in Ha My was saying "80 percent VC" with regard to Ha My's neighboring village Ha Gia, and this he did in contrast to Ha My, where only 20 percent of the population at most was VC, according to him. I asked some residents in Khe Thuong hamlet about the place's alleged "80 percent VC" historical identity. They agreed with people in Khe Thuan that the Americans mistook the non-VC Tu Cung (My Lai 4)—in which Khe Thuan and Khe Thuong are subunits—for the VC-strong area of Truong Diep (My Lai 3). This understanding, dominant among the people of My Lai, makes the massacre of My Lai doubly tragic, for the violence fell upon the wrong place. However, my informants in Khe Thuong strongly contested the idea that their community had been a VC stronghold during the time of the massacre. One of them was particularly angry and said, "That is pure nonsense. In my village there was no VC. In theirs they know very well that they were all VC at that time." His wife reminded him of his paternal uncle, from the same hamlet, who was a local partisan fighter. Turning his face angrily toward her, he said, "OK. Maybe 80 percent for them and 20 for us. Maybe, but not the other way around, absolutely not."

A former village chief of Ha My argued that there was not a single revolutionary activist among the victims of the 1968 massacre—they were all simple villagers, he said. Since 1995, when we first met, he has told me numerous stories that contradict his initial argument. He was well aware of the history of revolutionary activism of Ha My, in fact, more aware than most other former veterans. He introduced me to the village guerrilla fighter who underwent the unimaginable experience of enduring the staccato noise of the machine guns and the screams of the villagers from his underground hideout during the two hours of the Ha My massacre. This man knew that his wife and children, as well as his parents and grandparents, were among the victims. The village chief was proud, as were other village leaders, of the Hero Village title awarded to Ha My (and Ha Quang and Ha Gia) in 1989, and at public gatherings he used to speak of the village's long, exceptional contribution to the nation's history. He knew the names of the Monkey Year massacre victims who earned titles of revolutionary honor, and he was a close relative of some of the village civilian activists who perished in the massacre. He helped to write the local history of the women's struggle, in which the women of Ha My in particular appear to have played an exceptional role, and he collected historical facts about Ha My's distinguished place in the history of the Communist Party's organizational activity in the region. Why he asserted that there were "no VC among the victims" was a mystery to me.

Looking back, however, it appears that what the former village chief said was not a falsification of historical fact. The political identity of wartime Ha My depended partly on what the identification was for. Had I been an investigator from the provincial Department of Information and Culture dispatched to the village to collect data for a government publication on the local history of revolutionary struggle, the elder's description might have been entirely different. In fact, the local history project conducted in Ha My and elsewhere in 1999–2000 focused on the village's role in the wartime political-military campaigns, and it affirmed that many of the cited heroes of the anti-French campaigns were included in the list of victims of the Monkey Year tragedy.[78] In this context, the description "80 percent VC" can easily shift to become a statement addressing the collective historical identity of the self rather than others.

The former village chief is himself a veteran of the revolutionary war and has close relatives who worked as part-time peasant fighters within the village. His family provided these village fighters with food and shelter in difficult times; the fighters cultivated the land and helped build shelters in more peaceful times. These peasant men moved to the underground tunnel (or the village pond) when the situation was intense, but ate with their wives and children and lived lives that appeared normal on quiet days. This family had a neighbor who had been a laborer-soldier for the French army. He remained "neutral" throughout the war. The village communist cell did not trust him; he was too old for the Saigon army. He worked in the rice field and on the sweet potato farms on quiet days and ran away to the bush whenever the Saigon or allied forces came to the village. His family paid "tax" to the resistance war committee, just like many other village households at the time, and helped the partisan forces with food and labor. Most villagers did so, and it seemed natural to him that he should do it too. This man's neighbor had five children, all too young to join the army on either side, and her late husband had been an official in the South Vietnamese administration. She couldn't contribute much to the communist side, because she was very poor, and she hoped to evacuate to a city if possible. But she did help other villagers cultivate the communal land. The harvest from this land was shipped to the western mountain regions to feed the young volunteers from the north who were camped in the forest. Another neighboring family, the Tran family, were devout members of the local Cao Dai temple. Some of them had moved to the town of Hoi An and, unlike other villagers, did not return to the village in 1967 but managed to settle outside the refugee camps, partly with the assistance of friends in the religious sect. The town recruited the husband as an absentee village chief of Ha Gia and trusted him to report to the authorities the identities of VC-supporting villagers. It is unclear how sincerely he performed his duty during this time.[79] However, he regularly relayed information about the movements of Saigon and allied troops to his relatives who remained in the village. On at least two occasions, this information proved vital in saving human lives.

In this complex situation of war on a village level, "80 percent VC" and "20 percent VC" were indeed both realistic estimates. The truth of this illogical data and the collapse of the apparently enormous difference between two quantitative estimates are central to an understanding of the historical reality of the war in the village. The truth of 80 or 20 percent, and "No VC" or "All VC," for that matter, depended on whom the information was addressed to. The former village chief of An Bang hamlet succeeded in saving its two hundred villagers from the imminent threat of mass death by swearing to the foreign officer that there was not a single VC or VC supporter there. Shortly afterward, his sister joined a group of villagers gathered to welcome a delegation of party officials from the provincial authority. The man from the province asked the village women, "Are you all diligent workers for the glorious victory of our revolutionary war?" The village women said, in one voice, "Yes, Uncle, all of us. Yes, Uncle, our whole village."[80]

The identity of a community shifted between two opposite ends of the political spectrum depending on the situation and depending on the identity of the force that intended to classify it. Self-identity in this context oscillated across the frontier of Cold War and communicated with both regimes. It shifted from one to the other side of the frontier as the frontier itself moved between night and day and from season to season. The brutal force of bipolar politics influenced subjective identity and imposed upon it the cruel zero-sum theory. While the bifurcating system pursued the logic of zero-sum, people responded with the opposite logic of being both none and all. Whereas the system insisted on the homogeneity of space and the immutability of identity, the lived reality of the Cold War was "contradictory space" or "dialectical space,"[81] and identity in this reality was not an unchanging idem but a mutative entity whose transformability offered the only possibility for the preservation of life.

The village men, who fought in the fields of village war, oscillated between displacement from and placement in their native land. Apart from the few full-time guerrilla fighters who were removed entirely from the obligation of cultivation, most of these peasant fighters were also responsible for agricultural production and only occasionally mobilized to participate in a large battle beyond the boundary of their village. When the peasant fighters shook hands with the uniformed regular soldiers, endured the long tedious speeches by the political officers, and then ran swiftly home on moonless nights, it is not clear whether they were still soldiers. Back in their village, they received directives from the VC liaison, gathered in twos or threes to discuss the order, and shared their wisdom and experience—about an offense against the local military installation, about a particularly unsympathetic village chief, and about installation of booby traps designed to stymie search-and-destroy missions. The successful installation of a box of explosives within the enemy's Con Ninh base by three Ha My village partisan fighters is well known in the area. When they installed it, they were clearly combatants and had the spirit of combatants. At certain times, they farmed as ordinary villagers, and in less peaceful times, they took the water bucket and the carbine and hid in the underground shelter or in the old bomb crater filled with rainwater. When these fighters transformed back to farmers, it is not at all clear whether they were still combatants and considered themselves as such. When they hid underground, collected the food bundle, removed the camouflage of buffalo refuse, and ate the sticky rice brought from home, it is clear that they were not eating like other villagers and that they were not really ordinary villagers. However, when they finished the meal, lay down on the mat, and began to think about the new ducklings, the abdominal problems of the buffalo, and watering the vegetable plot—it is again unclear whether we can easily call them combatants of a war. These people were Vietcong fighters, and they were not. They were ordinary farmers and civilians, and they were not. Their identity shifted as they themselves shifted from the battlefield to village life and back to another battlefield again and again. They did not necessarily carry their village identity to the battlefield, and their fighter identity was not always carried to their deceptively quiet village social life. They were both soldiers and peasants, yet they could also be neither.

When a young village woman of Ha Gia was being dragged away by ROK soldiers in the dry season of 1967, she begged the soldiers to stop, saying, "No VC. No VC." The soldiers had found a carbine behind a false wall in her house. When her husband found the courage to come to the army base to make a plea for his wife, he said to the guardsman, "No VC. No VC." When he said it, it is possible that he really meant it. It is possible that the man was not a VC when he emerged from underground the previous morning and enjoyed the rare treat of a siesta in his own bed in his own home. It is possible that he was no longer a faithful worker for glorious victory when he was coaxed out of the suffocating underground shelter to spend the afternoon with his wife. When he left home to check the bamboo fish trap in the river, and his wife was gathering the rice-flour pastry left to dry on a mat, it is possible that neither of them had anything to do with either side of the war, at least for that sun-drenched afternoon. The old Viet Minh activists in Ha My and My Lai stayed put in the village, worked on the rice paddy, and gave rice to the village guerillas. It is possible that they did so as village elders, not necessarily because they remembered the doctrine of "Tinh quan dan nhu ca voi nuoc" (People are the water, and our army the fish). None of these old French War veterans, apart from a few exceptional cases, were recognized as war martyrs by the government after the war, nor were they considered revolutionaries by the villagers before the massacre. In village life, it is possible that people paid tax to the revolutionary authorities because they knew that peasants had paid tax for as long as they had existed. And it is also possible that people hid weapons more in fear of the mortal consequence of not doing so than because of any fervent commitment to the revolutionary war dictum "Each inhabitant [is] a soldier, each village a fortress."

The paid, uniformed, full-time, professional soldiers did not accept the fact that people could fight without a uniform, as a villager rather than a soldier. They did not understand the fact that, when these people fought, many of them fought simply to survive rather than to win. Because soldiers didn't understand this complexity, they could have seen the woman clearing the bed, where her VC husband slept, as VC, her children breaking coconut shells at the back of the house as VC, their house and their chickens and buffalos as VC, the tombs of their ancestors and the temple they worshipped as VC, and the entire world they lived in and relied on as entirely VC. Perhaps the soldiers couldn't see otherwise, since for them the meat they ate, the house that sheltered them, the temple they worshipped, and the entire world they belonged to belonged to one single inseparable complex—the army.

The cruel history of the Cold War is not a thing of the past in the villages that survived the war. The historical identity of the village still fluctuates in the violent memory of night and day, and between the hero and victim identities that together perpetuate this irreconcilable contradiction. In this double historical memory, Ha My and My Lai were both VC and "No VC" villages. Each harbored 80 percent *cach mang* (revolutionaries) and 20 percent Vietcong subversives. Pride and stigma, and honor and terror, tail one another and keep alive the magical realism in which a village is both VC and "No VC." Likewise, the collective identity of the victims of the village massacres remains unclassifiable. The victims were "simple villagers," and they were not. They were "heroic defenders of the native land," and they were not.

Just as their political identity could not be settled within the Cold War's zero-sum coherence, their moral identity continued to be unsettling in the domain of family ritual remembrance. A generation after the massacre, beginning in the early 1990s, the reburial of the improperly buried victims of war became one of the main preoccupations in Ha My and My Lai. In a mass exodus of the war dead to new places, the memory of mass death was revitalized too, and people invented creative new ways to deal with the grief of unjust death.

CHAPTER 3

A Generation Afterward

In Vietnam, household death-commemoration rites are a rich store of historical evidence. Numerous incidents from past wars are faithfully recorded in these rites, even though the archives and monuments may carry no trace of these incidents. On several occasions, including in the late 1980s and again in the late 1990s, village administrations in the provinces of Quang Nam and Quang Ngai collaborated with researchers from the provincial Communist Party on a survey of wartime casualties. They uncovered many previously unknown incidents, but these surveys left out as many cases as they revealed. People tended to report only the incidents of war death that they considered to be worth reporting or those they believed the authorities were interested in. Moreover, many incidents of routine killing, particularly those from the time of the French War, are unknown even to villagers themselves unless they lived in the immediate vicinity of the specific sites where these incidents occurred. However, if victims of war incidents left behind surviving descendants, the victims' identities and histories are very likely recorded in household death anniversary rites. Commemoration in Vietnamese domestic ancestral rites typically goes back three generations, although exceptions do exist. This custom of *cung gio* has resulted in the current situation, in which the history of violence of the last century that is kept in these private, decentralized sites of memory is far more comprehensive than in any other public records.

The domestic ritual calendars in places like My Lai and Ha My often are reducible to little more than a history of war, and they offer a panoramic view of the fluctuating production of violent death in past generations. The day before the twenty-fourth day of the first lunar month was evidently a special day in Ha My. Many families held death anniversary ceremonies on this day, and they did so simultaneously. Household commemoration activities on this occasion were not substantially different from death-day ceremonies prepared later in the year. Beyond the boundary of the household, however, the vista of commemoration on this day was clearly unusual. In Xom Tay, a subhamlet of Ha My, more than half the community's fifty households each laid out a magnificent table of food offerings, and the smoke from their incense burners practically enveloped the entire village. The atmosphere was festive on this day in which the Monkey Year massacre was commemorated. It was, as the villagers often joked, as if people were celebrating a happy day like the Tet, or Lunar New Year. The village was bustling with women returning from the market and preparing food, children hopping from house to house to collect candy, men crisscrossing the village on their way to visit friends and relatives, and a number of visitors from neighboring villages hoping to join the feasts.

The event was both particular and universal. The memorial was a specific event for each individual household, as in any other death anniversary, yet it had the appearance of a universal event. This was not exactly a collective remembrance or an enactment of collective memory of the sort that Maurice Halbwachs describes as an enduring "social framework" and a shared "perspective of the group."[1] Instead, the event was constituted by many separate and independent events taking place simultaneously. This multiple, simultaneous performance of commemoration is alien to the Vietnamese tradition of domestic death commemoration.

The French historian Pierre Nora argues that modern memory is fundamentally archival and monumental. On what he calls "archival memory," he writes, "Modern memory is, above all, archival. It relies entirely on the materiality of the trace, the immediacy of the recording, the visibility of the image."[2] The remembrance of death invoked in Ha My's ritualized, informal practices may not be an example of modern memory according to this definition and in the sense of not being incorporated into monumental and archival forms. However, an alternative definition of modern memory proposed by Paul Fussell and other like-minded historians of the First World War, may apply to it.[3] These scholars relate the rise of modern memory to the experience of mass grieving, and they relate the rise of "modern time" to "the simultaneity of multiple distant events that were shared by hundreds of thousands of men in battle and witnessed by the civilian population who attempted to draw those events together into a single coherent pattern."[4] In Ha My and My Lai, the anniversary of the village massacre enacts a temporal rupture within which separate households unite in practice as they prepare independent events. The preparation of independent events follows the tradition of *cung gio;* the unity in the practice goes beyond it.

Ritual death remembrance is an important source of historical fact, but it has one notable shortcoming when standing in for proper archival memory. Death in ritual remembrance tends to abandon its chronological identity. If I ask a villager about her ancestor who fell victim to a French village pacification mission in the 1940s, she will most likely tell me the precise day in the lunar calendar on which her family observes the anniversary of that particular ancestor's death. If I remind her that what I actually want to know is the person's year of death, however, she may have to make a special effort, and may even require assistance from other villagers, before she can remember the exact date. The historical circumstances of an ancestral death are normally well known to the descendants; the ancestor's precise moment of death is respectfully accounted for in the family social life. But this is not the case with the chronological identity of death. Ritual memories, Paul Connerton notes, "juxtapose with the structure of profane time a further structure, one qualitatively distinct from the former and irreducible to it."[5] Chronological order is at odds with Vietnamese ritual memory, and this may be because the two belong to different temporal structures, linear or cyclical. However, there is more to chronological amnesia in ritual remembrance than a question of temporal structures. The amnesia is an aspect of the living presence of the dead in the intimacy of domestic life.

Remembrance of death in the Vietnamese household not only looks to the past but also makes death an event for the future. The history of death is understood genealogically within a Vietnamese family, in the succession of generations. In ritual, however, the dead are invited to socialize with the living, and this sociability makes a death of the past an event for tomorrow. The death anniversary rite is usually performed on the day before the actual death day in the lunar calendar. The idea is that the rite prepared for ancestors should celebrate the actual living presence of the deceased, rather than their memory, as Le Van Dinh points out, "as if they were alive."[6] Commemoration is "the relationship between memory and identity," and, concerning death, it refers to the acts of honoring the beings of the past by enacting and reaffirming the importance of their memory for the identity of those who perform the act.[7] The dead, in this system, are expected to take part in the ritualized present by asserting their own particular historical vitality, expressing their aspirations and grievances, eating and talking together with the living, and sharing their sorrows and joy. Vietnamese popular culture emphasizes the supreme importance of remembering the dead, but its emphasis is on the dead person's *living* presence rather than the memory of this person.[8]

This social intimacy between the living and the dead in fact underpins the strength of domestic commemorative practices as a site of memory, something that the archival and monumental memories do not do. Around the seventeenth day of the second lunar month, the residents of My Lai prepared their private death anniversary rites for the victims of the 1968 massacre, but they also were expected to attend the official public ceremony prepared by the provincial Department of Information and Culture. This official ceremony is usually held in the landscaped park of the museum built on one of the massacre sites. The museum maintains several monuments dedicated to the victims and an archive of press material collected from around the world.[9] Because high-ranking cadres and the foreign press were to attend, the village officials were eager to have present as many survivors and villagers as possible. Most residents of My Lai were unenthusiastic about the official event and many sent schoolchildren as family delegates. Aware of this reluctance, the village administration put pressure on the villagers through kinship ties or sometimes by promising small favors. According to one relative of victims and former partisan fighter to whom I spoke about the issue, his lack of interest in the official memorial service was easily explained. The museum did not allow him to offer food and votive objects to his dead relative within its premises. One of his several relatives who had gathered in his house for a death-day anniversary rite added that it was embarrassing at best and offensive at worst to invite the dead for a get-together with the living without sharing food and intimate conversation.[10]

In the year 2000, a former village chief of Ha My concluded his speech with the following remarks, which I recorded from his written copy of the speech:

Today we gather here in the spirit of *ly huong bat ly to* [separate from the land but inseparable from the spirit of the land]. Everyone living afar from this land is thinking of the land that keeps the ancestors and the ancestral temples. A generation of thirty-two years has passed since the terrible destruction of our village. Like the green plants that grow on an abandoned grave, the village survived its death [destruction]. . . . After a generation of separation, the villagers have the opportunity today to eat together, to talk, and to share our sorrow and joy. Gratitude to those who traveled a long distance to join us. Gratitude to the dead who grant us, the living, this joy of being together.

Throughout the 1990s, there were many occasions in My Lai and Ha My when people gathered to eat and talk together, and to share their sorrow and joy, a generation after the war. This was a new phenomenon that the elders said they had not seen in their lifetime. The yearly reopening ceremony of the village communal house, when the former village chief read the above speech, was one of these occasions, but there were many more gatherings as well—for immediate families, extended families, lineage groups, the entire village, and even the entire historical population of the village across many generations. These reunions were sometimes held among the people who survived the war, and sometimes for those who did not; sometimes they were held for strengthening family feelings between the two historical groups, and sometimes primarily to appease the dead. People celebrated the renovation of tombs when the bodies of a group of war-dead relatives joined their long-dead ancestors. A large number of living relatives from distant places gathered together to establish a kind of "tomb group" to coordinate their efforts to renovate family ancestral graves, and they assembled again when their efforts came to fruition.[11] These events ended the long separation of survivors who had not seen each other since the war, but they were not meant only for that. The principal objective of the reunions was to end the long separation of the people buried in different sites, and those who came to renovate the tombs were clearly aware that they had gathered to help the dead eat together, talk, and share their sorrow and joy.

The end of a generation of separation took many forms, involved many people, and opened up a new perspective on reality. Above all, it meant the restoration of the right to approach the life-world as an encompassing reality that includes afterlife as well as life, and the right to move freely between the vantage point of life and the perspective of, in the words of Paul Ricoeur, "oneself as another." Ricoeur notes that "the selfhood of oneself implies otherness to such an intimate degree that one cannot be thought of without the other, that instead one passes into the other, as we might say in Hegelian terms."[12] Ricoeur develops the issue of agency implied in this expression of self-identity as a critique of the sovereign, immutable selfhood assumed in the mainstream tradition of Western philosophy and also as a way to reconfigure selfhood alternatively as a mutative, communicative identity. Jürgen Habermas writes in a related perspective that, in communicative action, "ego stands within an interpersonal relationship that allows him to relate to himself as a participant in an interaction from the perspective of alter."[13] This hermeneutical understanding of human action, in which the self appears to be "historical through and through," is helpful for determining how the dead generations from the past and the living generation become partners in social action.[14] The reburial movement of Ha My and My Lai, in my opinion, consists of a particular moral and esthetic principle of life manifesting in tangible forms—the idea that the community needs to modernize the afterlife, the life of past generations and that of the tragic war dead in particular, in order for the living members of the community to demonstratively improve their own life conditions.

Léopold Cadière claims that people in Vietnam operate in two worlds—the invisible (supernatural) world and the visible (natural) world.[15] A rising parallelism exists in the spatiality of domestic life between these two worlds of *am duong*.[16] The Ha My villagers began to improve their domestic environment, and they started by renovating the dwelling places of their dead relatives. The modernization of village life was initiated in both cosmological terrains, and the vision of a prosperous future materialized first in the place of the dead.[17] This reciprocal mode of demonstrating modernity made the past generation an increasingly active agent for the process of modernization.

TOMB RENOVATION

In the beginning of the 1990s, there were many family reunions in Ha My, and they were often emotionally intense occasions. During this period, the villagers gathered resources from a close circle of relatives and collaborated to remove the remains of their kinsmen from what they saw as improper graves. In most cases, the reburials concerned the unmarked, weather-beaten graves of the war dead. Those buried in the old, shallow graves in the flood zone were among the first to be moved. Some of these old graves held bodies that had already been moved once or twice. Having been interred hastily during the war, the corpses were moved outside the village to allow more space for cultivation or habitation immediately after the war. In 1975–1976, few of the many corpses had been identified. Often the only person who knew the identity of a corpse could not be found. The site of shallow graves, on which the survivors of the massacre had left a mark before evacuating the ruined village, had become a gigantic bomb crater filled with poisonous water. Young postwar volunteers from Da Nang and elsewhere had shown no respect for the excavated bones when they helped to clear stray ammunition and land mines from the farm fields. The state hierarchy in postwar Vietnam was determined to construct a new national culture that was "healthy" and "optimistic," one that inspired a "love of labor."[18] In line with this, the new postwar village administration had a strong commitment to economic reconstruction, and their dedication permitted little allowance for villagers still preoccupied with the remains of war, rather than with the prospect of a new life.

The state's approach to the remains of the war dead did not reflect a total absence of interest so much as a selective interest. After the war's end in 1975, the party and government took a keen interest in mobilizing the war's history for the purpose of incorporating the liberated regions in the southern half of the country. The commemoration of heroic war dead became a key part of this process of nation building. The bodies of the fallen heroes, and the war cemeteries that kept these bodies, became a principal site of national memory of the unified struggle against a foreign power.[19]

The Communist Party initiated a sustained body-finding campaign and encouraged citizens to take part in the sacred mission of recovering the remains of war heroes. The Vietnamese military sent former combatants and volunteers on body-recovering missions in the remote highlands. A large number of bodies were recovered when villagers returned to their war-torn villages and began to clear the rice paddies and rebuild houses. In the 1970s, it was an important civic obligation to inform the authorities if one discovered the remains of a revolutionary soldier. The villagers were given some basic instruction in how to single out the bones of a hero from others, and how to identify the bones of officers of the People's Army as opposed to those of the village guerilla fighters.[20] The bones that successfully passed the screening procedure were returned to the village of origin and reburied at the village's state war martyr cemetery. It was a central element of postwar body politics to place the heroic dead at the center of postwar village life and to promote civil interest in preserving their memory. In some northern provinces, the officials instituted a visit to the war hero monument as part of the wedding ceremony.[21]

Katherine Verdery writes that, although the political cults of the dead have "broad similarity internationally, their political meanings are more localized. The form may seem constant, yet each case has its own uniqueness."[22] In an important way, the official war commemoration in Vietnam was an imposition of a locally specific understanding of war upon other variant historical realities. Philip Taylor, in assessing recent social development in southern Vietnam, emphasizes that the northern and the southern regions had different economic histories and different orientations to commerce.[23] We must add to the regional variance another crucial historical dimension.

For the American public, death in the Vietnam War mainly meant the death of American soldiers. For northern Vietnam, death in this war primarily meant the sacrifice of its volunteer soldiers. For southern and central Vietnam, death in this American War could be the death of anyone. For northern Vietnam, the war was a "conventional" war with a relatively clear division of labor between the civilians, who participated in the war economy at home, and the soldiers who left home for distant battlefields. The war in southern and central Vietnam, however, was highly unconventional. It eliminated the division between combatants and noncombatants, as well as that between home and battlefield. For southern Vietnam, the conflict was a so-called people's war that idealized a total integration of civilians with soldiers within practical networks. In this total war, unarmed villagers had to fight as hard as any armed combatants, although many of them fought in order to survive the war rather than necessarily to win it.

This divergent historical experience of war between regions was not accounted for by the state-instituted war commemoration, which focused on the bodies of fallen soldiers, returning them to their homeland and defining their burial places as the embodiment of "revolutionary sentiment." In the northern region of Vietnam, this strategy made sense as it meant that the state, having mobilized the citizens for an honorable cause, returned their remains to the local communities after the war was over and collaborated with the latter in commemorating their sacrifice. The extension of this strategy to the liberated region below the seventeenth parallel, however, was highly problematic. In the southern and central regions, the return of village heroes to their home was not merely a celebratory event. As in Sophocles's epic tragedy of Antigone, which inspired Hegel in developing his philosophy of the modern state, many individuals and families in these regions were torn between the familial obligation to attend to the memory of the war dead related by kinship, and the political obligation not to do so in the case of those who had fought against the revolutionary state. Praised by Hegel as the "noblest figure that ever appeared on earth," Antigone is forced to choose between the obligation to bury her war-killed brother according to "divine law" and the reality of "human law," which prohibits her from burying an enemy of the state.[24] The people's-war version of Antigone had an added tragic dimension. While the remains of revolutionary martyrs were collected from nearby and remote battlefields and brought to the center of the village, the bones of ordinary villagers were being moved from the prospective paddies to the peripheral sandy wastelands. The concentration of heroic war dead at the center of the community coincided with the marginalization of village dead, and the Vietnamese cemetery architects followed the example of the north by designing the cemetery of war martyrs to be a place where the prosperous future is impregnated (see chapter 7).

It was illogical to unite civilians and the military in wartime and then divide them when memorializing the war. In the south, not only were the memorials fundamentally flawed in their accounts of historical reality, but they also complicated local efforts to come to terms with the reality. One result of imposing a standardized, formal scheme of war commemoration on southern communities was, somewhat ironically, a proliferation of the memorials for war heroes and informal practices of worship related to these places. The villagers incorporated the official monuments to heroic death into their domestic and public spaces, but they also built their own, unofficial cenotaphs and shrines. Unlike the state war monuments, these unofficial sites of hero worship were diverse in form and were used in actuality for remembering a wide spectrum of war deaths (see chapter 5).

The marginalized, informal remembrance of war dead benefited from the economic reform and political liberalization initiated in late 1980s. The economic reform program revitalized family-based agricultural and commercial activities, and it was accompanied by a growing tolerance for traditional religious practices. According to Hy Van Luong, political liberalization permitted the revival of family ancestral worship, through which the revitalized economic unit expressed its moral unity and developed practical kinship networks.[25]

From 1993 to 1998, when the reburial and tomb renovation movement was strongest in Quang Nam province, old corpses were moving in all directions. They moved from flood areas to hillsides, from private gardens to newly prepared lineage-owned burial plots, and from old agricultural cooperatives to the expensive private cemeteries of Buddhist temples. Some corpses left state war martyr cemeteries to join their kinsmen in recently purchased family plots in public cemeteries. The martyr cemeteries had to deal not only with occasional departures but also with a growing number of arrivals, which resulted from the upsurge in construction and road building. Some of the newly discovered skeletons of war martyrs took the places of comrades who had left for family grave-yards. In one case I encountered near Da Nang, two corpses practically swapped places. A lineage group purchased a plot of land from the district and had this place prepared for a family graveyard. Construction workers found the remains of an unknown soldier with his North Vietnamese army uniform relatively intact but no personal identification. After some negotiation with the district officials in charge of war martyrs and invalids, the family moved their relative from the martyr cemetery to the family graveyard. At the same time, they had the remains of the unknown soldier transported from their graveyard site to the war martyr cemetery. Thanks to the unknown soldier who took the place of their relative, the family told me, the reburial process had been easier because it required less paperwork.

The movement of corpses during this period was impressive in scale. The phenomenon appeared chaotic initially, but slowly a pattern emerged. The reburial movement of the 1990s aimed to concentrate the dispersed bodies in a new, common location under the proprietorship of a kin group. Just as the labor force was moving from the impoverished state sector to the revitalized private sector, so the corpses moved from the neglected margins of the centralized command economy to the center of the new private ritual economy. Poor families tended to enlarge an existing tomb site and turn it into a common family burial ground; finan-cially able families preferred to purchase a few hundred square meters in the public cemetery or an allotment on the premises of a Buddhist pagoda. More ambitious families turned their new family-owned burial grounds in public cemeteries into colorful theme parks boasting engrav-ings of phoenixes and twin dragons, and this sumptuous look became increasingly popular. Soon the public cemetery became a public place in name only, having been divided into many private burial plots, and looked like a gigantic imperial palace of the dead. Families revived the prewar house-style tomb structure consisting of a roof, columns, and a two-tier foundation. They also revived the complex spatial order of se-niority and the spatially demonstrated distinction between peaceful "death at home" and violent "death in the street."

My Lai joined in the general wave of corpse moving somewhat later than Ha My, moving hundreds of graves from the mid-1990s onward. In 1996, two brothers who lived in the hamlet of Xuan Duong, alongside the river My Khe, pooled their savings to renovate their mother's grave. They removed the fragmented bones from the old shallow burial site—

which was damp and suffering from buffalo traffic—and put them in a small clay coffin, bringing the coffin to a south-facing dry spot on a small hill overlooking the shrimp-breeding farms. Before the removal, the younger brother and a former guerilla fighter performed coin magic, called *jin jang,* at his mother's old unmarked grave in order to solicit her opinion about the move. Before flipping the coins, he told me, he had made this prayer:

> Mother, today I came to inform you that the eleventh day of the next month is a good day for you to move. Ong Minh read the book and told us so. It's been thirty years since you came to this place. You died without me knowing about what was happening to you. I was too busy with my army work, brother was away, and the world was so violent at the time. Please forgive us that we had to lay you here without a coffin, without funeral clothes. And please understand that your children were so poor that they couldn't offer you a better place. This place was flooded last year and the year before. You'd better abandon this place if you wish to live a peaceful life in all seasons. Ong Son offered you a piece of land above his peanut farm. Next year we will bring our sisters next to you if you move now. Will you agree to move on the eleventh day of the next month?

His mother's response to the removal plan, as revealed by the two old brass coins, was affirmative. The night after this communication, the man's wife dreamt about her mother-in-law. In her dream, a woman of middle age was carrying a bamboo basket. She lay down the basket in front of two small girls sitting on a dusty roadside. The three of them opened the cover, and there they saw white silk clothes, new shoes, and hats. They marveled at the clothes, took off their dirty and tattered pajamas, changed into the bright, shiny dresses, and started marching in a single file across the irrigation ditch. The girls were walking some distance behind the woman, and all three were moving toward what looked like Ong Son's peanut farm. A year after their mother's reburial, the brothers reburied near her the remains of their two siblings, aged ten and twelve at the time of the massacre, and thereby fulfilled their promise.

UNTIMELY DEATH

The deaths of children caused great difficulty in the Confucian ritual order and were traditionally unassimilated in the public spaces of commemoration—both the cemetery and the ancestral shrine. In Chinese Confucian tradition, for instance, it is argued that individuals should participate in a rite only if it concerns a person to whom they owe ritual obligation.[26] Thus the reburial of child victims by their surviving parents was not an easily accepted practice. The villagers of My Lai and Ha My—some more than others—were conscious of the fact that ritual order in ancestor worship discouraged downward commemoration. Although this rule did not prevent survivors from commemorating their war-killed children on a regular basis, it did contribute to making such practice strictly private.

Vietnam's eclectic religious tradition—or what some scholars call "unsystematic system of beliefs"[27]—has other ways to absorb untimely and genealogically disorderly death. The names and identities of dead children may be brought to a Buddhist pagoda, a Taoist temple, or the spirit shrine of a local medium. These institutions do not follow a genealogical ideology as strict as that of their Confucian counterparts, and tend to be more open to commemorating socially disruptive death. Describing the Taoist philosophical tradition in China, Roger Ames writes, "Order, far from overcoming and defeating chaos, is in partnership with it in producing usually familiar yet always novel experiences."[28] Taoist rituals in Vietnam likewise have developed elaborate liturgical categories that specifically address different forms of socially negative death, and Taoist specialists are frequently hired for such disruptive occasions.

In traditional times, some classical scholars were conscious of the problems that Confucian doctrines presented in terms of death commemoration.[29] While these scholars were serving the court, they were loyal to the ideology of genealogical hierarchy and the feudal political hierarchy that drew legitimacy partly from the genealogical order. When in exile from the courtly environment because of a political upheaval or purge, however, some of these mandarin scholars became critical of such a dogmatic genealogical order, and they produced literature and art that reflected this change of mind.[30] The career of Nguyen Du, the eminent mandarin scholar of the eighteenth century, is a good example of the classical scholar's shifting identity.[31] Estranged from the court, he adopted Buddhist lyrics and shamanist images, developing great poetic forms dedicated to the spirits alienated from the Confucian ritual order. His literary imagination culminated in the famous poem "Van Chieu Hon" (Calling the wandering souls), which bemoans the plight of the multitude of human souls that are excluded from the society. The work of Nguyen Du is partly about how a person in exile reflects on, and develops sympathy for, the displaced dead. His rendering of popular religious tradition and imagination enriched the tradition, and today his

poems are widely used in popular rituals as spirit-calling or spirit-con-
soling incantations.[32]

Buddhism also played a role in countering the rigidity of the Confucian ritual order. At the back of Vietnamese Buddhist pagodas, there
are usually auxiliary sites of worship, either attached to or separate from
the main temple building. These places are reserved specifically for death
remembrance. The ancestors of important families usually take possession of the central honorary locations in these places. In the space for
nhan dan, or "ordinary people," at each corner, however, people can
honor the memory of relatives by paying a small fee or donation. This
space is often filled with the pictures of former South Vietnamese soldiers, the names of women who died in childbirth, and the names of children who committed the Confucian moral offense of dying before their
parents. The group remembered on this people's altar is typically made
up of the young and old, of people from all walks of life, and of people
from different political-military backgrounds. Even portraits of uniformed U.S. servicemen missing in action may appear here. Buddhist
pagodas can host spirit consolation rites for those who died socially negative and disruptive deaths, and monks are dispatched to private homes
for the same purpose. Most established pagodas in central Vietnam keep
a few lay ritual specialists of a Taoist denomination and employ them for
organizing syncretic mortuary and commemorative services.[33]

Spirit mediums have been less visible in public than Buddhist or Taoist
practitioners, mainly because of the insistent, disapproving attitude of
the state authorities. However, they are very popular in urban backwaters
and in rural areas, and they play an important role in dealing with tragic
death. The moral rehabilitation of socially negative death in fact constitutes one of the core domains of contemporary Vietnamese shamanism,
and in the southern and central regions the rehabilitation often takes the
form of political reconciliation. An episode in which the spirit of a soldier
of the South Vietnamese army possessed the body of his younger brother,
who was a high-ranking official in the provincial Communist Party, is
well known on the streets of Quang Ngai. A local journalist who
attempted to write about it was reprimanded, and the story traveled even
more widely as a result of the publicity this generated. It is known that, in
a séance held with a local medium, the soldier spirit demanded that the
official pay respect to his elder brother. Many other related dramas of
spirit possession have taken place in the context of health or financial
problems within a family, and the solutions typically lead to the return of
the forgotten dead to the milieu of family ancestor worship.

In the above context, a solution for a domestic problem assumed a resolution of a global conflict. The bipolar political and military confrontation that overran the streets and villages of Vietnam from 1946 to 1975 was not an "imaginary war" (as in Europe), in which one arms for war in order to avoid it, or only a geopolitical, diplomatic affair between states and blocs of states.[34] For the individual actors who experienced the global confrontation on the ground, the war was waged at the heart of their most immediate, intimate sphere. The Cold War split traditional community and family life in Vietnam, and even the identity of individuals. The split historical identity of the Cold War continues to be an unsettling element in family commemoration. How to reconcile the heroic heritage of a revolutionary ancestor with another ancestor's stigmatizing legacy as a counterrevolutionary is a pressing question for numerous families in southern and central Vietnam. The counter-heroic ancestors may not be accounted for at all in household rituals, and this coerced forgetting is a critical problem in the popular spirit-possession dramas and ensuing curing practices (see chapter 8).

Another prominent aspect of contemporary Vietnamese popular religious culture is the transformation of the ghosts of small children into powerful deities and tutelary spirits. Cases of this kind are found throughout central Vietnam, particularly around the old imperial capital of Vietnam, Hue, and Hoi An, the ancient port town and once important base in the world's ceramic trade network. In the area of Hoi An, I recorded more than a dozen cases in the second half of the 1990s. When the spirit of a child transforms into a deity, it usually undergoes a process of "education" under the patronage of an established deity before it is established as an independent tutelary spirit. These nameless spirits, who are usually believed to have suffered a tragic war-related death at a young age, have an ambiguous identity. They learn the spirit's trade and become increasingly knowledgeable and effective in magical practices, but people believe that these small spirits still think and behave according to their historical identity, rather than their newly emerging transcendental status. Some of these small spirits become active in rehabilitating like spirits of the dead with tragic backgrounds. Lien Hoa, a young girl spirit in a hamlet south of Ha My, is such a case. This war ghost of a small child used to supervise a young novice female medium in the community, and while doing so, the spirit introduced several dozen child ghosts to the community. Most of these small spirits were from the area originally, and their related families gradually accepted them at the family altar and other ritual spaces. The lapse of a generation facilitated this process of assimilation. When the small sprits of the dead returned to their families, they became genealogically senior to the postwar generation. In these cases, the natural growth of the genealogical tree helped to overcome the negativity of genealogically unnatural death.

The postwar cultural politics of "a powerful, intrusive and atheist Vietnamese state," which opposed "vestiges of feudal, colonialist, and bourgeois cultures . . . [and] superstitions and other backward customs," made it difficult for people to resort to these alternative ways of commemoration when dealing with the ritual crisis caused by the war.[35] This politics of memory was an extension of the earlier "socialist struggle on the cultural front" conducted in North Vietnam as part of the land reform in the 1950s, and it instructed the population to challenge the rationality of their traditional religious ideas by redefining them as ideological elements of the repressive precolonial and colonial economic infrastructure.[36] This coerced disenchantment, or what Malarney calls the "desanctification of village space," resulted in widespread destruction of traditional places of worship and censorship of ritual practices.[37]

One exception in the war-caused ritual crisis was the large population of war martyrs. Within the political domain of heroic death, a reversal of the Confucian ritual order not only became possible but also took on a positive value. Although most war martyrs died in violent circumstances away from home, and thus should be considered to have suffered "bad deaths," according to traditional understanding, the moral negativity of their deaths was overturned by the positive political values—the merit of patriotic service to the country. Hence, the community elders could kowtow to the village youth buried in the village war martyr cemetery, and the image of the mother of war martyrs laying incense sticks on the altar of her dead children became an important postwar political symbol.[38] For the untimely tragic death that was not considered a heroic death, however, the genealogically inverted commemoration was problematic, and it continues to challenge the practice and morality of Vietnamese ritual commemoration.

The fact that the mass reburial movement was initiated a generation after the war is significant in this respect. The lapse of a generation between the death and the reburial made the young victims of the war no longer so young in the context of the family tree. Their surviving kin had produced a new generation to whom the young war dead were ancestors—not really "grandfather" or "grandmother," and too young to fit the conventional image of an ancestor, but nevertheless categorical ancestors. This was a significant change and resulted in a powerful shift in perspective.

After the brothers in Xuan Duong reburied their mother and siblings, the elder brother shifted his attention to the remains of his own two children, who also had died in the 1966 village massacre. He had hoped that his relatively better-off younger brother would continue to collaborate with him on what he saw as family work. A series of disputes between the two brothers arose when the younger brother refused to become involved in this work. This kind of family dispute was not at all uncommon. Vietnamese ancestor worship had specific rules concerning the tree of generations and encouraged collateral collaboration mostly for projects involving common ancestors and anterior generations. Later, the elder brother of the family in Xuan Duong relegated the reburial of his two lost children to his two surviving children, who were both married with children of their own. In the year 2000, the two children of the elder brother of the Xuan Duong family purchased a plot at the village's public cemetery. They then undertook the transfer of the remains of their siblings. Afterward, it became the responsibility of the grandchildren of the family to pay regular visits to the tombs to offer incense sticks. In the hands of these grandchildren, the family's tragic young war dead crossed the conceptual bridge from asocial death and obtained full commemorative status as a paternal aunt and uncle.

One of the youngest survivors of the Ha My massacre was aged three at the time and is now married with four children. When he married in 1993, he discussed with his elder brother the idea of dividing their household ritual. Before the marriage, it was his elder brother who held the annual death memorial ceremony for their father and a separate ceremony for their mother and three siblings. Their father died of an epidemic in 1960 and the rest fell victim to the 1968 massacre. After the birth of his first child, the younger brother was given responsibility for performing the rite for his mother and siblings. He was aware that some village elders disapproved of publicly worshipping people other than ancestors on the household altar. Other survivors, when they invited guests to their household death commemoration rituals, tended to keep the commemoration of the family's child victims for a separate occasion or to leave it unspoken during the rituals. The younger brother, however, insisted on remembering his siblings publicly. He installed a two-tier altar—the upper shelf for his mother, and the lower shelf, with three small incense burners, for his brothers and sister—and had his eight-year-old son participate in the ceremony.

The role of a new generation in countering the crisis in the ritual order is manifested in the actual practice of family commemoration. The fam-

ily in Xuan Duong, a few months after the reburial of the two small victims of the village massacre, held a Lunar New Year ceremony. A fairly
large group of relatives gathered for the occasion. On this occasion, the
victims' father, and then their surviving siblings, presented offerings to
the dead, addressing them as Uncle Phuong and Aunt Dung—that is, the
dead were addressed from the perspective of the grandchildren. This
demonstrated publicly that the family genealogical commemorative
order was reestablished, and the crowd participated in the process by
offering incense sticks and praying for the dead. In this context, the participation of the posterior generation was crucial, and their presence
made it possible to commemorate people who fell short of being ancestors, or even those to whom the commemorator himself would stand as
an ancestor. The genealogical order of family worship could be turned
upside down without actually violating the principle of the order.

The Vietnamese tradition of *cung gio* has a clear temporal order, and
this temporal order emphasizes social continuity and a peaceful transition between generations. The war changed untimely, violent death from
a relatively isolated event to a generalized phenomenon in the community, and a generation after the war, the young war dead have begun to
enter the private domain of family ancestors. So far, only a small number
have done so, and this movement is still hesitant. Nonetheless, impatient
family members are acting as if they were members of a later generation.
They wish to end their separation from the war dead who met an
untimely death and to have the opportunity to eat and talk together, to
share their sorrow and joy. In order to do this, they transform their siblings and children into the family's ancestors, or rather they adopt the
point of view of the generation after their own.

HOUSE RENOVATION

Nguyen Van Huyen writes, "In central Vietnam, the tombs constitute
sacred property and are profoundly respected. As a Vietnamese phrase
goes, 'The preservation of the tombs of ancestors is jealously carried out
with the greatest of care, more so than any other precious object.'"[39] This
scholar and former minister of education in Vietnam observed in the
1930s that the tombs were connected to other sacred objects in Vietnamese ancestor worship, notably the in-house ancestral altars *(ban tho)*.
"House," *nha* in Vietnamese, is both a built structure and a social unity,
and it can also refer to a collective unity or an individual identity. So, *nha*

tho means "a communal temple," and the term *Nha Nguyen* means "the Nguyen Dynasty," whereas *nha nong* means "farmer" and *nha van* "writer." In reburial rituals, the new tomb is referred to as the *nha* of a specific person. An old shallow grave, however, is rarely called *nha*. For the Vietnamese, to have a house is to have sovereignty, as in Nha Nguyen. *Nha* also means to become a sovereign individual with a specific place in the system of vocations, as in *nha nong* (farmer). Against this background, it was possible to imagine even the nation as a house, as one Vietnamese intellectual wrote in the 1920s: "The nation is a house, our House. And we are of the nation."[40] The same house-centered political philosophy applies to the dead. A dead person without a house, or tomb, is not an individual, and such incomplete entities do not easily enter the domain of ritual commemoration, which allows them to renew their ties with the living. And on the opposite side, it appears that the living, without the marker of sovereignty *nha*, may not establish a full communicative relationship with the dead. Thus, Vietnamese commemorative customs present house-making as a condition for ritual relationship and encourage the construction of the material basis of sovereignty on both ontologically distinct sides of the interlocutors.

In the second half of the 1990s, a number of residential houses in Ha My and My Lai underwent major renovations. This is evident in Ha My along the lateral dirt road from the seashore to its junction with a narrow road connecting Hoi An to Da Nang, which was built in the 1960s by the ROK engineering corps. By 1998, few of the old postwar, bamboo-pole, thatched-roof huts still existed along this road, a situation that also occurs in the more hidden residential compounds behind the bamboo, pine, and coconut trees. The People's Committee of Dien Duong, of which Ha My makes up one of four units, has been a rigorous propagandist for the renovation of roads and houses. The village in general has benefited from the committee's effective leadership, though it has received relatively little financial assistance from the district and provincial authorities. The village officials complained that the higher administration gave villages on the sandy soil of the coast less attention than they gave inland settlements built on rich red soil. Despite this view, the household economy of Ha My has been advancing since 1993, with an annual growth rate of 5 to 7 percent. Rice production has increased at an equivalent rate since the village agricultural cooperatives closed down in 1992 and individual families took over farming. Since then, cultivation has been rapidly diversified to include such commercial crops as coffee and peanuts. The renovation of residential houses took place in the midst of this rapid economic growth, and the refurbishment of the domestic ancestral altar was one of its principal elements. The renovation of the home, without an equivalent improvement in the domestic place of the ancestors, did take place, but the villagers considered the results of this one-sided renovation incomplete. Opposite cases existed, too. Disproportionately large ancestral altars appeared in some old one-room bamboo houses, making them look like wartime family temples, according to the neighbors.

Nguyen Thi Bon, one of the young survivors of the 1968 massacre and a mother of four children, was helped by a U.S.-based charity organization in building her new house. Bon undertook some complex negotiations with the charity about her idea of building an additional room to install an in-house ancestral shrine before she succeeded in persuading them that the extra space, for her, met the criteria of their category "essential requirements for a comfortable domestic life." Bon did not consider her hope for a new house to be an aspiration that belonged to her alone, or the house as a place to shelter herself and her children only. Bon's neighbors, speaking of her commitment to her house renovation, quoted the proverbial expression "Ancestors ate too much salt, so their descendants desire water."[41] This popular idiom about salt and water speaks of the historical nature of human motivations in the Vietnamese imagination—including the idea that the unfulfilled wishes of past generations are transmitted to and manifested through the living. Bon's brother, aged ten at the time of the massacre, survived the mass killing but was gravely injured. Bon's little sister, Bong, then aged two, also survived, although seriously wounded, thanks to the village mothers who died to save the village children. When the soldiers left and the world was quiet, Bon crawled out of the mound of dead bodies and walked toward her house to look for water. Many times during our conversations, Bon recalled a collapsing beam:

> I was cold, and so was my brother. Bong was crying, I can still hear her strange crying. Her chin was blown away, I could see her throat, wide open. Brother crawled into the house. The house was on fire, and outside it was raining. I followed Brother as I always had done before. I was thirsty, and I knew there was a water jar in the house. We had to warm our bodies. We were shivering. Brother yelled at me, "Bon, do not give water to Bong." Maybe he wasn't yelling. Maybe he was only whispering. But I heard him yelling, in a thundering voice. Then, the beam collapsed on him, and I could see nothing but the clouds of dust, yes, like the clouds of dust we used to see behind the tail of an American tank.

In early 1968, Bon's brother was in Da Nang, looking after buffalos for a distant relative. Just a few days before the massacre, his father brought him back to Ha My because extra hands were needed for the family paddy. The guilt of having done so remained strong with Bon's father until he died; Bon, to this day, suffers guilt for having encouraged her father to bring the boy home. The villagers, who had heard from Bon the story of the collapsing beam, heard it numerous times and anticipated that Bon would probably stop telling the story if she completed her new house. They said that the renovation was necessary for Bon to "share the sorrow." The day Bon opened her ancestral altar, according to the two elderly neighbors who took turns minding Bon's children while she worked in the paddy, she would call upon the village ritual specialist to invite the spirit of her brother to the new house, and the neighbors would join the feast to share her happiness. Then, they said, the pitiful little girl crying in the rain and in the clouds of dust, holding her bleeding little sister in her arms, would depart; they would no longer hear the story of the collapsing beam that killed Bon's brother once she had moved him to a new house.

When a house renovation was completed and a new ancestral altar installed, the family would hold the altar-opening ceremony, which was often chaired by a village ritual specialist, called *thay cung* or *thay phu thuy*. The ritual specialist, in a ritual procession popularly called *cau hon,* read the incantation that invites the spirits of the dead belonging to the family, encouraging them to settle in their new place.[42] After the procession, the ritual specialists were normally expected to inform the family of the conditions and wishes of the dead, as people believed the specialists were able to communicate with the latter. On a number of occasions that I observed, the ritual specialist made a specific suggestion about the organization of their clients' domestic ritual activity.

The Le family in Ha My, for instance, was advised by the specialist after the altar-opening ceremony that the family should extend the house renovation project and build an outdoor shrine facing northwest. According to the priest, the reason for this extension was that one of the family's ancestors had company. The specialist argued that an unidentified female ghost was showing signs of discontent during the rite, as she was unable to accompany the family's ancestral spirit to the domestic altar. He also explained that these two spirits appeared to him to be intimate with each other, and he warned that the nonancestral spirit might develop some negative feelings about her alienation. On another occasion, the Nguyen family was advised to build an outdoor shrine on behalf of someone who turned out to be their own ancestor. The host's father had been killed in a civilian massacre. The spirit of this ancestor, according to the ritual specialist, was reluctant to follow his incantation of invitation and remained restless outside throughout the ritual. The specialist argued that this spirit had company, and the host later identified the companion ghost as the host's elder brother, who had been reported missing in action in the Central Highlands. He explained that this young ghost looked happy to have been invited to the ceremony, and that he, unlike his father, was impatient to join the altar. Throughout the incantation, according to the ritual specialist, this young soldier ghost was tiptoeing, trying to see what was happening inside the house, but because of his reluctant father, he was unable to satisfy his curiosity. The village *thay cung* concluded that the soldier ghost, although he had spent all his youth away from home in the business of war, had remained respectful of his old village father. At this point, the family joined the specialist in reconstructing the magical reality of the ritual and concluded that the soldier ghost must have put aside his desire for the warmth of family life out of filial respect for the reluctant father ghost.

On these two occasions and many others, people understood the ghosts' inability to join the interior ritual space because of their history of tragic death—a violent war death, or the absence of the body, or the combination of these two negative conditions of afterlife. Besides these objective conditions, people also took account of the ghosts' subjective awareness of certain differences between themselves and the enshrined domestic ancestors and the way this was manifested in their unusual behavior. This was particularly evident in the episode of the father and son ghosts. The father ghost, unlike his son, was apparently conscious of the fact that the history of his violent death was a negative reality in domestic ancestral death commemoration. The way ghosts come to be seen as self-conscious beings is by no means through the mediation of ritual specialists only, and this process is in fact an important element of the cultural process of "liberation from grievance." The more that ghosts appear as though they are aware of their subjective conditions and identities, the more they come to take on the traits of a moral person. When this happens, the ghosts are already in a process of symbolic transformation.

The renovation of ancestral places in Ha My continued to create a place for unsettled ghosts. Many Ha My families, after completing the domestic ancestral altar, proceeded to build an outside shrine for wandering ghosts and began preparing two separate tables of food offerings on their ancestral death-day anniversaries. One table faced the outside shrine, overlooking the streets; the other was laid indoors in front of the ancestral altar. People were not sure whether they should worship some war dead at the inside or the outside shrine, so most families took to conducting a double commemoration. As the seasons went by, the place of ghosts became as sumptuous in appearance as that of ancestors, and the food offerings on the street altar as copious as those for the ancestors.

House renovations in Ha My, although there were exceptions, generally followed the completion of tomb renovation. Between these two activities, there rose another civil activity that aimed to reconstitute the family and community temples (discussed in more detail in chapter 5). Over the years, a general pattern emerged in the process of village social renovation. The dead were the first to benefit from the economic reform. This first phase brought a large number of displaced remains of the war dead to the family-held graveyards, and this encouraged the development of practical collaboration and moral unity within the families. It prepared the moral and organizational grounds for the revival of unity that was to be crystallized in the community-wide activities for the renovation of the ancestral temples. The temples reconstituted the autonomy of the traditional social organizations by providing them with historical depth. This later phase was related to the earlier tomb renovation because the ancestral temples were seen as the places to which the household ancestors were destined to move when their relationship to the living became more distant in the tree of genealogy. The temple, in other words, restored the past for the living and secured the future for the dead.

When these two related projects of tomb and temple renovation were in an advanced stage, the Ha My villagers turned their attention to their homes and began to form a relationship between the places of the dead and the places of the living within their dwelling space. Hence, the order of the village renovation can be summarized as a progressive diffusion of modernity from the tomb to the home in spatial terms, and from the past generations to the present in temporal terms. The village renovation in the 1990s proceeded from the tomb to the house, with the general objective of a circuitous social development across the differential cosmological environments. The villagers struggled to lift the tomb and the house from poverty simultaneously, and people's attentions shifted between the two domains, creating a way to see modernity from two respective positions. The Ha My villagers approached modernization as a process that concerned not only their future but also the future of the past generations. Their interests shifted between *am* and *duong*. The dead, in their imaginations, wished for a better life in their place of *am,* but they also wished for a better life in the opposite world of *duong*, where their descendants resided. In this emergent, doubly reflexive social reality, the warm wind of economic development seemed to blow from the opposite world, for the living as well as for the dead.

The mass renovation of tombs, temples, and domestic ancestral places in Ha My, My Lai, and elsewhere in central Vietnam was clearly a movement whose dynamics drew the general orientation of Vietnam toward a more decentralized market-based economy. Without the privatization of economic institutions, including the agricultural sector, as other observers have noted, it is doubtful whether a movement of this scale would have been possible.[43] Nguyen Van Huy and others observe, "The economic condition of the villagers improved in the reopened market economy, and people felt a need to revive their traditions."[44] It is undeniable that the economic confidence of the private sector and the state administration's political tolerance for civil activities of an apparently religious orientation were important factors in the development.

These factors alone, however, do not explain how the renovations in the village proceeded in this particularly encompassing way. The economic and political liberalization may have been the condition for the revival of traditions, but these certainly did not create the need for this revival. Hy Van Luong emphasizes in this regard the practical values of ancestral rituals—that is, their role in consolidating and expanding kinship networks and the advantage of doing so in family-based economic activities. He writes, "As the household regained its role as the primary production unit and gained more resources vis-à-vis the [agricultural] cooperative [superceding the suprafamilial relations within the production team and the village,] kinship ties became more important as a source of assistance [and the] reciprocal feasting system reinforced kinship relations in an agricultural community."[45] I do not doubt that there is a certain economic rationale in communal festivity, or that the formal transition from state-command economy to market-based economy constitutes the wider background of the renovation of the material culture of the dead. The transition in economic form, as I noted in the introduction to this volume, also corresponds to the shift in the focus of commemorative practices, from the national society to the familial and other local genealogical unity. Nonetheless, issues of moral economy are as much at stake here as those of political economy.

James Scott shows in his classical work on peasant rebellions, drawing partly on colonial Vietnam, that economic and political transformation in rural society is unintelligible without an understanding of the normative principles embedded in the life of peasantry.[46] Carles Salazar elaborates on this and demonstrates in his wonderfully named *Sentimental Economy* that the economy of family farmers in western Ireland is at once a social construct and a cultural experience.[47] Scott characterizes what he calls "the moral economy of peasants," following E. P. Thompson, in terms of their "subsistence ethic"—the idea that peasants have certain understandings of economic justice tied to the norm of reciprocity and the right to subsistence, and that they may rebel if these sacred rights are seriously violated.[48]

The notion of morality in Scott's scheme of moral economy is still an overtly economic concept, however, which means it mainly addresses the distribution of food and thereby reduces the moral identity of peasants primarily to the ego-centered purpose of the preservation of the self.[49] Nevertheless, his concept of the subsistence ethic can be instructive for understanding the reality of ritual revival, if we consider the concept from a more properly reciprocal perspective, and the idea of the self from a more sociologically realistic, historically grounded perspective, briefly discussed in the beginning of this chapter. The idea of subsistence, for the Vietnamese villagers, is not confined by the temporality of "from the cradle to the grave" (as is the case in classical political economy)[50] but reaches out to the sphere of life beyond the grave. Their understanding of moral economy incorporates communicative actions that render the survival of the historical other as part of the preservation of the self. Considering gender relations in Melanesia and analyzing them through a theory of gift economy, Marilyn Strathern concludes, "Imagining that the world is divided into 'two kinds of' things, relations, times, or whatever, is to imagine the person from two different vantage points."[51] This reciprocal perspective—which situates relations as part of a person, rather than (as in the commercial society, according to Strathern) the person as part of relationship[52]—extends to a conception of moral economy where rights to subsistence are an intersubjective normative principle. Strathern's idea of reciprocity, although identifying with the view of "relations in person" rather than that of "person in relationship," suggests further that the human actor must shift between (and exchange with others) these points of view in order to create relations.

A former partisan leader argued, in his joint-authored application letter to the district office for the reconstruction of his family temple, that the *viec ho* activity is being conducted according to the principle of socialist revolution, as it intends to share the benefits of economic growth with the past generations who experienced nothing but violence and deprivation in their historical life (see chapter 5). Ordinary Vietnamese may not argue the matter with such eloquence, but they are nevertheless cognizant of the particular idea of subsistence implied in the statement: subsistence, for the dead, means ritual remembrance, which guarantees their fundamental, inalienable right to exist in the social world. In Ha My and My Lai, the villagers' thirst for a better life and the desire of the dead villagers for a better afterlife were both real and urgent. What mattered was how to fulfill these separate desires in an integrative and interactive way.

The modernization of the village was a radical break from the vision of modernity that tore human desire and agency from its historical roots and denied economic and political rights to the historical generations. It is within this rising horizon of moral economy that I situate the memory of mass village death in Ha My and My Lai, rather than merely in the context of a changing political economy from one paradigmatic form to another. It is hard to imagine, in the latter case, what novel positive economic value there would be in reviving the ruins of tragic mass death, against the background of the death's negative political values prior to the market reform.

According to Nguyen Van Huyen, the "ancestors' presence in the domestic home is not in a mere passive state. The dead also act."[53] As the cosmologically parallel and esthetically correlative social development proceeded, the village ghosts of My Lai and Ha My came to take an increasingly active role in the process. The more visibly the world of *am* was renovated, the louder apparently became the voice of its population, and the more personal the messages it carried. Economic advancement seemed to stimulate political liberalization in the world of the dead, and this perceived development reinforced the commitment of the villagers to the particular, double-centered modernizing process they had embarked upon. Apparition, in this context, was not only a clear indicator of social transformation but also an important factor in bringing about that transformation.

CHAPTER 4

Ancestors in the Street

My Lai villagers vividly recalled the periodic lamentations of the village ghosts that they said echoed from the killing sites. A number of residents in Khe Thuan subhamlet claimed that they had seen old women ghosts licking and sucking the arms and legs of small child ghosts, and they interpreted the scene as an effort by the elderly victims to ease the pain of the wounded children. Some in Khe Dong subhamlet also graphically described several young women ghosts, each walking with a small child held in her arms and lamenting over the child's lifeless body. The mother ghosts were grieving, the villagers explained, for their dead children. One family living along the dirt road that leads to the seashore area once called Batangan Peninsula added that they had seen a group of child ghosts tailing faithfully behind a group of young mother ghosts. According to the family, this happened a night or two before the anniversary of the massacre. On this occasion, they could hear the ghosts having a jovial conversation—like "happy and excited birds in harvesttime."

The ghosts, according to the aged undertaker and cemetery keeper of My Lai with whom I often spoke, could lament their own physical pain or feel pain when their loved ones suffered pain; they might be sorrowful about their own tragic death or cry over the deaths of their children as if they themselves were not dead yet. Their moods and sentiments, and even their forms, fluctuated with the circumstances. The child ghosts appeared dead in their grieving mother's arms on a moonless night in a rainy season; the same children could be running after their mothers playfully in a pleasant evening before the anniversary day. It appeared to me that the village ghosts of My Lai led lives with their own ups and downs, and that the fluctuations of their lives were intertwined with the rhythms of life among their living neighbors.

These apparitions were initially confined to the sites of their deaths. After the remains were removed to the edge of the village in the postwar years, according to the undertaker, the ghosts traveled between their death sites and the new graves. He argued that human beings feel "inseparable from the spirit of the native land although physically separate from it"; the dead, likewise, have an enduring attachment to the place of their death even if their bodies have been moved elsewhere. This theory of enduring attachment to the place of origin (of life or afterlife) was indeed demonstrated by many stories of agile ghosts who, their bodies having been moved, hopped along the treetops to return to their place of death each evening. A ghost who flew head down, mutilated legs up in the air, used to be a familiar resident of Khe Dong. A longhaired, one-legged ghost of Ha My used to hover around the bridge of Cam Le and startle the village men returning from the marketplace drunk. One survivor family in My Lai used to be troubled by an entire ghost family of three generations. The old and young ghosts came to the family's courtyard each time the family organized a feast for their ancestors. Another survivor family told me about trouble with a clever ghost of urban origin who tried to outdo their timid ancestral ghost and settle in the ancestral shrine in her stead when the family held a spirit-invitation ceremony. The apparitions of massacre victims are known to have been most frequent in the second half of the 1970s and in the early 1980s, when the villagers were discouraged from practicing traditional commemorative rites. The village undertaker noted that these "invisible neighbors," as the Vietnamese often refer to ghosts, had become less active since the beginning of the 1990s, and he associated this with the rise of family and community commemorative ritual activities.

That the ghosts had become less active in the streets and the paddy did not, however, necessarily mean that they were actually vanishing from the village environment. In proportion to their allegedly declining presence in the public space, their appearance in the domestic and private sphere increased. This was a commonly held view among the ritual specialists in My Lai and Ha My alike. With the beginning of the 1990s, according to them, cases of spirit possession and affliction increased in number and intensity. Gossip about ghost-related dreams or intimate experiences with apparitions were frequent, and rumors of spirit possession circulated widely within and beyond the village.[1] It is possible that the ghosts appeared to be more intrusive than before because people felt able to talk freely about them. The general opinion of ritual specialists in My Lai and Ha My, however, was that there had been a definite increase in intrusive ghosts in the first half of the 1990s. Their stories seemed to indicate that the village ghosts were moving from the margins of the village to the interior spaces of the village homes. Just as the bodies of the war dead were moving en mass to the domains of kinship and community life, their spirits, it seemed, were making a transition from a distant existence to an existential proximity.

Crossing between the exterior and the interior of the house (not to mention the body) is a significant action that often involves a certain symbolic reversal.[2] The ghosts, if they intrude on the interior space, not only affect the order of the space but also become liable themselves to a vital transformation. The intrusive ghost is not the same as the passive, anonymous ghost in the distance.[3] The ghost in the street is part of an undifferentiated mass and is characterized, as Franz Boas writes in general terms, by "the lack of individuality."[4] Although the tree-hopping ghost of Khe Dong earned a certain identity among the villagers because of her unusual way of traveling, this being was still *con ma* and was not entitled to any kinship references that the Vietnamese normally offer to the familiar spirits. This characteristic anonymity and nonindividuality of ghosts changes in the event of an intrusion. Such incidents provoke fear, bewilderment, and curiosity, which prompt an attempt to identify the intruder's historical identity before a negotiation for a solution takes place. The ghost, through this process, typically abandons anonymity and recovers a personal identity. Tzvetan Todorov argues that personalizing the identities of the victims of mass killing is a way of countering the source of the violence, which is, according to him, fundamentally the modern mechanics of depersonalization.[5] The intrusion of ghosts, in My Lai and Ha My, was a signal for the commencement of this important process of individuation.

DEATH IN THE STREET

Intrusive ghosts create a particular condition of the body that the Vietnamese call *xac*. This concept, which literally means "corpse" *(xac chet)*, not only refers to the material condition of a body that is immobile and lifeless but also indicates the related but opposite condition of a soul that is free and vigorous. When the body dies, it is believed that the soul becomes free and can move between the place of death and the place of burial, as well as among other places of historical attachment and where its historical identity is remembered. The mobile soul of the dead may also appear in different places simultaneously, and this is recognized as a sign of its vigor and power, which the Vietnamese express with the concept of *linh*—meaning "forceful," "vital," or "auspicious."[6] When a spirit intrudes directly into someone's body in what we call "spirit possession," this mode of communication is called *xac* or *nhap xac,* which in this context means "the spirit enters the body." The two terms are also colloquial references for spirit mediums, that is, "people who lend their bodies to spirits [or people to whose bodies spirits import themselves]."

Just as there are two opposite conditions of *xac,* Vietnamese mortuary culture demonstrates two different ways of relating to death. One is an elaborate and complex system of dealing with the lifeless body. Here, the corporeal integrity of the deceased is of great importance, and proper ritual preparation of the body for interment is considered vital to the welfare of the dead and a precondition for a harmonious relationship between the dead and the living.[7] The place of the dead, such as the tomb, should be in order and permanent, and it should be marked by clearly identifiable structures and borders. Unless the bodies are buried in a proper place and following an appropriate rite, the commemoration of death is not possible or remains incomplete. Vietnamese mortuary tradition has developed a long, elaborate sequence of rites to separate the soul from the body. In this process, popularly called *hon bach,* referring to the dummy made of silk or paper used for capturing the freed soul of the deceased, it is necessary for the living to undertake the public lamentations called *khoc.*[8] The process is also imperative if the dead are to realize the radical transition of death and to start relating to the environment accordingly. This important process of making the physically dead find a different existence requires the dead person's body. This is why people missing in action from the battlefields became the object of great pity and concern, and why different institutions in Vietnam, from the family to the state, made determined efforts to find their remains.

At the other end of the spectrum, the idea of *xac* indicates that the presence of the dead can be permeable, unmarked, and unspecified, and may be thoroughly diffuse within the place of the living. It is believed that the spirits of the dead wander freely about the ditches, the footpath, the school building, the police station, the sand dunes, and the household kitchen areas, particularly at dusk. As Jennifer Cole says of ancestral memory in Madagascar, "Not only do the dead move among and watch the living but communication between the dead and the living is thought to be a normal—indeed necessary—daily occurrence."[9] Thus the dead are both mobile and sedentary at once, and this duality makes it conceivable that they may be multilocal at any given time.

On the first and fifteenth day of each lunar month, the number and intensity of traveling spirits may increase radically. This is what the spirit medium in Quang Ngai told me when he was trying to dissuade me from talking to him about ghosts on one of those days. In his opinion, speaking about ghosts attracts them, and he wanted to avoid the embarrassing situation of me turning into a *xac*. When a family holds an important death anniversary ceremony, such as the first year *tieu tuong* or the second year *dai tuong*, the entire ghost population of the area may hurry to the site of the ceremony and make it look like a crowded early morning marketplace. This is how a Ha My ritual specialist described his experience of such ceremonies. In popular knowledge, the dead who are properly entombed in an appropriate site according to ritual propriety are less inclined to roam about the streets than those who are improperly buried and did not benefit from remembrance rites. These hungry, thirsty, unclothed, unidentified wandering ghosts make up the majority of the traveling ghost squads.

The idea of forced mobility, which constitutes the identity of ghosts, is not entirely imaginary but rather relates to historical situations. In addition to the genealogical, temporal conception of improper death (see chapter 3), the Vietnamese have a place-centered understanding of the morality of death. *Chet nha* refers to death that occurs in a place that holds the deceased person's life history, namely, in his home and within his ancestral village. This "good death" constitutes all that is absent in the opposite concept of *chet duong*. The latter literally means "to die in the street," and it carries a number of added implications, such as "dying alone without the family to grieve," "dying violently" (for everywhere outside the home is considered less safe than within the home), or "dying accidentally" (rather than fatefully). The death of a soldier in the battlefield, in this dual conceptual scheme, is clearly a "street death"—the soldier usually dies away from his homeland and under violent circumstances. The death of a villager in her natal village in ordinary circumstances—this is "death at home." The mass death of the entire village population in their natal village, however, does not constitute "death at home" despite the fact that it took place at home. Nonviolent death in the street is still "street death," and death at home, if it is an exceptionally violent kind, becomes a "street death." In this case, the force of violence annihilates the boundary of home and turns the home inside out. The spirits of those who die a "street death," in popular belief, continue to live a form of life in the streets, being unable to anchor themselves to a specific place, and this continuity of the form of death with the mode of afterlife is in fact the core meaning of the concept *chet duong*.

This duality of death is manifested in Vietnamese ritual organization. Ghosts and ancestors constitute an elementary structure of Vietnamese domestic ritual. This is particularly the case in the southern and central regions, where the domestic ritual space explicitly incorporates a place for unrelated spirits of the dead as part of ancestor worship and in distinction to the ancestral shrine. The ritual space consists of two built structures, one of which is placed in the interior of the house, representing the permanence of family ancestry and household deities. On the opposite side of this *nha tho* (the house of ancestor worship), there usually stands a smaller outdoor installation, which may look like a large birdhouse, erected on a single column and as tall as an adult of average height. This place, called *khom* in the vernacular of central Vietnamese, is meant for unsettled wandering ghosts or for spirits that for various reasons are not free to enter the house of worship.

Places for anonymous spirits proliferate in the Vietnamese village and throughout the country. However, the fact that they constitute part of the domestic ritual space is unique to the southern and central regions. In the northern region, these "spirit shrines" (called *den* or *dien*) mainly refer to isolated places of worship scattered in the public space of the village.[10] The Vietnamese in the central region have various references for these shrines *(trang tho, am, or canh)*, depending on the specific shape or function of the shrine. In Quang Nam and Quang Ngai provinces, *khom* is the most popular term for ghost shrines, including the ones found in private houses and community temples. The equivalent term *trang tho* literally means "the shelf for worship," and the shrine takes the form of a piece of wooden shelving nailed to a small wooden stick that is inserted in the ground. On it, people prepare a bowl filled with sand in which they rest incense sticks. The humbleness of this "shelf," which alternately may take the form of an empty soft drink can attached to a tree, contrasts with "the house for worship" dedicated to gods and ancestors.

This horizontal, diametric duality of ancestral shrine versus external shrine for ghosts is a practical expression of the concentric dualism of inside versus outside. Conducting an act of worship in this structure requires a specific bodily practice—it requires the actor's body to turn and her perspective to shift. The ritual actor in central Vietnam, while she is engaged in the commemoration of death, places her body in the middle of this dual structure of worship—in between the two separate built forms and two different milieus of memory that they symbolize. The appropriate ritual action in this structure consists of reversing the positions between the outward direction and the inward orientation. The inward commemoration and the outward counterpart are different in technicality—the actor kowtows three times toward the ancestral altar and four times toward the shrine for ghosts, for instance—but also perhaps in meaning.

Within the house of worship, we may say, following Emile Durkheim, that commemoration renews the solidarity between the dead and the living, thereby affirming the historical continuity of the genealogical identity. The act of worshipping the sacred existence of the dead is, for Durkheim, an act of making the profane entity into a sacred one.[11] In contrast to these "true spirits" that constitute genius loci at the center of collective representation, Durkheim considered the ghost to be a sociologically irrelevant category and to be "a vagabond being with no clear-cut responsibility, since the effect of death was to set it outside all the regular [social] structures."[12] Léopold Cadière described the Vietnamese worship of ancestors and gods in a similar, positive light. With the external shelf for ghosts, following his binary scheme of *génies bons* versus *génies mauvais* (beneficiary spirits versus malignant spirits), the meaning of the act of worship swings from positive to negative. It denotes protection from the threatening unknown, according to his caricature of *génies mauvais* as spirits "taking pleasure in annoying and harming [the living]."[13] In this unrealistically simplistic scheme, the offerings made to the outward orientation amount to soliciting personal and communal safety from the malignant influence on the outside. Following Cadière, we may conclude that the house-side commemoration is for a stronger attachment with the dead, whereas its street-side counterpart expresses desire for detachment from the dead.

If we consider how relations with ghosts are represented in classical Vietnamese literature, however, it appears that the street-side worship is not to be dismissed from sociological imagination as Durkheim believed, or simplified into a negative, oppositional relationship, as Cadière paints it. As noted in an earlier reference to the poetic world of Nguyen Du, the moral identity of ghosts is relative to the existential condition of the living: people living in exile and people living at home do not have the same sympathy for displaced spirits. Nguyen Du's poems such as "Remembering Ten Forms of Death" are widely used today, in various modified forms, in ghost-related rites of consolation, and people believe that the cumulative effect of the incantation is to help liberate the ghosts of tragic death from their grievous state of existence.[14] Thus, it is possible to imagine ritual interaction with ghosts as an ethical engagement of a particular kind, and street-side worship as a form of human solidarity whose meaning goes beyond that of the kind of solidary relations that preoccupied Durkheim. As Edward Casey insists, *anima loci* (the soul of place) and genius loci (the genius or spirit of place, or Durkheim's "true spirit") are equally important for thinking about the spirituality of place, and understanding their relatedness is central to phenomenology of place.[15]

House-side ancestors and gods are called *ong ba*, whereas street-side wandering spirits are referred to as *co bac*. *Ong ba* (meaning "grandfather" and "grandmother") have names and specific identities, whereas *co bac* (meaning "aunt" and "uncle") have only an undifferentiated collective identity. *Ong ba* are beings permanently settled in the family graveyard, in the lineage temple, or on the household altar, and they are related in kinship to the proprietor of the place. *Co bac* are unrelated to the ritual place and are temporary visitors to the rite of worship held in honor of *ong ba*. Being unrelated, the *co bac* spirits are not invited to the interior of the house or the temple, and instead they are fed and watered in the open air, usually at the border between the garden and the concentric outside.

The "aunts" and "uncles" on the street include some who died bad deaths (defined in temporal and spatial terms), and they are to be kept away from the sacred and pure places of "grandfather" and "grandmother." In "the house of worship," the chaos and impurity implied in the notion of the "street" are considered incompatible with the values of continuity, peace, and harmony associated with "grandfather" and "grandmother." This conceptual scheme was probably a manifestation of the agrarian lifestyle, conducted in the enclosed, fortified settlement of *lang*, the rural village. Liisa Malkki notes that, among the Hutu in western Tanzania, a history of displacement is constitutive of their modern imagining of national unity. A similar idea applies to the Vietnamese historical imagination of nationhood.[16] The traditional bamboo-hedged rural Vietnamese village was developed during the fifteenth to eighteenth centuries, as a population migrated south to escape Chinese influence and occupied the territory of the indigenous Cham and Khmer population.[17] The rural village was a military unit as well as a moral unity, and an island of security opposed to the world of strangers *(nguoi ngoai)* outside the bamboo fence. The concentric worldview that distinguishes the peaceful, ordered interior from the dangerous, chaotic exterior applied also to the wider *nuoc* (country territories), on the one hand (thus *nguoi nuoc ngoai,* meaning "foreigner"), and, on the other, to the individual family home of *nha,* surrounded and protected by bamboo groves and cactus plants. The Vietnamese concept of *nha* in fact incorporates all levels of closed interiority, from the house, to the community, to the country. The Vietnamese house, as many observers have noted, is at once a place for dwelling and a place for the cult of the dead.[18] All the dead enshrined in the village temple, in the family temple, or on the domestic ancestral altar are cosmological insiders, and their places form the imaginary circle that the proper "death at home" should join and remain in. Outside, death was disorderly and potentially threatening, and thus it merged with the chaotic image of life beyond the bamboo hedge.

The Vietnam War made the traditional distinction between inside and outside practically meaningless and, in fact, turned the traditional communal "inside" into a fierce and confusing battlefield. This war was not a feudal battle waged against a fortified citadel or a bamboo-hedged village, but a peculiar modern war in which remaining inside the bamboo gate could be more dangerous than becoming a displaced refugee. In Ha My, nearly 80 percent of the inhabitants succumbed in a mass killing, and in the surrounding area half of the population succumbed to various forms of war-related violence in the period of 1965 to 1975. Given this historical background of social catastrophe, it is rare to find a pure domestic ancestor within the past two generations—an ancestor who had the good fortune of a peaceful death at home. Death in a civilian massacre, even though it took place in the homeland and sometimes even within the very house the victims inhabited, takes on the traits of "death in the street." This ambiguity in turn testifies to the scale and absurdity of the violence, which mutilated the traditional ideal of concentric dualism.

When we commemorate an ancestor who died a tragic death, in which direction do we turn—the ancestral side or the ghost side? Our ancestors—are they in the house or are they out in the street?[19]

This is an urgent question, as I indicated earlier, for relatives of the massacre victims when they set out to rebuild their domestic ritual space. The memory of mass death, or violent death at home, rests neither at home nor in the street; the memory of individual victims is neither easily placed in the domain of ancestors nor conceptually part of the milieu of the wandering ghosts. This "neither/nor" opposition defies attempts at classification and may, as Zygmund Bauman writes, militate against "either/or."[20] The ambiguity of mass death in the traditional structure of worship complicates domestic remembrance practices, but I agree with Bauman that it is in this ambivalence that the wounds of modern violence (the Holocaust, in Bauman's work) are truly witnessed.

The difficulty in commemorating the victims of mass death within the domestic ritual relates further to the materiality of the dead bodies. In the view of the villagers, the bodies in the mass grave are in disorder, undifferentiated and unclassified. The corporeal collectivity of unrelated people in kinship, although it can sometimes unite different families in commemorative activities, makes it practically impossible to bring the dead bodies to the domain of kinship, which is a necessary condition for the commencement of proper ritual remembrance. The bodies in the mass grave, in this sense, form a material condition whose meaning is opposite to that of people missing in action. The latter complicates domestic ritual with the absence of the body to be reburied; the former with the presence of too many bodies to rebury.

During the ritual, the actor's movements relate to this materiality of war death. The actor shifts his position between the house of genealogical memory and the outer terrain of anonymous death and, by doing so, creates an alternative spatiality of memory. This interstitial space between "house" and "street" is not merely a distance between two established sites of memory, the ancestral shrine and the shrine for wandering ghosts, but it itself provides an arena in which kinship memory of tragic death can be located with its full bifocal ambiguity of being near and distant at once.[21] Although it is here that we find a clash between culture and history—the modern war created death that goes beyond the traditional classification of death—it is also in this arena of active remembrance that we see the power of human action to create leeway (or an interplace) for the unsettled memory.[22]

The concentric dualism of inside and outside, or genealogical center versus anonymous periphery, is an established theme in the study of Southeast Asian cultures and considered by scholars to be an unequal, but dynamic, structure. The exemplary center in this scheme is considered inactive, and the active periphery is associated with the structural dynamic.[23] The Vietnamese notion that ghosts are mobile beings not only implies the existential inferiority of being placeless, in contrast to placed ancestors, but also relates to this idea of active periphery, and the same applies to the phenomenon of intrusive ghosts introduced earlier. When the ghosts import themselves into ritual interiority, this becomes a sign for their potency—the power to transgress the rule of classification. When this happens, the arena between "house" and "street" becomes vital for the interaction between the mobility of ghosts and the movement of ritual actors.

PATERNAL FEELING

Ba Lap is one of the eldest survivors of the Ha My massacre and her family has one of the largest houses in the village.[24] Her family completed their house renovation project more quickly than most other families in the village thanks to financial support from her youngest son, who is settled in Australia. Lap's new house is audacious in design. Surrounded by immaculately landscaped vegetable gardens and fruit orchards on four sides, the house is prominent with imposing marine architecture on its front side. Lap's youngest son is one of several from the village who escaped by boat in the mid-1980s. Having a kind of mental fixation on the European cargo ship that rescued the sinking escape boat in the open sea, according to Lap's neighbors, this man insisted on incorporating his memory of the benevolent cargo ship into the family's new house. Overlooking the terrace that is supposed to resemble the upper deck of the cargo ship, Lap's family has built a spacious common room on two floors and installed a new, tilted ancestral altar on the upper floor. Lap's daughter-in-law, the wife of her eldest son, regularly prepared incense, garden flowers, and rice gruel on the altar on behalf of her late father-in-law and sometimes for her husband's three younger siblings, whom she had never met.

A brother of her husband, aged eight, was killed at the 1968 Ha My massacre. His then-five-year-old sister survived the massacre but did not survive the hospitalization that followed. Another sister died of malnutrition and related illness just before the massacre. Although Lap herself performed a ritual for them occasionally, it was mainly her daughter-in-law's responsibility to care for these small spirits of the dead. When she was busy in the paddy or the marketplace, the daughter-in-law relegated this responsibility to her twelve-year-old daughter. This girl, like other village girls of her age, was the most regular practitioner of the family's daily ritual routine. She changed the flowers on the altar, cleaned the surface, and joined her friends on trips to the cemetery to distribute incense sticks. While doing their duties, the girls usually sang their favorite popular songs and exchanged views on the poetic quality of each song. The village undertaker and gravedigger once told me that the dead villagers in the cemetery, in his opinion, preferred this cheerful group of visitors to their silent, grim-faced adult relatives.

Ba Lap's late husband had worked for the South Vietnamese administration as the village chief of Ha My before he was reported dead in mysterious circumstances. Lap was informed that the communist *dac cong* (special agents) had assassinated her husband, but she did not believe this explanation. Her husband's body had disappeared from the alleged site of assassination, and the officials were unable to identify the date and the hour of his death, thereby making it impossible to settle the date for a death anniversary ritual. This was 1963. It was not uncommon at that time for people to disappear from home or from the fields to be later found dead. But it was rare for the family of a Saigon government official to be unaware of the death day of the victim. When the VC special agents kidnapped and executed individuals whom they considered to be enemies of the people, they informed the families of the precise time of their death. This information allowed the family to prepare the death-day remembrance. Because of this, Ba Lap was convinced that her husband's death had not come at the hands of the VC.

In 1993, Lap's eldest son, Van, came to discover the truth about his father's death. The following account of the events that led to this discovery is reconstructed through a series of my recorded interviews with Van and his wife held in May 1996 (again in February–March 1999 and January 2002) as well as casual conversations with his family and neighbors. The first event happened the morning after the fifteenth day of the third lunar month, 1993. The night before, Van had prayed to his father's ancestral tablet, and later distributed incense sticks to the few unknown graves in his garden. During the following morning, as he lay daydreaming in his bed, something came to him, and Van dashed outside as if, in the words of his wife, he were running away from a poisonous snake. He began drinking water from the well, bucket after bucket, as if he had not had a drop of water for the last hundred years. Having emptied three large buckets of water, Van ran toward the paddy. He said to his wife, "I'm going out to find my father's body." His wife, thinking that Van was play-acting, told him, "Please do as you wish. You'll fall and break your nose. Do you not remember you're a blind man?" Concerned that her husband might actually fall into the ditch, she decided to run after him. She found him collapsed in the bamboo grove across the paddy. Later, the two of them returned to the same spot, this time bringing Ba Lap with them:

At two o'clock in the afternoon, we all went back to the place. There, he jumped on to the spot where he had earlier collapsed unconscious, and sat down, cross-legged. We lit incense sticks, and Mother said prayers. Husband said, "I'm buried here, right here, underneath." He then rubbed his face with his hands, as if he were washing his face, and passed out. Father was gone. Husband didn't remember a thing when he came back to himself. Mother had a hard time coming along with us on her artificial leg, but it was worth the effort. She was so happy to hear Father's voice after the many years of separation.

After this incident, Van had regular visits from his father's spirit, mostly in the late morning or early evening. Meanwhile, he hired two laborers, had them dig the spot in the bamboo grove, and found a set of bones there, which he believed belonged to his father. Three days after the reburial of the remains, Van said, he had an important conversation with his father about his death. This conversation took place between the "father," who possessed the body of his eldest son, and his daughter-in-law, who faced the body of her husband but spoke to her "father-in-law." Her interlocutor revealed that Van's father had succumbed in an assassination plot organized by two South Vietnamese officials who allegedly had been jealous of his position. The conversation was followed by a long monologue by the father's spirit in which he spoke of his sentiments for his family and his dead children.

The Ha My villagers who heard about the incident of possession speculated about the meaning of "jealousy" in the drama of assassination. It could mean the kind of jealousy among competing officials within the state organizations. Van's mother accepted this interpretation, believing that someone in the wartime state bureaucracy had attempted to obtain her husband's job by eliminating him. Other villagers subscribed to a more historically specific notion of jealousy in wartime. In the 1960s, the attempts by village officials to protect their villagers against abusive military actions could lead to difficulty for individual officials. The reluctance of low-ranking officials to cooperate with the village evacuations was viewed as sabotage or even collaboration with the enemy. In the environs of Ha My, there were several cases where the village chiefs, after having tried to mediate between the villagers and the army, were dismissed from their positions and had received death threats. When the threat became a reality, the incident typically was blamed on the communists. Most of the villagers who took part in the reburial of Van's father interpreted the story of his death along this familiar plot line—the tragic fate of a sympathetic wartime village administrator. Ending his absence of thirty years, Van's father not only joined the domain of family life at last but also made a decisive comeback to the moral world of his natal village.

When the dialogues with the "father-in-law" were disseminated to the community, they were removed from their supernatural origin and often became indistinguishable from other ordinary family conversations.[25] Hence, two village women working in the sweet potato field described the new tomb of Van's father across the field: "That one over there [belongs to the husband of Ba Lap]. . . . He was missing for many years. He was assassinated and his body was abandoned." I asked them how the family had brought him back. One woman said, "The man decided to return to his family and told his eldest son to help him. He came home one day, spoke to his son, and showed him where he was."

As the peculiar bodily reunion of generations between Van and his father continued, and the stories about it circulated in the village, Van's father became an increasingly active participant in the family and community affairs. The ghost of the man was becoming more of a living ancestor. When Van's younger brother in Australia was facing business failure and divorce, it was rumored that the father ghost told his eldest son that the breakup of the marriage was inevitable. The villagers interpreted this statement in two different but related ways. Some took it to mean that Van's father, like other Ha My elders, did not approve of his city-born daughter-in-law. When he had escaped the country, Van's younger brother had eloped with a girl from Da Nang, the daughter of a former officer of the Saigon army. Some of Van's neighbors speculated that the girl, like everyone else from the city they knew of, must have jealously withheld her husband's Australian money from his family in Vietnam. They also speculated that, after the divorce, Van's brother would be free to devote his love to his native land. These speculations provoked animated conversations among the villagers and helped bring the spirit of Van's father even further into the milieu of village life. The ghost was acting like a typical head of a village household and an elder in a lineage association, who would view the village's connections to far-away places with a self-centered perspective.

The intrusive spirit in Lap's family, in the process of transforming into an ancestor, accumulated the traits of a moral person. The more the spirit appeared to be a willful and intentional social actor, the further removed from the history of unjust death he became. The ghost's transformation to an ancestor was a gradual process that involved not only the reburial of his physical remains but also his participation in social affairs. The transformation, moreover, was more than a unilateral transition from anonymity to identity and from the exterior to the interior of domestic ritual space. The mobility of village ghosts troubled the general spatial and ritual social order. In this situation, one could imagine the unusual circumstance of a ghost worshipped in a house as easily as the opposite event, of ancestors wandering in the street.

A year after the reburial of her husband's remains, Ba Lap organized a death-day anniversary on his behalf and invited the village ritual specialist, Thay My, for the occasion. On this occasion, Thay My proposed to Van that the family erect an outside shrine for wandering ghosts. The shrine, according to the priest, should be under the old bamboo tree kept at the edge of Van's garden on the east side and should face eastward—toward one of the sites of the Monkey Year massacre. The priest explained that the shrine would be for three unnamed ghosts. Lap was curious about the identity of the three ghosts and tried to return to the subject on several occasions during the meal after the ceremony. Each time she did this, Van told me, the respected Taoist master politely declined to satisfy his mother's curiosity. Thay My simply kept listing the families who, he argued, had benefited in health and economy after they had built a ghost shrine according to his instructions.

After that, Lap's family, like many other families in her neighborhood, prepared offerings on the external shrine, which Thay My had told them to build, each time they had an occasion to do so on the domestic ancestral shrine. The neighbors speculated that the three ghosts in the house of Ba Lap were her own three lost children. Van and his wife thought so too, although they were cautious not to mention it at home. Their aging mother believed that she had reclaimed all her lost children and settled them in the tablets next to their father, according to Van, and it would be sad for her to know that they were still in the street. A few years later, however, it turned out that the three ghosts who allegedly frequented Lap's outdoor shrine in fact included the spirit of her recently reburied husband.

The day before the annual death anniversary of the Monkey Year massacre, several survivor families were gathered at the house of Thay My to discuss the idea of holding a community-wide "spirit consolation" rite on behalf of the victims of the mass killing. Later in the evening, a few fishermen from Ha My's seashore community were also present in the gathering, having come to discuss the safety of their next fishing trip. The evening's conversation was partly about Van's father. People praised his sacrifice for the villagers during the war and his sacrifice for his children. Thay My told them that the spirit of Van's father had appeared in his dream and thanked him for helping his family. According to the priest, it transpired that the father ghost wished to stay with the ghosts of his tragically killed children, and that this was why Thay My had been inspired to suggest a shrine to Van's family during the ritual a few years back. The priest said that Van's father, although he was happy with his reburial, was unhappy to see his two children still wandering in the street. The father ghost decided to remain in the street, too, in order to care for them, he explained, until an opportunity came for his children to benefit from a reburial. In another dream that he had, the priest said, the ghost of Van's father had two small, timid children with him, each one holding his hand, and that he looked proud that both of them were wearing new shoes and clothes.

In Van's home, the day after, his mother and his wife had prepared an attractive table of food, sweets, clothes, and paper votive money facing the ancestral altar. I asked Van's children who the table was for; they said it was for their aunts and uncle. On the external shrine, Van's wife had prepared a smaller table of offerings. Later in the evening, when her mother-in-law had retired to her bedroom, Van's wife moved some of the sweets and money from the ancestral altar to the shrine underneath the bamboo tree. Van asked me to escort him to the ghost shrine, where he lit a few more incense sticks and made this prayer:

> Co Bac, if you're related to this family, please accept this food and help this family.
> Co Bac, if you're unrelated to this family, please accept this food and protect this family.
> Co Bac, related or unrelated, we welcome you and are happy to relate to you.
> You are welcome to carry some food with you, if you wish.
> We pray for you, we pray for you.

The experience of Van's family did not surprise the villagers; instead, it provoked intense speculation and debate about how to interpret particular apparitions and dreams. Through this interpretative process, a ghost came to have its own moral dilemmas and aspirations. When a ghost was talked about as if it were a living moral being, its transformation had already begun. The ghost, in the process of transforming into an ancestor, accumulated the traits of a moral person and behaved in the way he would have had he been alive. The more the ghost resembled a moral person, the further its life was perceived to have moved away from the displaced life of a wandering ghost. And the more it became a willful and intentional actor, the further it was removed from its history of tragic death.

Many families of Ha My, like Van's family, did not think of their external shrines as places for unknown ghosts only, although they described them as such. A number of them built their shrines under specific instructions from the ritual specialists on behalf of their war-killed relatives or those who fell victim to the massacre. Once built, however, such a shrine was believed to be not only a place for their unsettled ancestors but also a place for all sorts of other unrelated anonymous ghosts. In popular idiom and imagination, ghosts constituted a composite group of diverse historical backgrounds.

An old mandarin ghost could have as a companion a young *hat giong do* ghost—"red born and bred," referring to a dedicated communist activist. This unusual pair was often reported in the community of Cam An. A group of child and young mother ghosts moved in company with amputated solider ghosts. Several villagers of Thuy Bo claimed that they had seen this refugee group composed of civilians as well as combatants. The residents of My Lai remembered not only the lamentations of mother ghosts grieving for the dead children in their arms but also the swift movements and whispering noises of three American GI ghosts near the shrimp-breeding farm. The neighbors periodically made small food offerings to these ghosts, and when they did so on their external shrine, the food and money were meant for the GI ghosts as well as the native mother and child ghosts. On seasonal ceremonial days, people in an isolated neighborhood of Ha My distributed incense sticks on the grave of an anonymous girl ghost, at the edge of a children's playground where they believed lay a Viet Minh patriot, and at the village pond, where people sometimes saw an agile ROK Marine ghost.

The attention given to these differential historical beings was equal, unrelated to their particular social status or political affiliations, for the simple reason that these beings existed in the environment. Don Lam claims the Vietnamese "cult of deities is an open system marked by some democracy. It admits both female and male divinities, young and old, of aristocratic (kings, queens or mandarins) or plebeian origin (peasants), even the souls of beggars, thieves and enemy soldiers falling in battle in our country."[26] Indeed, it seemed that, just as the living have their inalienable human rights, so do the dead—the right to be remembered—and that the ghost shrine is an open memorial representing this universal ethic where ancestors and ghosts may share their sorrows and joys, free from the moral hierarchy of death that separates them. The choice made by the spirit of Van's father to remain in the street, and his paternal feelings for the ghosts of his children, which prompted him to make that choice, had been for this spirit, unlike for an ancestor in the ritual structure, a way of becoming a real ancestor in the moral world of Ha My. This was the magic of giving a place to ghosts, of giving ghosts the freedom to choose a place for their memory.

Earlier I mentioned the reciprocal perspective of the rising cosmological parallelism in village social renovation. In this chapter I have suggested a further parallel development in the renovation of the place of the dead. In his essay "Versions and Visions," Nelson Goodman writes, "So long as contrasting right versions not all reducible to one are countenanced, unity is to be sought not in an ambivalent or neutral *something* beneath these versions but an overall organization embracing them."[27] This principle of esthetics applies to the theme that concerns us here. Both the moral hierarchy of "house" versus "street" and the fact that this cosmological structure is anachronistic when applied to the memory of violent mass war death are real in domestic death commemoration. Between the cultural rule and the historical reality, unity was made possible in a practical organization that integrates the dual structure of worship with the shifting, "ambidextrous" bodily practice encompassing the bipolar moral spectrum of death. The movements of the body in this social practice cannot be considered merely a reinforcement of the symbolism of center/periphery or a demonstration the preeminence of genealogical memory. The renovation of the ancestral place, in the work of this active remembrance, also materialized its opposite symbol and revitalized the marginal identities represented by it.

The ghost of Lap's husband allegedly chose to remain in the street as long as his children were there. We can conclude that the magical drama of this ghost's homecoming was an expression of human agency, which, in commemorative practices, strives to account for historical reality within the given structure of norms and by imagining it from the point of view of the historical other. Ancestor worship that rises on the ruins of mass death—perhaps this *had* to be an "open" system of practices acknowledging the ambiguity concerning ancestors and ghosts and honoring the intimacy between them. Otherwise, the ancestral memory enshrined on the altar would be too far removed from the history of tragic death to merit worship.

CHAPTER 5

Heroes and Ancestors

Ancestors and ghosts are not the only categories of death found in Vietnamese domestic ritual space. In traditional times, these two categories might have been sufficient for conceptually organizing the cosmological mirror of the living world. The rise of the modern nation-state, however, has added a novel category of death to the traditional cosmology of death. Called *liet si* in Vietnamese, it refers to the heroic death of fallen soldiers who sacrificed their lives for the sacred purpose of protecting the nation. Historians suggest that the institutionalized commemoration of this category constitutes the core of "modern national memory."[1] In western Europe, mass death in the First World War invigorated the traditional belief in martyrdom and resurrection, and the tombs of fallen soldiers and the cenotaphs that keep their memory became forceful emblems of national unity (see chapter 1).[2]

The state commemorative art of postwar Vietnam adopted many esthetic elements from the Europeans, but Vietnam's institution of heroic death does not represent the "invented tradition" in the way this is defined by the historians of European experience.[3] The European art of war heroism drew heavily upon the traditional symbolism of Christian martyrdom. In contrast, the postwar Vietnamese state, like other socialist states that aspired to develop revolutionary esthetic forms free from the legacy of a backward past, censored the elements of traditional religions when it developed its modern institution of heroic death. It enforced the borrowed esthetics of hero worship in place of the traditional religious practices. However, the Vietnamese state institution of heroic death was an "invented tradition" in a novel way and a different sense. In his classic account of the modern process of national integration, Benedict Anderson highlights the technology of printing, which disseminated the language of the state. The development of "print capitalism" enabled, through literature and literacy, the fictional unity of the nation-state to take root in the minds of the people as a given reality.[4] Anderson focuses on the fact that commemorative oratory about war martyrs such as Jules Michelet's was distributed widely in France, enabling people to understand the imagined community of a nation-state as "a collective subject to whom the actions of the state can be internally connected, in creating, or trying to create, an experiential 'we.'"[5] Although the postwar Vietnamese state hierarchy, too, has produced a large volume of literature on war heroism, its principal instrument for making people think of, and experience, the nation has been ritual rather than literature, especially in the countryside.

Shaun Malarney describes this ritual politics of nationalism in the context of postrevolutionary northern Vietnam. He shows how the domestic ancestral shrine was transformed into a place of revolutionary leaders and war heroes, and how the equivalent process took place in the public space of the village: the state substituted war monuments and martyr cemeteries for the family ancestral graveyards and village communal houses as the village's sacred places.[6] In the southern regions, a core part of the postwar social mobilization was the replication of this ritual politics. The villagers "read" and experienced the nation-state within their most intimate sphere of life and on an everyday basis. The mass-produced portraits of national leaders and the death certificates of revolutionary soldiers replaced the tablets and other memorabilia of ancestors. The official village assembly hall of the People's Committee, similarly decorated, replaced the traditional communal house that used to hold the inscriptions dedicated to the founding ancestors. This was an invented tradition of a particular variety: the traditional religious institution became the technology of national integration. Imagining the nation-state became a matter of thinking about dead war heroes within the familiar system of ancestor worship.

I have described how traditional ancestor worship has reemerged into this hero-centered political culture and how ancestors and ghosts once again have become formative categories. This political transformation can be examined in the light of the shifting places of war heroes. Understanding the cult of ancestors in modern life, and the life of ghosts for that matter, is impossible without an understanding of the cult of heroes. The two ideologies share the same infrastructure.

THE POLITICAL HISTORY OF TEMPLES

Household ancestors in Vietnam do not remain in the house forever. A few generations after their deaths, when their relationship with the living inhabitants of the house becomes distant, these ancestors must hand over their place to the ancestors of newer generations and move on. This usually takes three generations for a novice ancestor, and the place he moves on to is normally *nha tho toc*—the ancestral temple of his patrilineage or the lineage hall. Following the renovation of ancestral tombs, the Ha My and My Lai villagers began to concentrate on reconstituting their family temples and the village communal house of *dinh,* the shrine that commemorates the village's founding ancestors.[7] From 1993 to 1997, the lineage groups *(ho* or *toc)* of Ha My competed with one another on this collective project and completed more than fifty temples by the spring of 1997. The district of Dien Ban, where Ha My is located, counts 957 lineage groups within its boundaries. About 600 of them completed their family temples by 1999.[8] When the renovation of individual family temples was well advanced, the lineage associations collaborated on the restoration of the village communal house. By 1999, the three hamlets of Ha My, Ha Gia, and Ha Quang had completed their communal house.

In 1996, when the temple renovation movement in the region was at its height, the early morning gatherings in town coffeehouses and the midafternoon tea gatherings in rural houses were abuzz with news about new family temples. Everyone, particularly the men, was talking and thinking about *nha tho toc.* The general meeting of the members of a lineage group initiated a family temple association consisting of the elders and the eldest male descendants, and this group organized the villagers, tapped the network of relatives in the cities or other provinces, and sent letters of appeal for financial support to overseas relatives. The lineage groups that had affluent overseas relatives were the first to complete their temples, and these tended to be superior in size and architectural grandeur. Groups such as the Nguyen family of Ha My, on the contrary, faced great difficulty in raising money. Having suffered a particularly heavy loss of life in the Monkey Year tragedy, the elders of this lineage experienced frustration during their five-year preparation for a small one-room temple. The members complained of the relatively large donation expected of each family. When their temple finally opened in the year 2000, the opening ritual was unremarkable according to the established local standards.

These restored sites of communal identity and solidarity took on an architectural form that corresponds to the dual structure of ancestor worship discussed earlier. A typical new family temple in Ha My consisted of three rooms, the middle one of which held the ancestral shrine. The building had carved images of ascending dragons on the rooftop and along the central columns. On the opposite side of the building was a simple stone or concrete wall and an incense burner in front of it. This wall was a structural equivalent to the external shrine in the domestic setting built for the displaced spirits of the dead. The external shrine at the temple, likewise, represented the unnamed, unplaced, and unbounded elements of the past—the structural opposite of the identified, located, genealogically enclosed historical identities held in the interior. The place of ghosts in the temple, however, took on a dimension unknown in its domestic equivalents. The new temples incorporated a monument for war martyrs and integrated this monument with the shrine for wandering ghosts.

The ancestral temples in central Vietnam played an important part in wartime revolutionary politics (see chapter 1). Political ideas and military plans were frequently discussed in temples. Experienced communist cadres chose to meet village elders in their family temples, knowing they were more likely to gain community support for high-risk mass action if they discussed it inside a sacred place. They believed that unfamiliar political ideas were more easily introduced to villages if disseminated with the appearance of ancestral endorsement.[9] Partisan fighters from distant places slept on the floor of the village communal house. For generations, Vietnamese rural village temples provided temporary shelter for *nguoi ngoai* (travelers or strangers).[10] The U.S.-Saigon war administration understood the importance of rural ancestral temples in reproducing kinship and place solidarity, and the local troops took the view that ancestral temples in rural Vietnam bred subversive activities. In the 1960s, many temples in Quang Nam and Quang Ngai provinces became legitimate targets of destruction under village pacification programs. The destruction of ancient temples by explosives, together with the desecration of ancestral graveyards by armored vehicles, was recalled by Ha My and My Lai villagers in particularly strong language charged with expressions of anger and bitterness (see chapter 7).

It is ironic that these ancestral temples, which had made a distinguished contribution to the war effort, were singled out as symbols of political impurity and cultural backwardness when the war ended. According to William Duiker, this is related to the shift of focus in the nation's political leadership, from a mobilization of all resources for the nationalist struggle during the war to a focused ideological struggle against "vestiges of feudal, colonialist, and bourgeois cultures" after the war.[11] As town youths in southern Vietnam were being chased by the officials who tried to rid them of their decadent hair styles, village ancestral shrines, together with Buddhist pagodas and animist temples, were hammered down from 1975 to 1977 against the expectations and wishes of the returning villagers who had survived the war elsewhere. A construction worker and former partisan fighter in Quang Ngai recalled a prayer from this period when he helped destroy three temples in the area of My Lai:

> Ong Ba, please have mercy on this poor man. I apologize to you, and my ancestors apologize to you, that I ought to do this terrible thing to your honorable place. Please see with your clear eyes that it is not me who is doing this to you. My hands are only hired hands, and the hands that are trying to bring your place down are elsewhere. If you feel indignant, I beg you to make sure that you're not angry with a wrong person. I apologize to you. Please accept this small offering as my apology.

My Lai villagers told many stories of vengeance related to the destruction of temples. In these stories, indignant ancestors or an animist deity took direct action against the culpable person—usually a state functionary or a war veteran being overzealous in the antisuperstition, moral purity campaign after the war. Some of the men who actually destroyed temples went insane, according to the construction worker cited above, and some of the officials who orchestrated such immoral acts suffered accidental death under the influence of vengeful spirits. In a less calamitous case, the family of a culpable party official was obliged to hold a ritual of reparation on behalf of the offended animist deity. This man was lucky to save his life this way, said a resident of My Lai and a distant relative of the official, and subsequently became a secret follower of the deity. In the past, these postwar confrontations between the political activists with their excessive ideological commitment and the supernatural actors with their excessive mandate for retribution circulated the village only in whispers. Today, one can hear such stories of magical battles openly at any family gathering. In a particularly engaging episode that entertained the entire crowd gathered for a funeral, an elderly relative of the deceased spoke about the Tiger Spirit (Ong Cop) giving a history lecture to a party official and an author of the party history. The official, suffering from a symptom of mental disorder, came to visit a local medium in order to convey to the animist deity his regret at having dishonored the deity's home, Mieu Ong Cop. The elder said that the deity had asked the medium to deliver to the culpable the following message:

> Seven men and women of your sort [communists] used to sleep in my house. They cooked meals in my house, washed their clothes in my backyard, and helped themselves to the fruits on my table. I was not pleased at all with their rude behavior, but I said nothing and did nothing. I tolerated them, even when the females washed their dirty clothes in my place, and I even helped to save their lives when they were in mortal danger. The day when the soldiers surrounded my house and were firing at it, the seven men and women were in panic. They were in fear, and two of them prayed to me for mercy. I took pity on them, particularly the young woman from the highlands. She used to pray for my forgiveness when her friends took fruits from my table without a word of excuse. I helped them escape—the seven men and women, all of them. And you, ungrateful man, now come to break my house? After all that I endured for your people?

Stories of this kind tell about a contest of power between state ideology and local morality and the community's commitment to the places that define its unique identity.[12] The traditional Vietnamese village had "a personality with its own individuality," and temples (the specific configuration of their interrelationship) represented this "village personality."[13] Nguyen Minh Dat, the village poet of Ha My, describes the prewar identity of Ha My:

> The Banyan tree in front of the village *dinh* had survived many generations.
> Do you remember the Mieu Cop in the middle of the village?
> Below it was Ba Su, and above it stood Ba Dong.
> Do you remember Ong Phu in the paddy?[14]

In the countryside, the network of temples distinguished a village from others. In the town, the community temple dedicated to a specific genie or deity made the neighborhood a place with distinctive, memorable characters. And the particular traits of a community deity affected people's perception of the place. The Tiger Spirit, Ong Cop, and the Whale Spirit, Ca Ong, for instance, are known to have different personalities and orientations. Among many stated differences, the Tiger Spirit is considered to be impulsive and quick-tempered, easily provoked but easily reconciled with, whereas the Whale Spirit is relatively more patient but ferocious once a taboo is broken. Tiger temples tend to be interrelated in a form of descent—between the parental site and the offshoot "child" temple. By contrast, each whale temple, even the smallest unit, is strongly autonomous but still forms a symbolic affinity with a temple that worships a different deity. A whale temple is typically situated in a seaside fishing hamlet, where there are abundant taboos in relation to maritime production activities and an exchange relationship with the agricultural neighbors is encouraged. A tiger temple, however, is often found in an area likely to expand, such as a busy crossroads.[15]

Traditionally, rural temples and their urban counterparts had different infrastructures. The former stood on communal land *(tu dan dien* or *tu dan tho)* and drew from it the necessary resources for ritual activity.[16] Urban community temples lacked such an economic basis and tended to support themselves with contributions from community members. The postwar Vietnamese state administration made rural communal lands into state property and leased them to agricultural cooperatives and later to individuals. In urban areas, many community temples that survived the war and the postwar demolition have been leased out to small businesses. Today, the state has legalized the private ownership of land and is selling to private bidders what used to be the inalienable property of the village communal house or other community temples. Although few people took issue with the postwar transfer of communal land to state ownership, most villagers spoke bitterly about the land being handed over to private owners. This view was prevalent in Ha My, where they used unusually strong words to condemn the transfer of twenty-eight acres of historic communal land to several rich individuals and outside speculators.[17] In response to this grim prospect, a number of urban communities made efforts to reinstate the prewar communal ownership. In 1998, the neighborhood of Phan Boi Chau Street in a town in Quang Nam province prepared its fifth petition to the provincial government:

> We, the Funeral Organizing Committee of our community, make this plea to the National Assembly of the Quang Nam Province on behalf of the community and in order to preserve the community's most precious heritage site. Our community has an ancient temple, which was beautifully built on 522 square meters and has rich old relics. At the time of the collectivization, the salt-manufacturing enterprise Hai Nam took over the temple site. They used the holy shrine for storing sea salt. The state enterprise is now selling the land and the building to a foreign individual. Most people in our community have no specific religious affiliations. We only worship our ancestors who set foot in this land and built a beautiful community. On the twentieth day of the seventh month, the community holds a ceremony to honor the memory of our Tien Hien. This ceremony preserves the colorful, rich tradition of Vietnam

and is an opportunity for the residents to enjoy festivity. On the fifth day of
the fifth month, the first and the fifteenth day of each month, and during the
Tet, the residents wish to light incense and candles in the temple. Many wish
to rent the temple to hold a funeral as in the old times. . . . When we prepare
our incense burner on the street toward what turned into a salt storage, we
see that this is not a civilized way of honoring our ancestors. This impropri-
ety makes us feel sad and shameful to our ancestors. . . . Now our temple is
about to be taken over by a private individual who is not even part of our
community. Everyone in our community believes that this is unacceptable.
What will happen if the temple becomes someone's private property? We
wish to hold ceremonies in the temple, not on the street outside the temple.
Please show your sympathy to our deep commitment to the most important
basis of our community.[18]

Even without the question of communal land, the renovation of a
temple was a politically sensitive issue. Tan Viet writes, "Although our
party leaders have not yet formulated any precise political line on the rising work of ancestor worship, it is obvious to everyone that they are also
descendents of a family line. Our party leaders have their placenta buried
somewhere just like anyone of us. Some high-ranking cadres have volunteered to participate in the work of ancestor worship. They have done so,
because they knew the wide public opinion, and this way contributed to
the advancement of the general *viec ho* movement. . . . Family feelings
are a natural feeling."[19] Tan argues that the *viec ho* activity of family
ancestor worship encompasses all sectors of the society and transcends
the differences in class *(giai cap)*, social status *(vai tro vi tri)*, and social
systems or ideologies *(che do xa hoi)*. He asserts that "family feelings"
are "natural" and a universal phenomenon, and that they were sup-
pressed by the adverse circumstances of foreign domination and violent
wars. He also argues that ancestor worship—*ve chau to* (to gather to
serve the ancestors)—meets favorable circumstances today.[20] According
to Tan, these consist of the political foundation of national independence
achieved by the liberation war, on the one hand, and the current economic development that promotes the liberty to practice cultural life, on
the other. The mass struggle for independence from 1945 to 1975 under
the leadership of the Communist Party, Tan argues, contributed to
achieving the favorable circumstances for ancestor worship.

The revival of ancestor worship was a thorny political issue, as Tan
implies with his tactful remarks about the party leaders' placentas, and
required a redefinition of tradition within revolutionary state politics.
The temples in a Vietnamese community invoked the historical memory
of multiple episodes of destruction by not only foreign aggressors during

the war but also the victorious political authorities after the conflict was over. For the community, restoring such a place meant transcending the history of war and deprivation. For the state, it meant a return to backward cultural tradition and a challenge to the modern secular national identity. Against the background of a "contest between official and vernacular memory," the state apparatus of Vietnam initially maintained a critical distance from the *viec ho* activity.[21] Village officials kept out of the family temple project, although some officials and party cadres were informally as enthusiastic about the project as the ordinary villagers.

By the early 1990s, nearly all agricultural cooperatives had collapsed in Quang Nam; by 1992, production by the private economic sector had risen to represent an astonishing 80 percent of the gross national product. Family-owned businesses mushroomed in the towns, and agricultural production was practically handed over to family units, who were entitled to the use rights to farmland, including the right to inherit, sell, and mortgage it.[22] Private ownership of land was still illegal, but only nominally so, as various public institutions, including even the army, were selling the use rights to state property to the private developers. The state administration encouraged this trend and was eager to administer it. The return of the market and private economy was celebrated as a social advancement; that of ancestor worship was not. Concerned party functionaries complained about the rise in ritual expenditure, which the earlier postwar state administration had successfully discouraged in the second half of 1970s. The popular revival of ancestor worship frustrated the political leaders who saw it as hampering the prospects of an economically prosperous nation.[23] The state's economic policy intended to impose on the unproductive sectors a system of higher efficiency and to not waste capital on ritual activities for the nonliving. The political reform policy was meant to open the nation's front door to advanced ideas and foreign investment, not its back door, which led to the ruins of history. The family worship practices and the popular ritual economy appeared to some officials to be the apparition of an old ghost that would hinder the nation's forward march into the prosperous commodity market economy. Indeed, a party official and author of party history whom I knew once referred to Marx's comment about the ghost of the ancient regime corrupting the spirit of the French revolution, when we met by accident in a beer bar in Da Nang and talked about the issue of temple renovations.

In the early 1990s, local party officials held meetings to discuss the growing number of applications for permission to build family temples, and the rank-and-file party members were ordered to neither endorse nor participate in ritual ceremonies. A newspaper columnist denounced, in carefully chosen words, the parochial nature of ancestor worship and contrasted it—"the prerogative of upper classes"—to the intimacy of the masses with the allegedly equalitarian Buddhist tradition.[24] These somewhat paranoiac reactions from the state officials were modified to a more accommodating form by the end of the 1990s. An official publication from Da Nang in 1999 presented an orthodox neo-Confucian argument that family solidarity is the backbone of national unity.[25] And a report in an influential provincial journal of Quang Nam argued, in a somewhat ironic way, that family ancestral temples could be mobilized in effective collaboration with the administration's social campaign against superstitions and magical practices.[26]

One notable reaction by the state hierarchy to the popular religious revival was the intensification of civic morality programs. The programs included renewed attention to the social welfare of war invalids and families of war martyrs. The nationwide promotion of "Heroic Mothers of Vietnam"—the mothers who lost three or more children to the liberation war—was vigorously carried out at the provincial, district, and village levels. The village administration held banquets and title-awarding ceremonies for the village's mother heroes, oversaw the building of one-room pension homes for the solitary mother heroes without a surviving child, and organized large crowds for the funerals of Heroic Mothers. Hue-Tam Ho Tai relates the promotion of Heroic Mothers to the weakening of the earlier triumphalist official war remembrance in the new reality of a general economic and political liberalization. She believes that the feminine symbol of the Heroic Mother represents loss and grief, rather than glorious victory.[27] Considering the maternal icon from a different angle, and as a symbol relating to kinship ideology rather than as a gendered symbol, however, we can also argue that the icon provided a solution to the genealogical problems in the conventional war hero worship.[28] The Heroic Mothers produced the youths who gave their lives to the nation; honoring their identity was an ultimate tribute to the memory of their dead children, as this act meant a substitutive fulfillment of filial obligation by the nation on behalf of the nation's fallen heroes. This symbolic mediation of the Heroic Mother in war hero worship made it possible to commemorate the young war dead within the norms of Confucian morality. Acknowledging maternal sacrifice, in other words, helped to conceal and neutralize the conceptual and moral crisis embedded in the political institution of war hero worship.

The state administration also revitalized the body-finding missions for the recovery of revolutionary martyrs missing in action and expanded the categories of war martyr and war invalid to include heroic prisoners of war and other relatively marginal revolutionary activists. A number of previously untitled villagers in the environs of Ha My and My Lai benefited from this trend and earned sealed certificates of honor from the state or even a small state pension. The revitalized production of war heroes also applied to collective units. Many rural villages, including Ha My, were nominated to be "Hero Villages" in the early 1990s, and this was followed by the addition of the categories "Model Village" and "Model Neighborhood" (in an urban community), which became popular in the mid-1990s. The criteria for a "Model Neighborhood" varied from province to province but emphasized "general moral purity" and included "healthy family life," "healthy communal harmony," and "the absence of unhealthy social practices and elements." The Department of Information and Culture and other related civic relation departments throughout the state hierarchy, from the village to the province, expanded in the same period, and they tried to recruit young, competent university graduates. This boom of patriotic individuals and communities inflated the frequency of public meetings on the legacy of the liberation war and stimulated official research and publications on the local history of war.

The result of this official activity was that, at the village level, it appeared as if the state's hero worship and the village's ancestor worship were prospering together in the 1990s.[29] The village was busy with preparations for ancestral temples; the village and district administrations were preoccupied with events celebrating the heritage of the patriotic war. This had a positive effect on the temple renovation project, for the project involved a particular group of villagers who moved relatively freely between official and communal activities. Rumors about their activities circulated across villages, and these rumors in the politically controlled rural environment, as James Scott argues, were "a kind of democratic voice" and "a partisan effort."[30]

The veterans of the American War have considerable moral authority in Ha My and My Lai. Many of them are experienced in oratory and network-type organizational work, and they are respected by the villagers for their knowledge of the world beyond the village. Having gone back to agricultural or horticultural work immediately after the end of the war, these former partisan fighters participate in various informal mutual support networks among the villagers and often play an important role in deciding family and community matters.[31] These veterans joined their lineage association for the local temple project, helped draft the application for the official permit, and lobbied the party officials on behalf of the association. One application letter drafted collaboratively by a local poet and former partisan leader states, "Thanks to the successful economic reform, our villagers now live better and can think about cultural prosperity. Our work represents the villagers' love of their native land, and the national independence, achieved under the leadership of the Communist Party, forms the basis on which this work can be realized. The village's contribution to national liberation is signified by its entitlement of Hero Village."[32]

The coauthor of this letter was a former partisan leader living in Ha My. He was intensely interested in village affairs, and his house was frequently crowded with visitors. In 1996, this elder was actively involved in his lineage association and was also receiving many invitations to state ceremonies. The ceremonies included the annual assembly of war veterans and invalids, the Heroic Mother nomination ceremonies, the new interprovincial feasts in celebration of wartime solidarity, and the celebration of a new publication on the local history of war. Through these events, the elder renewed his contacts with the acting party officials and exchanged village news with veterans from other places. From one official gathering, he brought home to the members of his lineage association a rumor about Ong Bua, the renowned former partisan leader of the Cam An–Cam Chau area, two miles south of Ha My, who, after retiring from the army, now supplies tiles and bricks to local builders. At the time, the Ha My association faced difficulty in obtaining permission for the temple; the district office had ignored the application, and the lineage elders were looking for a way to end the delay. The family of Ong Bua had had a similar problem, and the rumor was about how he persuaded the skeptical party officials to move forward with the construction of his family temple. In their next application letter, the Ha My family repeated the words that the eminent former partisan leader had used in his: "It is according to the principle of our revolution to share wealth and happiness with the generations of war dead who knew nothing but poverty and suffering. The nation's prosperity should benefit all the generations of Vietnam, not merely those who are alive."[33]

The participation and moral authority of people like Ong Bua encouraged the lineage associations and helped to legitimize an activity that the state saw as a revival of the backward past. When the delegates of a lineage association went to the district office to discuss a temple renovation project, they brought prepared references to successful projects in which the families of war martyrs and the heroic mothers were actively involved. They used the statistics of war casualties to demonstrate that the family was entitled to worship their ancestors who had produced many distinguished patriots. In speeches to his lineage association, the above-mentioned elder of Ha My clarified the dialectic between national history and local heritage. I quote from his notes for a speech he made during the early preparatory stage of the family temple:

> On behalf of our temple association, I wish you all great happiness and thank you for coming to join us to remember the great people who discovered this land and planted life here. . . . Our ancestors made a distinctive contribution to the nation's history. Many were brilliant in scholarship and sacrificed for the independent Dai Viet. As the saying goes, "If the names of ancestors are written in the national history, their descendants earn good reputation." Our ancestors did not leave us with a citadel or great monuments of high architecture. Even if they had, the civil wars and the liberation wars of the past ten centuries would have all eaten them up. But they left us with a precious heritage—that is, tradition, and tradition lasts forever. This is their victory. There are these old words—"The birds have a nest, the people have a place of origin." By commemorating the first settlers and the ancestors who opened the land on the day of *cung gio* or *ton tao phan mo*, the descendants reveal the deep past and renew their relationship with the past—this is what our ancestors paid for with their blood and bone. . . . The war of the past fifty years destroyed all our places of worship and desecrated ancestral tombs. Few traces of our ancestors remain. What is left is only us. We are the most precious remnants. . . . At wartime we dreamt about family reunions such as today's, always. Today is a good day, an auspicious day in the year of the Cock. For two decades our country has been in peace; so have been our people. We have the fortune to be in the birthplace,[34] thanks to our ancestors' blessing *[phuc duc]*. Thanks to the *cong duc* of our founding ancestors, we endured the many ups and downs of the country. The *cong duc* of our ancestors is such that their bone and blood contributed to the defense of the country, its development, and the prevention of natural disasters. Now we are proud of this ancestral history and promise to keep the history forever.

GHOSTS WHO WORSHIP ANCESTORS

The parallel development of state hero worship and communal ancestor worship affected the material forms of the renovated ancestral temples. As noted earlier, the renovation of temples, like the equivalent process in the domestic ritual space, entailed creating both an interior ancestral temple and an exterior shrine for ghosts. The renovation of temples developed an added complication, however.

In 1995, residents of the hamlet of Ha Gia completed a shrine for ghosts on the opposite side of their newly refurbished ancestral temple house. The completed wall-shaped shrine for ghosts included an esthetically opposite vertical structure—a replica of the kind of Gothic patriotic tower found in the cemeteries of war martyrs—with the inscription "To Quoc Ghi Cong" (Your Ancestral Land Remembers You). The style for ghost shrines had changed when Ha Quang built its communal house in 1999. On this site, a tall marble tombstone was erected behind the low wall-shaped shrine for ghosts, and it listed the names of several hundred of the village's war martyrs. The seaside communities in central Vietnam have a specific temple that honors the community's founding ancestors and the fisherman's guardian spirit, the Whale Spirit. The most sacred object in this temple is the coffin that contains the bones of a whale found beached nearby. In the whale temple of An Bang, as in whale temples elsewhere near Ha My, the villagers prepared next to the sacred coffin a smaller coffin with the inscription "Your Ancestral Land Remembers You" on it. It has also become a custom in these villages to have one of the seasonal temple-opening rites fall on July 27, the National Day of Invalids and War Martyrs.

The background for this syncretism includes circumstances both recent and distant. On the one hand, the villagers were conscious of making the place of their ancestors acceptable to the state's revolutionary politics and were particularly concerned about the revival of rituals. Most temple associations had a plan to hold a full-scale ancestral rite when their temple was completed. When they gathered to discuss this matter, the elders were not sure how the state authorities would react to such a public demonstration of an explicitly religious orientation, which required official permission. The idea of opening the temple without a magnificent rite was not an option, for the renovation of the temple meant, for the villagers, the restoration of a communal ritual activity. In this context, grafting a monument of war martyrs onto the place of ancestors could have been a convenient solution for strengthening the legitimacy of the place, much like the incorporation of former partisan leaders into the lineage associations.

On the other hand, the fusion of war heroes and community ancestors has a long history in Vietnam.[35] The communal house of Ha Gia, for instance, has the distinctive legendary background of a warrior cult. In the prewar period, the temple kept a model battle junk in the back of the building in memory of a village ancestor who had won a naval victory in the fourteenth century. The village used to perform a mock naval battle scene as part of their community ancestral rite. In light of this, the architectural form of the Ha Gia temple can be seen as introducing new historical material into an ancient cultural scenario. Sherry Ortner discusses a similar example in Sherpa religious history in the Himalayas.[36] As the Ha My elder's speech indicates, the village's ancestral history becomes powerful because it records a distinguished contribution to the country that has been recognized by the state, and because this recognition, in turn, has been inscribed in the local historiography. Only through this two-way process of recognition does the ancestor's contribution to the nation transform into a blessing for the descendants.

The state of Vietnam places the heroes of war in their place of origin; yet a genuine return of these heroes to their place of origin, from the perspective of the village, means the assimilation of their legacy into the domain of kinship. In the village, national history that is not incorporated into local history is not history. Heroism becomes a meaningful ideology only if it enriches the community's genealogical heritage. Within the spectrum of ancestor worship, war martyrs become genuine heroes only when their histories, having been incorporated in national history, are incorporated back into the place of village ancestors.

However, the memorial to war heroes that is assimilated in the space of ancestor worship is not the same as its formal state-administered equivalent. The latter is a religious symbol of nationalism and an instrument of state control; the former can be a pliant instrument of the community used to circumvent the state control of memory.[37] The communal house of Ha My has a unique history in this regard, which goes back to the period immediately after the liberation of the village in March 1975. At the end of this year, the Ha My villagers made a collective decision to rebuild the ruined temple of founding ancestors and petitioned the district party authority. This was an extraordinary move on the part of the villagers, considering that, during the period of 1975 to 1979, religious practices were strongly discouraged. In the neighboring villages and towns, Buddhist pagodas, animist temples, and roadside shrines for ghosts were being dismantled or closed down. No official permission could be granted for what was then regarded as a highly contentious idea, but a solution had to be found to satisfy the insistent village delegates. The fact that some of the core cadre leaders of the liberated village were also close relatives of the insistent villagers helped. After a series of informal meetings between the village's officials and the elders, the district party office granted permission on the condition that the temple would be used for honoring the memory of the village's revolutionary war martyrs. Completed in 1976, the communal house of Ha My had a prominent neo-Gothic "patriotic tower" of the sort normally seen on war monuments. On it, a village calligrapher has written "Our Warriors" in Chinese letters.

Over the years, this war memorial in the ancestral shelter became a singularly important public place in Ha My. The returning villagers, having no other place to commemorate their dead relatives, came to the patriotic tower to make offerings. The survivors of the Monkey Year massacre grieved the mass death at this place; the families of the war martyrs joined them there to do their death anniversary ceremonies. Returning war veterans came to the tower to light incense in memory of their wives and children; orphaned boys and girls brought fruits for the ghosts of their parents and siblings. Unlike the state memorials, the patriotic tower of the Ha My ancestor temple was open to all forms of war death and drew no boundaries between heroic death and tragic death.

How local communities reclaimed their sacred sites from state control is dramatically expressed in the following contemporary legend. When the renovation of the village's communal house was completed in 1995, the various lineage associations of Ha My collaborated to hold a community-wide rite in order to initiate it. The village ritual specialist Thay Sang was invited to oversee the rite. While Thay Sang was reading the incantation of spirit consolation while facing the tower of "Our Warriors" after having completed the part for the village ancestors alongside the temple, a large crowd of ghosts suddenly appeared in his sight. The ghosts were in families, young and old together, and there were also mutilated soldiers in tattered uniforms. Instead of receiving the tray of food laid out for them on the open-air altar in front of the patriotic tower, these ghosts rushed to the ancestral temple on the opposite side—the temple that smelled of fresh paint and attractive engravings. The old ghosts examined the building in delight, and the young soldier ghosts listened to the whispers of these grandmother ghosts. The young female ghosts began to kowtow, and the mother ghosts encouraged their child ghosts to do likewise and pay respect to their great ancestors. The boy and girl ghosts were reluctant to do what they were told and kept eyeing the tray of food and offerings on the other side.

The legend says that, at that moment, Thay Sang felt the urge to stop reciting his great poem "On Behalf of Seventy-two Different Deaths and

Invitation of Wandering Ghosts." He felt the urge to follow the ghosts' footsteps, walk toward the temple of the village's founding ancestors, and join the crowd of ghosts. He was reading good poems, and people were offering plenty of food for the wandering ghosts, and yet the ghosts were ignoring the food and money and were huddling behind the praying villagers, facing the opposite direction.

Each time someone recounted this dramatic scene in which the ghosts and the villagers were standing back to back and kowtowing in opposite directions, people laughed. According to the story, Thay Sang realized that his prayers had no recipients, and that they were being made to the empty space. Recalling this event just before he passed away, Thay Sang told me that the ghosts of that day must have been ghosts from Ha My, not wandering ghosts. People who so respect their original ancestors that they graciously honor them even after death, he argued, must be ghosts of Ha My origin. They were not tourist ghosts, but *ma que*—"the ghosts of the native place."

The fantastical ritual landscape painted by this story should be considered in comparison to the real landscape of commemoration that is regularly held in state memorials, where the crowd is gathered to honor the memory of fallen soldiers and the pure spirit of the nation they represent. In the magical landscape of the ancestral rite, the spirits of fallen soldiers are no longer on the opposite side of the crowd. Instead, they join the crowd and become part of the community of descendants, living or dead, who together commemorate the truly important heroes of the place—the legendary ancestors who planted the seed of life in the village (although the story is careful to have the dead descendants still maintain distance from the living descendants by giving the two groups opposite orientations). The transformation of war heroes from passive objects of commemoration to active participants in local memory was an effect of bringing the war memorial to the domain of kinship. The ghosts of war heroes may join the domain of ancestors; yet, the place that safeguards the pure spirits of the latter does not allow their commingling. Moreover, the institution of war heroes excludes the ambiguous war dead from its pure territory, although it experiences a certain amount of flexibility when dealing with heroes of the people's war.

CHAPTER 6

Grievous Death

"The bodies are all naked and they are all wounded," a woman in My Lai said of the mass grave near her house. She meant to draw attention to the fact that the victims of the massacre had been buried without coffins or funeral clothing, and that the broken pieces of individual bodies had not been put together before burial. Other relatives of victims in My Lai also spoke of the village's mass graves in graphic terms and with forceful indignation. A survivor of the Le family told me that thinking of his relatives enduring the terrible conditions in the mass grave induced physical pains in his own body. Partly for this reason, the victims' close relatives living in the village rarely visited the mass graves or conducted *chap ma,* the regular practice of weeding, cleaning, and repairing the tomb. Those who lived elsewhere did pass by the grave when they came to visit the village, and some of them left on it small gravestones with the names of their relatives written on them.

In Ha My, the narrative of the atrocity inscribed on the memorial stone speaks particularly bitterly of the desecration of the fallen bodies. The museum authority in My Lai regularly arranged for a few survivors to present their oral histories of the massacre to important visitors. When a narrator told of a village woman trying to gather the fragments of the bodies of her children in her bamboo basket, it had a strong effect on the audience. In both Ha My and My Lai, the survivors still suffer from the regret of not having had the opportunity to separate the bodies of the victims and bury them individually before they abandoned the village. After

the war ended and they returned to the village, it was difficult to be physically close to the mass grave and impossible to imagine any decent life
for the entombed in such a condition. The chairman of the Survivors'
Association in Ha Gia told me in 1997:

> When the floodwater subsided, we saw many skulls and bones. I did not
> know whether the skull belonged to my mother or my neighbor's sister-
> in-law. That's not a proper life; that's not a life at all. The authorities were
> not interested in correcting the situation. And I must be true to myself, too.
> We were busy with our daily life and trying to survive the hardship after
> the war. I tried to ignore the situation and tried to look the other way. Once
> in a while, particularly the first lunar month, the shame came back and in-
> duced unbearable pain in me.

The material conditions of an improper, collective burial complicate
commemoration. As I mentioned earlier, it is believed that the spirits of
the dead, in such negative physical circumstances, continue to relive the
dreadful drama of violent death, and that they are unable to find a way
out of it on their own. This is how ritual interventions become necessary
to break the perpetual captivity. Reburial in this context contributes to
dividing the life of the dead into past and present. The ritualized spatial
movement of the body creates a sense of temporal rupture between the
time before and the time after and enables the soul to feel that its painful
experience has become a thing of the past. This production of historicity
is central to the Vietnamese practice of reburial and tomb renovation.

In sociological literature, the meaning of reburial is often expressed in
the idioms of social transcendence. In Madagascar, for instance, ancestors are buried twice, first in a temporary place and then in the collective
tomb of ancestors when the bodies have thoroughly decomposed. Bloch
interprets this custom as a triumph of the potency of the sacred, symbol-
ized by the bones assembled in the ancestral tombs, over the impurity of
the mundane, which he argues the decomposed flesh represents. Placing
the fleshless ancestral bones within the collective tomb, he explains,
demonstrates the ideal of a transcendental social order, which in this
case is the lineage.[1] This interpretive strategy of mortuary culture follows
Durkheimian sociological tradition that separates social life into two dis-
crete spheres, the sacred-transcendental and the profane-immanent. The
strategy has its merits—it does not separate the ritual from the political,
for instance—but suffers from limiting analytical interests to the politically dominant symbolic processes only. Edmund Leach writes that
Durkheim "believed that collective representations were confined to the
sphere of the sacred, and since they held that the dichotomy between the

sacred and the profane was universal and absolute, it followed that it was specifically sacred symbols that called for analysis by the anthropologist."[2] Bloch himself notes that villagers in Madagascar exclude the remains of "bad death" from the sacred place of the dead. His analytical interests exclude the important question of how some social actions, in pursuit of a transcendental social ideal, create exclusion and marginality, and this is because the analysis pursues a goal similar to the social facts it draws upon. This is evident in Bloch's later works in which he presents a more generalizing argument that the "conquest" of the mundane by the sacred vitality is a human religious universal.[3] The construction of a transcendental modality, either analytical or empirical, ought to exclude unfitting elements.

The practice of secondary burial is known to the Vietnamese mortuary tradition, although it has nearly died out. In the past, the bones were separated from the decomposed corpse and reburied in a designated lineage burial ground. In the fishing communities in central Vietnam, the corpse of the whale, the community guardian, still undergoes a complex ritual of delayed burial. This mortuary tradition may be described using a language of social transcendence. In the realm of mass-produced tragic death, however, it is difficult to see how the idioms of symbolic conquest can work. An ideal reburial for the victims of tragic mass death is the opposite of the reburial for the ancestors of good death. The remains of those who died in a mass death do not await the joining of a collective entity but are already in a collective and, in the minds of the living, hope to get away from it, although this individuation apparently may involve participating in a form of collectivity such as the domain of ancestor worship. There is a certain drive toward individuality in the commemoration of bad death, and this orientation must negotiate with the dominant ideals of a coherent social whole. Most critically of all, removal of the remains of mass death is meaningful in a Vietnamese village not because of the identity of its destination but because, through the act, the death has the opportunity to depart from the tragic history. The meaning of reburial, for bad death, is personal liberty rather than collective identity. "If memory is seen as the continuous traversal of the space between what goes without saying and what cries out to be said," as Paul Antze and Michael Lambek insist, the sociology of death cries out for a theory of marginality that can balance the preponderance of the theory of sacred social center.[4]

A certain historical episode demonstrates these ideas. There is an unusual grave in the War Martyr Cemetery of Ha My. This Collective

Tomb of Thirty-Five Victims of Crime of War holds the victims of the massacre in Ha Gia, one of the communities that neighbor Ha My, and has a compelling history. If visitors look at this site without knowing the historical background, they may get the impression that, in this place, civilian death turned into a military death, and tragic death transformed into heroic death. This impression would not be entirely incorrect, for the state administration resisted removal of the corpses, viewing it from a related transcendentalist perspective. The mass grave, however, presents an entirely different picture if we consider the intentions and motivations of the Ha Gia villagers who actually fought to move the corpses to the symbolic center of revolutionary politics. In order to understand their intentions, we must first come to terms with the idea of *chet oan*— "grievous death"—and the idea of justice implied in this important native category.

UNJUST DEATH

In traditional Vietnamese belief, the morality of death was understood not only in temporal-genealogical (see chapter 3) and spatial-concentric terms (chapter 4) but also in a legal language. Death could be "just" or "unjust," in a metaphoric reference to the heavenly imperial authority that was believed to determine the cycle of life. Unjust death—in the milieu of this dualist worldview and belief in the afterlife organized under a vast bureaucracy equivalent to the feudal political order of this world—was the antonym of *chet nghiep* or *chet so*, meaning roughly "fateful death." The Vietnamese notion of "fate" *(nghiep)* refers either to "occupation" in the stratified Confucian hierarchy, with its mandarin scholars at the summit and traders at the bottom, or, as in other cultures influenced by Indic tradition, to the Buddhist doctrine of karmic continuity and accumulation. Thus, "fate" means a fixed place in the hierarchical order of things (either in this or that world), and "fateful death" an ordered, anticipated death in the great cosmic scenario of the cycle of life—that is, a determined place in the transition from this to that world. The other expression of fateful death, *chet so*, is less philosophical and refers specifically to the book of life and death kept in the Registry of the Other World (for the purpose of taxation, in ancient imagination).[5] Hence, it literally means "death according to the book [of fate]"—that is, a proper, orderly death, from a bureaucratic point of view. Vietnamese folklore has numerous examples of this "faithful death" or "preregistered death."

One such example tells of a man who had the fate of *chet troi,* meaning "to be drowned and drifted away." Aware of his fate, the man never went swimming, and he avoided any work or activities that involved contact with water. He even refrained from wet-rice cultivation because of his fear of water. One day, he was washing his face in a bucket of water, trying to refresh himself in the summer heat. Instead of using his two hands to splash water on his face, as most people would do, he hurriedly plunged his face into the bucket. The story says that this man could not avoid his fated death of *chet troi* and he died in the shallow water of the bucket. Another popular story is about *chet ho,* death by man-eating tiger. A man found out from a fortune-teller that his unpleasant destiny was to die at the age of forty-one in the mouth of a tiger. Unlike the man whose fate was *chet troi,* this man avoided all forested areas, said no to all temptations to hunt or gather medicine, and lived a life strictly by the water. One day, tired by the heat, he went swimming. While he was bathing in the water, he saw a tiger approaching the seashore. He let out a scream of shock and collapsed in fear of his fateful death.

If "fateful death" assumes an order in the cosmic cycle of life and death, "grievous death" *(chet oan)* speaks of ruptures and failures in the cycle. The result of such a failure is *oan hon,* "the spirit of a victim of an injustice," and these spirits of the dead are believed to suffer from the memory of "unjust misfortune" *(oan kho)* or "gross injustice" *(oan khuat). Oan hon,* and also *oan tinh* or *oan uc,* speaks of forms of worldly injustice that cause death and that continue to shape life after death. The dead person experiencing this condition of afterlife is believed to perpetually reexperience the agony of violent death.

That the dead can feel physical pain relates to the idea that the human soul is a divided entity. It has the spiritual part of *hon,* which corresponds to *spiritus* as against *anima* in the European philosophical tradition,[6] as well as the bodily, material part of *via.* The material soul, or what others translate as "vital soul," senses and feels, whereas the spiritual soul ("pure soul") thinks and imagines.[7] In a good death—at home, under peaceful circumstances, surrounded by loved ones, and after a long life— the material soul eventually perishes together with the decomposing body. Only the spiritual soul survives a good death, and it is believed that the ritually appropriated pure spirit travels across the imaginary threshold between *am* and *duong* to eventually join the pure domain of ancestral worship. The soul of one who experiences a bad death, on the contrary, remains largely intact and keeps its predeath dual formation because of the absence of ritual separation.[8] The material soul is believed to linger near the place of death and the place where its decomposing body is buried. It feels the discomfort of improper burial and awakens the spiritual soul to the embodied memory of the violent death. The material soul's bodily pain and the spiritual soul's painful memory communicate with each other, and this communication between the two kinds of souls can generate the perilous condition of "grievous death."

Being captivated by the memory of injustice, the soul experiencing "grievous death" is unable to depart to the other world until the situation is corrected by the intervention of an external power. The concept, although it signifies a state of imprisonment within the vexing and mortifying memory of experiencing an unjust event, also has a progressive connotation that points to concrete measures against captivity. This symbolic state of imprisonment is described graphically as *nguc*—"incarceration in medieval pillory"—and the countering act of liberating the soul from the memory of injustice is called *giai nguc*, "breaking the prison."[9]

The death of an armed combatant and the death of an unarmed civilian in war should be differentiated, according to the above conception. The latter may be a "grievous death," whereas this specific idea normally does not apply to the former. This differentiation does not mean that the soldier's death is in any way less tragic than the civilian's death. Instead, it relates to the issues of whether the death was objectively justifiable and whether the tragedy was subjectively intelligible to the victims. The soldier's death in the battlefield, called *chet tran*, is tragic but not illegitimate; the death of ordinary villagers in the chaos of a war is both tragic and unjust.

Thay My, one of Ha My's ritual specialists introduced in an earlier chapter, suggested the example of a road accident when he tried to clarify for me this particular ethics of war in popular culture. He said that all accidental deaths on the road are tragic, but only some of them result in the grievous death of *chet oan*. If a man is driving his scooter at a speed that is not permissible, he is doing it in the knowledge that his action could lead to a fatal accident. If he crashes into a tree trunk and dies on the way to the hospital, his death is not a grievous one, according to Thay My. This man did not intend to die, but he created the circumstances of a possible death. Hence, the death that is circumstantially expected circumvents the cultural category of unjust and grievous death. The road accident of a prudent schoolgirl on her bicycle is, on the contrary, clearly a grievous death. She is not responsible, Thay My explained, for the tiredness of the overworked truck driver who crashed into her bicycle from behind. She neither created the circumstances of the road accident, nor expected any such tragedy on her usual journey back from school. Accidental death in these circumstances was not part of the person's self-awareness, and it therefore induces grievous feelings in the spirit of the dead.

The same logic apples to the soldiers and the villagers of the people's war. Whereas the soldiers fought with a certain awareness of the risk of their activity, the villagers supported their fighting without, in principle, having to risk their lives for doing so. Death of the armed soldiers was anticipated, whereas the unarmed villagers were expected only to till the soil, raise the pigs and children, and protect their families and village. For these two groups, war death takes on different meanings, and the civilian death becomes ritually more complicated to deal with than the soldier's death because of its added meaning of unjustified, grievance-causing death.

A large-scale civilian killing in a confined place is clearly a tragic event, but it becomes an "unjust" event through a specific cultural understanding of the ethics of war. This understanding resonates with the legal concept of "noncombatant immunity" in the theory of justified war,[10] but the "injustice" of death in Vietnamese conception relates further to the morality of commemoration. According to a song called "Come and Visit My Hoi [the old name of a subhamlet]" in My Lai:

Let's listen to a story of a crime.
When the night's fog is still glittering the bush,
Birds are singing, hens are calling chicks.
Diligent children have already begun their play.
Farmers chase their buffalo toward the horizon.
Old women and men, and children,
Who earn a living from the soil—
Who wants to kill them?
Does the nation know about it?
An American crime has just been heard.
Some lost parents.
Some left no trace, entire families, leaving nobody to wear the white ribbon
     of mourning.
This is *grievous death*.
You ask me how many, I don't know how many.
You keep asking me the number, How many?
I do not know how many were killed.
I do not count how many incense sticks I ought to burn.
Let's go see My Hoi, Tu Cung.
People! Remember My Hoi's blood.
Stop the hands of killing.

I recorded this song from a village elder after hearing it sung on several occasions. The song attributes grievous death specifically to death in a massacre that resulted in the discontinuity of family lines. The same is true in Ha My and other places affected by large-scale civilian killings in central Vietnam. In his memorial speech in 2000, the former village chief of Ha My listed the following names as the most grievous victims of the 1968 massacre:

> Nguyen Miem was a partisan. His wife and four children were killed in the village. A month later he himself died in combat. His whole family is now traceless. Nguyen Thao, although old, joined the revolutionary war after losing all his children to the massacre. He was killed shortly after. The family of Le Khe lost their first child to the enemy. He was killed himself in November the following year, followed by his wife and remaining four children shortly after. . . . Trian Nhieu joined the national struggle and was killed on October 27, 1967. On the 24th of the first month 1968, his wife and four children were killed by the mercenary army. The entire family has no trace now. Nguyen Kien's wife was killed on the 24th of the first month, 1968. Their one-year-old daughter survived. Kien came back, buried his wife, carried the baby on his shoulder. Like the legend of Pham Cong, he carried arms in one hand and a baby in the other. He was killed in action a month later.[11]

The decimated family genealogy provoked the strongest sense of injustice and moral indignation in the victim communities that I visited. The grievous death in the song of My Hoi refers to the tragedy in which the loss of human lives took place together with the loss of the institutional basis on which to lament the death and console the dead. A grievous death in this context is not only the destruction of innocent lives but also a crisis in the social foundation of commemoration, and the idea of justice implied in the category points to the right to be commemorated and accounted for. According to this cultural conception of human rights, the right of the dead to be liberated from the violent history of death is inalienable, and the protection of this right depends on the secular institutions of commemoration. Kinship is the basis, in this conception, of ensuring that these rights are respected. Religion is a technical means, for it provides the practical, instrumental knowledge for the actual performance of commemoration.

REBURIAL IN HA GIA

In September 1986, the relatives of the victims of the 1968 Ha Gia massacre were invited to the civic relations office of the village People's

Committee. The meeting was held to discuss the future of the remains of
the thirty-five victims. Earlier that year, the district authorities had
announced plans to renovate the irrigation system in several relatively
underdeveloped villages of the district, including Ha Gia. All the villagers welcomed the news, negotiated with the village authorities about
the portion of their paddy or garden to be given up for the project, and
cooperated with the authorities in organizing the necessary labor force
for the construction. All had gone smoothly until the villagers realized
that one of the irrigation channels was to cut through the mass grave.
This was the place where the ROK Marines brought the thirty-five Ha
Gia villagers and massacred them with handheld grenades. This was in
the spring of 1968, just after the massacre in Ha My. The fragmented
bodies of the victims were buried on the site, and a small cluster of pine
trees had grown there by 1986. The Ha Gia villagers wanted to know the
fate of the mass grave before they went any further on the irrigation project, and they organized the Survivors' Association of Ha Gia to represent
their view.

The village elder who led the association in its early years kept de-
tailed minutes of the meeting. The document listed the delegates from the
Survivors' Association: the former Ha Gia partisan leader; the village
chief of Ha Gia at the time; representatives of the Pham, Le, Dinh, and
Nguyen families; and a woman from the Pham family. The woman lost
both sides of her family *(ngoai,* maternal side, and *noi,* paternal side) to
the massacre and volunteered to join the meeting. The families of the
thirty-five victims had presented to the People's Committee and the Community Party their proposal to remove the corpses to the Revolutionary
Martyr Cemetery situated at the center of the village. Ong Thanh, the
former guerilla leader, spoke first in support of the proposal:

> *The former guerilla leader:* I remember the situation. I was the one who en-
> couraged and ordered the villagers in Ha Gia to stick to the "Defend
> Your Village" strategy. I was the one who persuaded the victims to
> remain in their homeland so that our men could rely on them for food
> and shelter in order to carry out our fight against the enemy. The vil-
> lagers indeed provided us with food and help. They protected us in
> the underground shelters, hid our weapons, risking their lives to do
> so, and brought me information about the enemy troops. I can con-
> firm in retrospect, first, that our men, including me, survived with
> generous assistance from the villagers and, second, that the efforts
> of the Ha Gia villagers to keep the village were equal to our efforts
> to deter the enemy troops. They were equally important for the revo-
> lution as any men of arms.

The village chief of Ha Gia: If the guerilla leader had not asked them to remain in the village and to stay where they were, the villagers would not have been killed by the foreign troops. They faithfully followed the Communist Party's appeal: Mot tat khong di mot li khong roi [Do not move a yard away, do not go an inch away from your homeland]. For this reason, I believe that the victims of the massacre are entitled to be entombed in the martyr cemetery.

The secretary of the People's Committee: The Ha Gia villagers were killed by the Korean troops; they didn't kill the enemy troops. They can't be martyrs, for our martyrs are those who fought directly against the enemy. Suppose we agree on moving their remains to the martyr cemetery, what will then happen to the remains of victims in Ha My? We move them too? What about the victims in Ha Quang, Ha Loc, and other places? We move them all to the martyr cemetery? If this should happen, we will be obliged to expand the martyr cemetery to be as big as our village. This can't happen. Our revolutionary martyrs are pure and should remain so. We cannot agree on a wrong policy. I suggest that we move the remains to *rung* [burial sites in the woods].

The representative of the Le family: We don't want our relatives buried in the martyr cemetery. But we don't have a choice. There are some old revolutionary martyrs among the victims. Since their bodies were buried carelessly en masse, it is impossible to sort out the bones of the martyrs from the rest. Do you see the situation? We must honor the martyrs by bringing them to a proper place where their bodies belong, but we must not make the mistake of bringing wrong bones to the place. If we can't sort out the bones, it is better to bring them all to the martyr cemetery rather than make the mistake of burying the martyrs in the woods.

The representative of the Nguyen family: Our relatives stayed in the village to support the revolution. They drew enemy fire to their bodies on behalf of the revolutionary fighters. When they were captured and about to be killed, where were you, the so-called freedom fighters? You had run away, leaving the old and helpless abandoned without protection. You saved your life because there were people like us willing to give their lives for you. And now you say you can't admit us to the martyr cemetery. What nonsense! This is [an instance of] "Do vat chanh bo vo" [Take the juice from the lemon and discard its skin].

A member of the Pham family: If they can't enter the martyr cemetery, do not try to remove them at all. They've suffered many humiliations and may endure hardship a bit longer. Meanwhile, their living relatives will make a case with the district authority. If the district cannot solve the issue, the relatives will appeal to the province, the central government, all the existing authorities on earth, to do justice to their deaths.

The secretary: I can assure you that the higher authorities will never agree with your unconventional, unjustifiable action.

The village chief: On behalf of the people in Ha Gia, I will be willing to talk to the highest authority if necessary about the intentions of our villagers. The simple fact is that the victims could have avoided the tragedy had they not listened to the guerillas. If they had abandoned the village after the Ha My incident, which I believe many would have gladly done had not the guerillas forced them to stay on, they would have survived. This proves that the thirty-five people died for the revolution. They kept the village for the army, and their struggle was as strong and important as the work of combatants. The army should be grateful to these innocent civilians who sacrificed for the nation, not discriminate against them.

The former guerilla leader: The real issue is that, among the victims, there were some former partisan fighters who defended the village against the French and also several civilian supporters. All these people deserve recognition from the government. First of all, they deserve to be honored by being moved to a place of heroes. If you agree to bury them in the martyr cemetery, no outside authority can go against your decision. The policy of hero entitlement is such that it should be flexible depending on the specific situations of a village. The village party cell and People's Committee should listen to the voice of the people.

I discussed the details of the meeting with a number of members of Ha Gia's Survivors' Association, individually as well as in group. Our conversations were often intense, particularly during my visit in 2001–2002, when the members were advancing an initiative to erect a stone in memory of the victims of the village massacre, prompted by the successful memorial project in neighboring Ha My (see the next chapter). They had prepared documentation, including the above minutes, and were debating how to concretize their own memorial project. Their new initiative was eventually frustrated for complex reasons, but their solidarity was strong and they had villagewide support.

Their solidarity for the memorial project was rooted in the series of events since 1986, when their meeting with the village officials failed to reach an agreement. A few months after the meeting, the Ha Gia villagers heard that the irrigation project had been modified and that the removal of the mass grave was not necessary. It was not until two years later that the mass grave again became a critical public issue. In the spring of 1988, a prominent war veteran of the Pham family of Ha Gia returned to his homeland, ending his years of postwar work in the north of Vietnam. This veteran had lost six members of his family to the 1968 massacre and had outstanding political credentials. The families of the victims united around this man, revitalized the Survivors' Association and reopened the case on the removal of the mass grave. They secured financial support from the village's cooperative farm and sent a delegation to the district office of the Communist Party. A schoolteacher and member of the association organized the parents of his students to support the reburial; the former guerilla leader of Ha Gia organized the veterans in Ha Gia, Ha My, and Ha Quang; and other participants of the association also widely disseminated the news of their activity. This widespread activity and prolific networking contributed to persuading the village administration in 1988 to permit removal of the mass grave to the village war martyr cemetery, on the condition that the actual removal would be conducted with no formal commitment from the village administrative authorities.

The reburial procession attracted the entire village of Ha Gia, and the association carefully planned the occasion so that it looked identical to a government-sponsored burial ceremony for war martyrs. The officials of the village administration refrained from taking part in the procession, and only volunteers from the village conducted the removal. The Ha Gia and Ha Quang villagers contributed financially to the event, and the village youth association provided pallbearers. The village women's association prepared food for the participants, and the village association of elders volunteered to oversee the ritual procession. The village chief of Ha Gia was aware of the event's political implications and made a carefully crafted speech before the excavation started. I quote from his handwritten notes:

> Today, the village of Ha Gia and the People's Committee of Dien Duong are happy to remove the old remains of the thirty-five victims of the 1968 Ha Gia massacre to the village's revolutionary martyr cemetery. We are very happy to recognize you as soldiers of the liberation war. The enemy captured you, killed you brutally, children included, tore apart your bodies, and then destroyed the Family Temple of Dinh Family with their flame thrower. . . . We the descendants are honored to bring you to the place of the nation's heroes. This is the intention of the People's Committee and the result of their correct policy for war invalids and martyrs.

Despite the efforts of the Ha Gia villagers to make their reburial procession look officially endorsed, the event provoked disapproving remarks and gestures from certain sectors of the state administration. A few days after the reburial, a district official in charge of war invalids and social welfare came to inspect the cemetery. On arrival, he hired several war veterans and ordered them to dismantle the collective tomb in the war martyr cemetery. One of the veterans informed his wife about what was happening, and she immediately relayed the news to her relatives in Ha Gia. Within an hour, a large crowd of Ha Gia villagers gathered in the cemetery, some armed with sickles or clubs. I was told that one woman in the crowd confronted the official with these words: "If you intend to touch the bodies of our relatives, that makes you our enemy. You will have to fight us first."

The above episode exposed some of the contradictions inherent in the postwar Vietnamese cult of war heroes and, in particular, the ambiguity concerning civilian death and the legacy of the war. The war in Vietnam, for the Vietnamese, was theoretically a people's war, which advocated a total fusion of the army with the people. The theory idealized this unity as a sublime social form, as can be seen in such famous slogans as "People are the water, and our army the fish" and "Each inhabitant [is] a soldier, and each village a fortress." The unity did not last. After the war, the dead "inhabitant-soldier" lost the flip side of her identity and became a mere inhabitant.

The death of a combatant (or a party activist) during his or her active patriotic duty earns the honorific reference of *hy sinh* (self-sacrifice), and the dead the formal title of *liet si* (revolutionary martyr). In public communication, the Vietnamese villagers rarely hear the expression "self-sacrifice" addressed to the civilian victims of the war, nor would they easily use the expression themselves mistakenly. As a formal concept with a precise meaning, "self-sacrifice" refers to certain rigorously defined categories of death, and it is the state that holds the right to control the referentiality of the concept. The martyrs of the liberation wars, the party activists killed in duty, the patriotic heroes in anticolonial struggles, the exceptional Heroes of Vietnam, the Heroic Mothers of Vietnam, and other designated patriotic servants of the nation constitute the category in contemporary language.[12]

In the vernacular, however, self-sacrifice appears to be a much more complex and context-specific concept. Ba Lap's late husband, whose story is featured in chapter 4, was an employee of the South Vietnamese administration. When Ha My villagers spoke about the circumstances of his assassination, which were allegedly related to his objection to the brutal treatment of his villagers by the army, his death was a *hy sinh* (self-sacrifice) for the village. The deaths of the mother victims of the 1968 massacre, who fell on the village children to try to shield them from gunfire, were spoken of as self-sacrifice by the villagers who gathered for their death-day anniversary. The former partisan fighters of Ha My were clearly aware of the specific meaning of *hy sinh* and addressed their fallen comrades in these terms when they participated in the annual memorial in the war martyr cemetery. When they visited the graves of their own family members who had succumbed to the massacre in their absence, they lamented over *hy sinh*. In this context, the deaths of their wives and children were a sacrifice in exchange for the life of the grieving veterans.

The disputes between the Ha Gia villagers and the village administration concerning the reburial were partly caused by a difference in the definition of *self-sacrifice*—a difference between popular understanding and the official language. The villagers supported a wider definition that could do justice to the role of unarmed civilians in the historical reality of the guerilla warfare. For them, the unity of the army and the people not only justified the prospective incorporation of the thirty-five civilian victims among war heroes but was already a given reality among the victims. The village delegates pointed out that the mass grave was a politically mixed grave containing the remains of revolutionary martyrs as well as those of ordinary villagers and insisted that this justified the collective reburial in the war martyr cemetery as it was impossible to separate out the martyrs' bones.[13] The officials understood the state of political mixture but still rejected the idea of reburial, viewing it from an opposite standpoint. Above all, the reburial episode illustrated a conflict between two perspectives—the state's perspective of the dead as passive objects of political control and the popular perspective in which they were conscious historical subjects. In the former, we may say, following Henri Lefebvre, that the place of sacrifice maintained its centrality by expelling peripheral elements according to the economic principle of scarcity of space. This economic rationality, as Lefebvre points out, "lays claim, implicitly or explicitly, to a superior political rationality" of the state.[14] For the relatives of the victims, the corpses were all distinctive individuals, with names and concrete historical identities, who should have been rescued from the state of enmeshment. The villagers took part in the reburial movement in the hope that their dead kinsmen would have the opportunity to escape their tragic conditions. This was a common objective for all in the association, and whether they were related to a martyr or an ordinary civilian was far less relevant in this moral unity. The unity was based on the shared understanding that a proper burial and an appropriate ritual commemoration are two primary conditions for the welfare of the dead. If the dead are buried in an improper place, it is important to generate those two conditions through an act of reburial. The reburial creates a break in the life of the dead, thus enabling the dead to be separated from grievance as their bodies are moved to a new place, and when the act concerns a mass grave, it also allows the dead to recover their individuality. These two works of reburial—creating a sense of temporal removal in the life of the dead and individuating their identities—were the primary intentions of the villagers of Ha Gia who participated in the reburial of the thirty-five victims. One participant and active member of the Survivors' Association recalled the reburial as the two of us toured the war cemetery together. Resting on the stairs leading to the war hero memorial tower at the center of the cemetery and overlooking the collective tomb, I felt that the relatively large tomb looked somewhat out of place in the midst of the hundreds of identical graves all symmetrically laid out. I asked him if he shared my impression. Saying that the tomb, in his opinion, was actually too small for twenty adults and fifteen children to lie comfortably in it, he told me:

> We had prepared thirty-five coffins, for each skull, small or large. Since we didn't know which skull was for which family, we naturally decided that each one of us would consider each skull as if it belonged to our family. So, the event meant that each family kowtowed to thirty-five individuals, and each skull had many families to clean it. I knew my mother, my sister, and my sister-in-law were among them and were happy that they finally had their own coffins. . . . I had prepared sweets and clothes for my little sister, but I didn't know which coffin she was in. So we pooled our paper money and offerings and burned them together. We were happy that our families were in a new place. Although I would have liked to know which coffins belonged to me, I am glad that we did the removal together. The dead were all together; we had to be together to bring them to a new place.[15]

The event in 1988 was not the first attempt to rebury the victims of the Ha Gia massacre. At the beginning of the 1980s, a family of Ha Gia held a ritual called *chieu hon luyen cot*—"calling the spirit to a substitutive body"—in order to remove their ancestor from the mass grave. The substitutive burial was a modified form of the ritual of *chieu hon*, which typically deals with the death of fishermen whose bodies are lost at sea. Known as one of the most complicated ritual procedures, it involves communicating with sea spirits to obtain permission to return the souls of the dead, preparing a dummy body (*luyen cot*), and performing the main rite, which invites the spirit of the dead person to the new body. When completed, this procedure is followed by a funeral procession and the interment of the dummy body. Fabrication of the dummy requires special materials and is restricted to specialists with exceptional ritual knowledge.[16] The most difficult part of the substitutive burial is the induction of the spirit of the dead to the clay body. It is believed that, when the spirit is summoned, a number of other wandering ghosts may accompany the invited spirit. The ritual specialist and the hosting family must legitimize the act of returning the spirit of a particular individual to the group of ghosts, who may otherwise prevent the individual from departing from their group. For this reason, it is known that the ritual of substitutive burial tends to be successful if it is undertaken for a senior or prominent individual among the group of the dead, or as a part of a series of rituals that aim to return an entire group of spirits that died in the same circumstances. This knowledge is based on the premise that the ghosts are cognizant of the social order of seniority and thus are more likely to tolerate the return of an aged ghost.

The family that undertook the complex and costly ritual of substitutive burial was prominent in the community, having a mandarin heritage and a high-ranking official in the provincial party, and the beneficiary of the reburial was the most senior among the victims and also a veteran of the anti-French armed struggle. The Ha Gia villagers saw the mass reburial of 1988 as an extension of this earlier substitutive burial. The substitutive reburial frustrated other families of victims, who could not afford the cost of an equivalent ritual, and stimulated them to look for an alternative solution. The member of the association whom I quoted above said about the substitutive burial: "It was not fair that some lived in a nice place while most others continued to suffer. They could do *luyen cot* because they had friends in high positions. People like us were not allowed to do it even if we had money. The police would not have tolerated it. When everyone is in hell, you sigh and try to cope. When one of them escapes hell, you must find a way to help them all escape."

For the people of Ha Gia, the removal of a French War veteran to an individual tomb in the family graveyard and the removal of thirty-five untitled individuals to the collective tomb in the state war hero cemetery were identical in meaning—in each case the act liberated the dead from the grievous history of mass killing. Here, the spatial destination of the dead, ancestral or heroic, was not important, but their liberation from the historical origin of death was. Transcendence, in this context, was immanent in the movement of corpses, not determined by the identity of the place where their movement ended.

The war hero cemetery in Ha Gia was a sacred place in two different senses: it excluded impure elements, and its sacredness transcended the secular politics of body and economy of space. The theory of symbolic conquest, which drew upon the politics of purity too exclusively and too uncritically, had to be given a broader perspective, one that incorporated

the sphere of human actions that do not reduce human body to an instrumental object of social construction. This applies not only to the administration of war graves in Vietnam but also to the analysis of African ancestral tombs. For, as Georg Simmel writes, "the unified act of life includes
both the state of being bounded and the transcending of the boundary,
despite the fact that this seems to present a logical contradiction."[17]

CHAPTER 7

The Stone of Fury

The moral identity of mass village war death was ambivalent. It shifted between tragic and heroic, as illustrated by the Ha Gia mass reburial described in the previous chapter. Finding a place for the identity of an individual victim was also uncertain: some believed it should be in the ancestral memorial, whereas some chose its structural opposite. In preparing for a domestic ritual, people imagined that ancestors who experienced tragic death were hesitating between the ancestral shrine and the shrine for ghosts. The memory of mass civilian deaths created relationships with the domain of political hero worship as well as that of family ancestor worship, but the relationships remained awkward and quarrelsome. In each domain, tragic mass death encountered a formidable force of exclusion.

Vietnamese ancestor worship is based on a particular temporal and spatial order; it sits uneasily with radical social ruptures and does not easily accommodate deaths that fall outside the spatiotemporal order. The state apparatus of Vietnam attempted to centralize commemorative practices away from the village and the family; the imposition of this command economy of memory, which concentrates on the heroic and regenerative deaths of revolutionary combatants, complicated the commemoration of civilians in the southern and central regions. Neither the dominant traditional culture nor hegemonic revolutionary politics welcomed the memory of village victims of mass war death.

Did the commemoration of mass civilian death require a place of its

own, separate from the established sites of worship? In Ha My, the construction of a public memorial to commemorate the mass death of 1968,
and the reburial of the bodies of the victims, presents this idea as an independent solution. As in the case of the Ha Gia reburial, the most significant aspect of this story is the conflict between cultural norms and political ideals. The memorial project in Ha My involved initiatives from
international actors, and the finished object was intended to be a symbol
of peace and reconciliation. Thus it contrasted with the reburial in Ha
Gia, which resulted from local initiatives and brought the civilian dead to
an emblem of nationalism. Underneath these formal differences, however, the two events demonstrated a common, substantive issue. Placing
the dead was at once a political action and a cultural practice, but the
cultural practice had a normative quality that transcended the politics of
space.

HISTORY OF WAR MONUMENTS

The Memorial for 135 Victims of Ha My opened in December 2000 in
the middle of a paddy, which had been one of the sites of mass killing.
The opening ceremony attracted a large crowd from Ha My and the
neighboring villages. Relatives of the victims arrived from distant places,
and party officials from the village, the district, and the province were
present. Most notably, a number of people from Ha Gia, Ha Quang, An
Bang, and elsewhere brought with them votive papers with the names of
people written on them. They presented at the memorial's altar these
names of the dead—victims of incidents other than the one in Ha My—
believing that they might benefit from the occasion.

The finished monument consisted of a three-meter-high stone with an
inscription that listed the 135 victims, a roof structure on four columns
to protect the stone, and two collective tombs for the remains of the victims. Elevated on pillars to avoid flooding, the memorial is the largest
built structure in the village. Some war veterans of Ha My disapproved
of the fact that the memorial, built for civilian victims, outdid the war
martyrs' monument in size and grandeur. Many survivors and relatives of
victims did not share this opinion but felt that the memorial was too
imposing for family-based commemoration. They were concerned about
the village elders being willing to come there to make their small, individual offering to the dead. The names on the stone begin with the eldest
victim, born in 1880, at the top corner of the far left column, Tran Thi
Tu. They end with three infants who had nicknames (they were too small

to have real names), Nguyen Thi Hong, Nguyen Van Teo, and Nguyen Van, all born in 1967, and three *vo danh* (unnamed) infants at the opposite corner. The reverse side of the stone displays full-blossomed lotus flowers—the Vietnamese symbol of peace and harmony—engraved in marble.

In Vietnamese war monumental art, the "tragic death" and the "heroic death" are clearly differentiated. Among many installations that I have seen throughout central Vietnam, no other example captures the contrasting symbolism of war death as explicitly as the twin installation in Thuy Bo. Thuy Bo is situated at the foot of Bo Bo, one of the battlefields of the so-called Hill Fights between the U.S. forces and the regular communist army, twenty kilometers west of Ha My, and the place is famous in the province of Quang Nam for the quality of the chicken meat it produces. This small village, hidden behind a marketplace on one side and open to the rapidly rising hills of the Central Highlands on the other, has two prominent neo-Gothic monuments on the main dirt road. One of them is the Memorial of Thuy Bo, dedicated to the 145 victims of the 1967 village massacre, and its northern neighbor is the Monument of Victory, situated in the expansive state cemetery of the village revolutionary war martyrs.

The Thuy Bo war crime memorial was built in 1977, and it consists of a tall central Gothic tower and two horizontal wings that extend from the lower half of the vertical tower. The form is known as "bird" to Vietnamese monumental artists. One horizontal wing depicts wartime village life. A group of children is cheering a group of uniformed soldiers and resistance fighters in civilian clothing. The soldiers are marching; the partisan fighters are in combat motion with their carbines or handmade explosives. In the background, women are tending a rice paddy, one of them with a rifle slung on her back. The opposite wing depicts the scene of mass killing and the end of the youthful struggle depicted in the first wing. Here, the women are under imminent threat of death—with the muzzles of carbines pointing to their necks. The child held in the arms of an elderly woman droops, lifeless. A soldier wearing the helmet with "US" written on it is holding a club in one hand and a baby by its leg in another. The grin on his face is chilling.[1]

The memorial to victory in Thuy Bo's war martyr cemetery is identical in structure to the war crime memorial. It consists of a pointed neo-Gothic tower and has two wings unfolding from the lower level of the pillar. A large traditional incense-burner and an altar are placed between the two wings and in front of the tower. The classical dictum of the official Vietnamese war commemorative art, "Your Ancestral Land Remembers You," is inscribed on the surface of the Gothic tower. Above the inscription, a sculpture depicts a family of three. A man in uniform holds the single-star flag of Vietnam, and a small boy who also holds the flag-pole with his small hand stands beside this man. Behind the boy, a woman holds a gun with one arm and rests her other arm on the boy's shoulder. The self-sacrifice of this revolutionary nuclear family constitutes the radical symbolic transition between the imagery depicted by the two wings. The wing on the left, from the perspective of the spectator, like that in the war crime memorial, paints a historical reality of the wartime village, although it does so with a much more panoramic vision. It depicts soldiers in full-scale combat gear, rather than village sappers, and heroic scenery from the famous Truong Son (Ho Chi Minh Trail) in the Highlands. The latter imitates printed imagery from school textbooks of modern history. The wing also shows the national war heroine born in the district who is known to have stood against advancing enemy tanks. The depiction of the war on this wing, compared to its counterpart in the war crime memorial, is much more imaginary, mixing elements of village history with those of national history and incorporating legendary national heroes. Moving to the opposite wing, the landscape changes radically in scale and temporality, depicting a peaceful, prosperous view of postwar village life. Children march to school, women become school-teachers and mothers, men become doctors, farmers sit on tractors, and a soldier of the People's Army stands at the margin of the thriving village, rather than at its center. Modern housing blocks can be seen in the distance, and the village People's Committee building is at the heart of the landscape, surrounded by lush forest and expansive farmland.

This installation situates the memory of heroic death as the threshold through which the violent past of a war transforms into the prosperous communal life of the future. The villagers' self-sacrifice for the ancestral land enables this transformation. The nuclear family at the top of the tower signifies the transformation of the military command of "All Forward!" into a forward movement in economic development. This motif of regeneration, dominant in Vietnamese war hero memorials, is absent from the war crime memorials. The latter provide no indication as to how the deaths should be assimilated into the linear temporality and forward vision of the future. There is no future in the landscape of a war crime.[2] On top of the vertical column, Thuy Bo's war crime memorial presents the sculpted bodies of victims. An infant clings to the breast of a fallen young mother. Next to them, an angry young woman raises her clenched fist to the heavens. This symbol is based on a real individual, the Thuy Bo villagers insisted, although similar statues of "fury and defiance" are found in the memorial in My Lai and elsewhere. The memorial in Binh Son, Quang Ngai, adds a narrative to its statue of fury and defiance: "The memory of this heinous criminal act will be held in the innermost part of our body, and our fury stretches to and pierces the heaven."

The memorials in Thuy Bo, My Lai, and Binh Son belong to a particular style of monumental art called "Stone of Fury." Built during the first decade after the end of the war, this style is distinguished from the later "Stone of Spirit Consolation" adopted in the second half of the 1980s. The Stone of Fury displays, as its name suggests, the experience of horror and an expression of indignation in graphic form. The statue of a female victim in the My Lai memorial site is holding a dead child in one arm and making a gesture of defiance with another. The Stone of Spirit Consolation of the 1980s departs from the realism of the earlier style and is usually made of a simple tombstone that inscribes the history of mass death and feelings of abhorrence in a narrative form. The Ha My memorial follows this style and has the following inscription on the back of the stone:

> History writes that this land was opened by the descendants of Nam Nong, who five hundred years ago crossed the Marble Mountains and migrated southward to erect a memory of the country. These ancestors built a village in Ha My, plowed the land, fished in the sea, and grew vegetables. This way, a life of harmony began in this land where the rivers meet the sea. This life lasted as long as heaven was quiet and the land was in peace. . . .
>
> Then came the thunderstorms and the pitch-dark clouds. They desecrated our land, imprisoned us in the strategic hamlets, forced us to abandon our ancestral land, and transformed our fertile land into a wasteland, abandoned and barren. We lost our land and sea, endured the pain of our intestines torn to pieces. There are not proper words to describe the cruelty of the war. Numerous heads fell off to the ground, their blood joined to form a river stream, and the palm trees too dropped their dried leaves and perished away as if they were the lifeless hair of a dying body. While our tears filled the village pond, our temples turned to ashes, the lush forest of Ha Gia became a dark skeleton, and corpses crowded the Khe Long dock. . . .
>
> In the spring of 1968, on the 24th day of the first month, the soldiers of Blue Dragon massacred our villagers. The village land turned scarlet red, the immolated corpses became inseparable, the bones sank into the sand, our houses disappeared. We cannot forget the smell—the smell of burning blood. We cannot forget the ants—their voracious appetite for the flesh of our children. The collapsing roof in flames broke the bones of our elders,

those who tried to run were shot one by one, and the babies were still sucking the breasts of their dead mothers. The cruelest of all the cruel deeds was
to desecrate the graves. Darkness fell upon this village. Even the weeds
turned yellow. The grievous spirits of the dead were abandoned, having
no place to rest, and our fury reached the skin of heaven. . . .

Absolute darkness, however, is not known under heaven. It has been
twenty-five years since our land regained peace. Potatoes and rice grow
again on this land, the shrimps and fish crowd our sea again. Following
the leadership of the Communist Party, we transformed the wasteland into
a prosperous land. This land is an old battlefield and remembers a lot of
human suffering. The foreign soldiers recognized their misdeed of the past
and offered an apology. This stone is built on the foundation of forgiving
and the fundamental humanitarian feelings that we all share. From now on,
the sand dune and the trees that grow on it will remember the history of the
tragic killing.

The Stone of Spirit Consolation incorporates the Stone of Fury within
a modified scheme of collective memory. It relegates the towering "fury
and defiance," which was the dominant and most demonstrative element in the previous monumental style, to the rear side of the stone and
to the past tense. A caption on the My Lai memorial states, "Hold the
memory of this crime as deeply as possible in you." In Thuy Bo one can
read the inscription "Hold the hatred of the perpetrators of this crime as
deeply and fiercely as possible in you." The equivalent emotion in the
Stone of Spirit Consolation appears within a historical narrative and
within a framework that projects a certain detachment from such a deep
remembrance. The stone in Ha My is inscribed: "The sand dune and the
trees that grow on it will remember the history of the tragic killing."
Some of the bodies of the victims had been removed to the sand dunes
after the end of the war, before being taken back to the site of mass
killing in 2000, on which the memorial is erected. When the remains
were reburied, they had a place to rest, a stone that details their identities, and a memorial that narrates their history. The sand dunes were
their old home; the memorial is their new home. The plight of the victims
was neglected when they were in their old home; the new home recognizes their suffering and its injustice. The poetic idea of the sand dune
remembering the dead relegates the grievous emotions to the time before
the reburial and to the place prior to the memorial. Following the movement of the bodies of the victims, the spectator is encouraged to move
from the deep grief of remembrance to a place of reconciliation, relegat-
ing the obligation of deep remembrance to the pine trees that grow in the
sand dune where the bodies were.

LOTUS FLOWERS

The Memorial for 135 Victims in Ha My was dedicated to the village by a group of ROK veterans. It was an extraordinary event that the former soldiers, some of whom had been directly involved in the military operations that resulted in the massacre, came to honor the village. The initial reaction from the Ha My villagers to the news about their unusual visitors was disbelief and shock. People spoke quietly about feelings of anger and fear; a number of survivors complained of sleepless nights and appetites lost because of flashbacks. Several survivors told me that, during the two years from the first visit of the delegation of the ROK veterans until the day the memorial was opened, they had numerous dreams about the killing. Sometimes these were nightmares about the faceless and red-eyed soldiers, the strange quietness after the killing, the chilling laughter of the soldiers, and the unforgettable smell of burned bodies; sometimes they were auspicious dreams about their dead relatives who appeared less troubled, about the foreign soldiers who used to amuse the village children on their shoulders, and about the rice and C rations the villagers used to barter with the soldiers in the Con Ninh base.

The actual circumstances that brought the veterans to Ha My were complex, but there is no doubt that their initiative involved the spirit described by Brian Willson: "Veterans are in a unique position to initiate courageous leadership in a national healing process. This requires speaking the truth about what we know, including the fact that all people and the earth are intimately interconnected. Our souls, and the soul of our country, are at stake."[3] It is also clear that the decision was influenced by a formative change in the international arena. By the end of the 1990s, the history of war crimes in Vietnam once again became an international issue. That My Lai was only one of many similar incidents was news to the U.S. public. An article in *Newsweek* questioned how the crimes committed by America's allied troops had been kept concealed from the public for three decades.[4] The media in South Korea ran a series of stories on the hitherto unknown history, attracting violent responses from certain sectors of the country's Vietnam War veterans. The scale and brutality of the intimate killings—an estimated nine thousand casualties—astonished the public in Korea, who had no prior knowledge of the tragic aspect of what they were told was a legitimate war against communist aggression. The Committee for Truth in the Vietnam War was launched, a network of nongovernmental organizations that initiated a nationwide campaign for a public inquiry. A former Korean "comfort woman" for the Japanese

Imperial Army in Manchuria attracted public attention by contributing to the campaign all the compensation money she had received from the government of Japan.[5] Meanwhile, a popular Vietnamese youth magazine followed suit and published a number of pieces on the mass killings, as well as interviews with Gu Su Jeong, a Korean historian based in Ho Chi Minh City who played a pivotal role in unearthing and disseminating the facts about the killings.[6] The public in Vietnam, particularly the postwar generations, was astonished and asked how a tragedy of this scale could fail to enter the official war history. It became apparent that the My Lai incident was only one part of a gigantic human tragedy, and public interest in the hidden history of the Vietnam War and the wider implications of the war crimes were explosive on both sides of the China Sea.

Both governments reacted swiftly to the eruption of public awareness. The Vietnamese government discouraged further communications about war-crime history and issued a series of requests for cooperation to the domestic media. I was told that one of the stated justifications for this censorship was that "Vietnam must transcend her tragic past, although we must not forget it," and this statement circulated widely through the official channels.[7] I also had an opportunity to have a similar message personally recited to me, when a senior provincial official politely rejected my application for further research in the My Lai area on the grounds that the aims of the research did not match the authority's intention to move beyond past tragedies in foreign relations. While I was walking along the office corridor in dismay and disappointment, a junior official followed me and offered his kind advice that I should resubmit my application through a foreign trade organization, changing the theme to something on economic development strategies. I reminded him that I was not an economist, and he said that it shouldn't matter. I did not know how to pursue the matter further.

In the meantime, on the Korean side, the foreign office quickly initiated a program of "humanitarian aid" and began pouring resources into the five provinces of central Vietnam. By the year 2002, this program had resulted in around forty new school buildings and several hospitals in the districts known to have suffered mass civilian death at the hands of the ROK troops, although the aid was nominally meant for any places in Vietnam in need of these facilities. The heads of the two states met in the same year and exchanged an agreement on economic cooperation. By this time, politics in South Korea was struggling to make a clean break with the legacy of the previous authoritarian, anticommunist regimes, whose leaders with military backgrounds had advanced their army careers in the Vietnam conflict. The president of South Korea expressed regrets about the conflicts of the past; his Vietnamese counterpart accepted this statement and returned it with courteous remarks about a constructive future relationship between the two nations.

These currents of political reconciliation, or what Jacques Derrida calls "geopolitics of forgiveness," brought the officials of the ROK embassy in Hanoi to Ha My.[8] The day these diplomats arrived in the village in order to inspect the new school building built on the old military base of Con Ninh, the village administrators of Ha My escorted them to the construction site of the memorial, which was then nearly completed. To their great surprise, as they later told me, the diplomatic officials were outraged with the "aggressive and belligerent" statement they found on the back of the memorial stone. The visitors argued that the stone expressed hatred and demanded that the village officials change it to a message of reconciliation and peace. Back in Hanoi, the embassy officials repeated their protest to their contacts in the Vietnamese foreign office.[9]

The whole affair culminated in a general meeting of the families of the 135 victims in September 2000 at the village People's Committee. In this meeting, the Ha My villagers had the rare opportunity to talk face to face with high-ranking government officials and to openly argue their point with them. The official delegation suggested changing the stone; most villagers insisted on keeping it the way it was. The villagers had had no part in designing the memorial in the first place. It was the village cadres who had formulated the design, with the collaboration of a local building company, and they solicited the controversial inscription on the stone from a journalist, following the advice of a provincial official. This journalist was based in the provincial capital and used to contribute poems of commemoration to the newspaper and to official meetings on the national anniversary days for war martyrs and invalids. This man was familiar with the Stone of Fury style and had been involved in writing inscriptions for memorial stones before Ha My. The villagers knew that the party officials were embarrassed about arguing against the Stone of Fury, which was their idea in the first place, and especially under the foreign influence of diplomatic officials. I was not able to join the meeting but was told immediately after that the provincial cadres had taken turns making elaborate speeches about "transcending the tragic past without forgetting it." The representatives of the families of the victims raised their voices in favor of "defending the village heritage from foreign influence." One family representative called the idea of changing the stone a "second massacre"—killing the memory of killing.

When the memorial officially opened in December 2000, the obituary on the back of the stone had vanished from sight. It was buried underneath lotus flowers that had been carved in marble and fixed onto the stone. The new stone obliterated the traces of "fury and defiance," celebrated reconciliation without evidence of grievance, and claimed to remember the unjust killing without telling the history of injustice. It invented a new style that corresponded to the new doctrine of "transcending the tragic past without forgetting it."

The controversy over the memorial stone exemplified the limitations of state institutions in conducting a genuine process of reconciliation. As Edward Relph writes of "place making": Places "have to be made largely through the involvement and commitment of the people who live and work in them; places have to be made from the inside out."[10] James Scott has written a damning indictment of how the large-scale social experiments in the past century have failed because of a systematic exclusion of practical knowledge from the top-down decision-making process of the state bureaucracy.[11] An event such as the alteration (or defacement) of the memorial perhaps would not have been necessary had the villagers been allowed to participate in the first place. Most survivors and relatives of victims were in fact surprised to see the inscription on the finished stone, considering the unusual circumstances in which the idea of the memorial came to existence in the first place. The local Vietnamese state officials paid no attention to these particular circumstances and imposed on the stone what some might see as an idiosyncratic narrative of "fury and defiance." The diplomatic officials had no interest in knowing the truth of the narrative and imposed on the stone a banal symbol of reconciliation.

Although the memorial stone suffered an intervention by state powers and, more fundamentally, a geopolitics of reconciliation not accountable to local experience and voices, the opening turned out to be a positive event for Ha My and for the commemoration of the Monkey Year. And this was, somewhat paradoxically, partly because the memorial soon became a relatively insignificant locus of memory.

THE VANISHING MONUMENT

In the city of Harburg, Germany, there is a memorial stone that remembers a memorial. The Monument against Fascism, an obelisk-shaped structure made of hollow aluminum coated with a layer of dark lead, was installed in a busy suburban shopping area of the city in 1986. Visitors were invited to inscribe on the surface of the memorial their thoughts and messages, and when the surface was filled with graffiti, the memorial was lowered into the ground to provide a fresh surface. Designed to be a "vanishing monument," the memorial was lowered on several occasions and finally disappeared from view in 1991. After that, the artists who designed the memorial left a stone in its place to remind visitors of the "death" of the memorial. This avant-garde installation was designed to be a "self-destroying" object and, as such, was intended to challenge the ontology of traditional monumental objects, which is, according to the artists, the idea of permanence. By challenging the property of permanence, the artists also intended to democratize memory: "The best monument may be no monument at all, but only the memory of an absent monument. . . . If it were truly consumed, no longer visible or conspicuous . . . it would actually be where it belongs—that is, within the people for whom it was created." The Harburg memorial tried to reconcile the need to remember a tragic past with the need to distribute the practice of remembrance to the wider public. By keeping the memory of the vanished sculpture and what it stood for, the artist said, "the public becomes sculpture."[12]

Public memorials in Vietnamese villages can also vanish from sight or die. They may be part of the physical environment without being part of the landscape of commemoration. They may be ephemeral objects in the reality of social life despite their materiality of permanence. In daily life the Vietnamese villagers maintain no intimate relationship with the war monuments and memorials, and this inevitably results in a gradual decay of the built forms unless the state intervenes. The impermanence of the memorial is in turn partly a product of state control. Hue-Tam Ho Tai writes that the "Vietnamese state was able to exercise complete control over the commemorative project in terms of design, location, budget. This contrasts with the politics of commemoration in countries such as the United States, where monuments are often the products of compromise between the public agendas of officials and the more personal concerns of ordinary people, where the nationalizing visions of élites must be reconciled with the more parochial horizons of local communities."[13] And John Bodnar notes that the experience of the Vietnam War contributed to strengthening this "vernacular memory" (as against official memory) in local communities of the United States.[14] Because of the state's dominance, public memorials in the Vietnamese community can live or die depending on whether they attract sustained interest from the state hierarchy. The memorial of the village massacre in An Bang, a neighbor of Ha My, is a dying monument. Built in the mid-1980s with the sponsorship of the district authority, the site had quickly disintegrated and become unrecognizable by the beginning of the 1990s. The memorial in Thuy Bo is also a striking example. The village's memorial for war martyrs is in excellent condition. The district authority employs a salaried guardian for its maintenance and periodically organizes workers and students to weed and repair the premises. For the students, the activity is part of their civil ethics course and is important for those who wish to obtain the credentials of a model pupil. The village's war crime memorial does not benefit from any such institutional support and is practically in ruins.

The general museum of My Lai is a unique heritage site in Vietnam that is, together with the former War Crimes Museum in Ho Chi Minh City, maintained by the state, unlike other installations dedicated to the civilian victims of the war. The museum in My Lai has an exhibition hall dedicated to the history of the massacre, and its three-hundred-acre landscaped garden displays a number of statues depicting scenes of killing. It attracts thousands of visitors every year, and the official annual memorial event attracts the foreign press and party officials. While I was there, during the week before the event, the village loudspeaker urged the villagers to fulfill their civic obligation by attending, and the chief of each hamlet was called upon to encourage as many people as possible to attend. Most villagers, including the relatives of the victims, were apathetic and prepared various excuses for their absence. In the past, the museum had maintained several graves of victims within its grounds, and their families used to visit the premises for the death-day anniversary. All the remains had recently been moved to family burial grounds against the wishes of the museum authority, which considered the bodies to be historical evidence, and, since then, there has been no tangible contact between the museum and the villagers. The province of Quang Ngai is hoping to extend the museum and has claimed several hundred acres of fields for that purpose. Several U.S.-based nongovernmental organizations have been active in the area, providing humanitarian and medical assistance to villagers, and there are many unresolved issues in the village relating to the legacy of the American War, such as the plight of the surviving victims of chemical military devices. Improving the museum might help to attract international attention to these pressing problems. The land acquisition, however, had caused considerable discontent among the villagers, who complained about beautifying a place that had no relevance for either the victims or their families.

My Lai is not the only place where public memorials have failed to be integrated. The memorial of Ha My has two collective tombs at the corners of its walled compound. While the memorial was under construction, the villagers brought to it the scattered remains from the sand dunes, the bamboo forest, and elsewhere. Later, Ha My villagers rarely visited the graves, apart from the opening ceremony and the few occasions when they accompanied outside visitors. In Thuy Bo and An Bang, commemorations of the victims of the village massacres were conducted in private, either individually or collaboratively, and this everyday practice was not extended to the public monuments. When the families in Thuy Bo observed the death-day anniversary for the victims in 1999, they chose to hold it together at the house of a village elder. His house was a stone's throw from the Stone of Fury in the village war crime monument. The participants presented votive papers with the names of the victims written on them. They conducted a simple ceremony in the elder's courtyard, offered incense sticks in the direction of the monument (which was also the site of the killing), and later burned the papers together with other votive objects. After the meal, when most of the guests were gone, the hosting elder headed toward his lineage ancestral temple, laid fruits on the altar, lit the candles and incense sticks, and reported to the ancestors, "Honorable ancestors: Your children held a memorial this morning. Please show your sympathy to their sorrow if they are still in sorrow, take care of their pains if they still have them. We pray for you." On our way out, he cleaned the surface of the outdoor shrine, placed a few fruits on it, lit the incense, and whispered a prayer while kowtowing four times to the shrine for ghosts.

Placing a permanent memorial in a community, moreover, inevitably provokes a sense of inequality in relation to the neighboring communities. The villages near My Lai all suffered large-scale incidents of killing during the earlier village pacification campaign of 1966, but none of these many incidents are accounted for in monument form. For people in these villages, this inequality adds further injustice to the injustice of killing innocent civilians. When construction of the Ha My memorial was under way, there was widespread discontent in the neighboring villages that had suffered like incidents of face-to-face killing. There was discontent within Ha My as well. The relatives of victims of relatively small incidents of killing were saddened to the extent that one of them told me, "If you have the terrible fate to die in a massacre, you have to avoid a small massacre at the least." The presence of a monument elsewhere heightened the absence of such an object in the vicinity, and people expressed their bitterness in a graphical language that painted a growing alienation among the dead.

In the villages near My Lai, people told stories about how they believed the spirits of their ancestors were jealous of those of the victims of the My Lai massacre. The imaginary situation they depicted drew upon the organization of a domestic ritual familiar to them: the memorial in My Lai is closed to the victims of war crimes other than those of the My Lai massacre and relegates them, during ceremonies, to the position of anonymous ghosts. Just as a domestic ancestral ritual classifies death in the duality of kinship and anonymity, so does a memorial divide tragic death into placed identity and placeless nonidentity. The memorial, in other words, creates a further category of ghosts in the category of ghosts of tragic death. In popular imagination, the spirits of the dead are cognizant of the nature of the place to which they are invited for a ritual. If the place is a site of kinship, those excluded easily reconcile with the exclusion, for they are aware, as it were, that this is the nature of life. A public commemoration, however, complicates the picture. The memorial event in My Lai is instituted by the provincial authority and thus should be open to the victims of all massacres within the provincial territory. The memorial, however, recognizes only a particular incident. Given this disparity between the locality of memory and its social institutional basis, the villagers near My Lai have come to believe that the ghosts of victims of mass killings outside My Lai are excluded from public commemoration events in My Lai, and that they have built up grievous feelings about this alienation.

Despite this problem of alienation and that of gradual decay that I pointed out earlier, the completion of the memorial turned out to be a significant event for the families of the victims. Public recognition of the tragic history by the state or other external institutions proved to be crucial for the incorporation of tragic death into local ritual.[15] Although not involved in the construction of the memorial, most families actively participated in the reburial of the remains. They had prepared 135 coffins and distributed among them the bone fragments collected from the outskirts of the village. This individuation of the victims' bodies, although it was merely symbolic, was a critical act, which demonstrated to the dead, as noted earlier, that a new life was beginning for each of them. The participants later told me that it had been a moving experience to touch each of the many skulls in turn, thinking and wondering which one would belong to their relative. It was also a satisfying experience to express sorrow freely and in public, which some said had not been possible for the past generation.

For a period after the completion of the Ha My memorial, many rumors of apparition also circulated the village. A woman of Ha My origin returned to the village after decades of absence. Having lost her husband to the massacre, and having been settled in a city since 1968, this woman was concerned about the health of her son from her second marriage, suspecting that his illness might be related to the death of her former husband in Ha My. Following the advice of a relative, she came to consult with a female fortune-teller *(thay boi)* about her recent experience. While in Ha My, she dreamed about her former husband. In the dream, the husband reproached her, saying she had neglected to visit him at his new place.[16] The medium's tutelary spirit advised the woman to pay a visit to the memorial as a gesture of bidding farewell to her late husband. Because she was remarried and not able to commemorate her former husband at home, it was agreed that the medium would perform death-day anniversary and other periodic remembrance ceremonies for the husband on her behalf. These substitutive kinship memory practices were an important domain of work for this *thay boi* and other ritual specialists in Ha My and My Lai.

In another incident, it was rumored that the spirit of Van's father (and husband of Ba Lap) had suggested to his family that they conduct his death anniversary ceremony on the internal ancestral altar rather than at the external ghost shrine. People who heard this incident understood that the spirit was happy and finally at peace to see his children reburied. The villagers also talked about the spectral group of a mother with two toddlers who used to frequent a road in Ha Gia, and how they changed in appearance from war refugees to a wealthy family. Some children told stories at home of small ghosts from the village primary school who, according to them, used to steal pencils and paper from them. Some time after the opening of the memorial, they claimed that they had seen the ghosts huddled in the corner of the school corridor arguing among themselves. They said that the ghosts had a large amount of paper and sweets in front of them. The villagers, hearing this from the children, assumed that the child ghosts of the school were happy with the votive gifts they had been offered.

These incidents of apparition, widely disseminated within the village, were a conclusive sign to the villagers proving that the dead were content with the reburial, and this awareness affected how future domestic commemoration events were organized. In 2001, the families of the victims assembled together to initiate an informal association and discussed the possibility of holding a collaborative rite. The idea was to consolidate the individual domestic death anniversary rites for the victims of the massacre and to have the families take turns organizing them. The participants persuaded an elderly village ritual specialist to take part in the group in the hope of having his services for the interfamily domestic rite. Meanwhile, the domestic ancestral rites began to incorporate the identities of the massacre victims explicitly. Van left the tablets representing his siblings on the family's ancestral altar when the family was preparing the Lunar New Year feast. One of his neighbors hung the picture of a young woman next to her brothers. The woman was killed in the 1968 massacre, and the two men were martyred in the battlefields the same year. This rehabilitation of tragic death to the domestic ritual sphere had a contagious effect on other neighbors, and it included not only the victims of the massacre but also other stigmatized identities (see chapter 8). The decision to disclose the hitherto concealed identities in the family's domestic ritual space was a private matter, but the private display was also a public statement of the family's new moral identity.

Whereas remembrance of the mass death came to take on increasingly more explicit forms in the domestic sphere, the public memorial built to keep the memory looked abandoned a year after its completion. Villagers rarely visited either the walled memorial compound or the two collective tombs located in it. Some victims' families said they felt too intimidated by the imposing monument to conduct routine prayers there. Other families added that they felt uneasy doing ritual offerings to their relatives, knowing that the recipients cohabited with many others in the monument. The family of Ba Lap pointed out that it was not possible for them to ritually associate with all the victims, and that only people having no victim relatives could pray for all the names inscribed on the monument.

The memorial failed to do what it was built to do: to provide a place for remembering the dead. Yet precisely because of this failure, it contributed to the vitalization and distribution of the memory across many places. Within the village reality, the identities inscribed on the memorial stone were transformed from an anonymous mass into concrete historical persons at specific places elsewhere. The victims finally had individual coffins, although they still shared a collective tomb. Accordingly, their families began to collaborate on a wider communal rite that would parallel their individual domestic rites. In this way, the living generation invented a new social network of commemoration to account for the new reality of the dead generation.

The memorial stone did not mark the final resting place of the Monkey Year victims, nor was it a place of symbolic closure. Because it failed to concentrate and settle the collective memory of the victims, the stone emerged instead as an important catalyst for remembering the victims as individuals. Public recognition of the victims' collective existence liberated them as individuals and contributed to making their laborious homebound journey less arduous.

CHAPTER 8

The Decomposition
of the Cold War

Heroes, ancestors, and ghosts coexist in the village environment. While revolutionary politics and traditional religious heritage separate them, the three social classes in afterlife associate in popular ritual practices. Although they constitute a hierarchy, the hierarchy that structures their relative values varies at different sites of memory. Their status changes between the state war memorial and the community temple, and the war heroes who occupy the symbolic center in the former are relegated to the margins, outside the village ancestors, in the latter. The position of ghosts also shifts in this movement of memories. The memory of tragic death is left in a void in the monument of heroes, whereas in ancestor worship it becomes an essential part of the spatial structure of worship, representing a generalized anonymity worthy of a particular kind of respect. Social hierarchy in the afterlife, therefore, is not fixed in today's Vietnam but is variable relative to the specific locus of memory. In this plural, dynamic environment of commemoration, the political identity of the dead is constantly in fluctuation as it moves from place to place, and this mobility makes the space of commemoration, according to José Ortega y Gasset, proliferate with a multitude of perspectives.[1] In this reality of relativity and multiplicity, determining the absolute identity of heroic death, or that of tragic death, has become impossible.

The revival of the cult of ancestors was an important part of the changing political relations of the dead. Localized ancestor worship emerged as a powerful paradigm of history in place of the dominant national hero worship. Although war heroism and the ancestral cult share many common ideological and esthetical elements, these two social forms also have a few distinctive orientations. Vietnamese war heroism cuts through regional differences, creates homogeneity across differential local unity, and its management is centralized. The Vietnamese ancestral cult, on the contrary, emphasizes regional specificity, reinforces local unity, and its management is highly decentralized.

A further difference between ancestor and hero worship must be noted: the difference in how each cult claims its centrality. As systems of values, ancestor worship and hero worship are both based on an elaborate mechanism of exclusion. The domain of ancestor worship is closed to the genealogically unrelated and those who died a socially disruptive death. The domain of hero worship rules out those who died a politically incompatible or unproductive death, thereby clarifying, according to Katherine Verdery, "who is to be included in or excluded from the new national society that is being made."[2] As Peter van der Veer puts it, "Power works not only positively to inculcate certain truths, but also negatively by systematically excluding, forbidding, and denouncing."[3]

In today's Vietnam, these two exclusive systems of values coexist, and each contests the other's relevance and strength. The rule of genealogical exclusion and that of political exclusion can collude as well as collide. Remembering mass civilian war death was a problem in the domain of ancestor worship partly as a result of the role the latter plays in empowering the genealogical legacy that the state defines as meritorious. Unlike hero worship, however, ancestor worship demonstrates the reality of exclusion explicitly within its built form. I introduced the spatial structure of "house" and "street," or the central ancestral temple versus the peripheral ghost shrine, as an example of the esthetic dualism of ancestor worship. A centrality such as that of modern hero worship, according to Henri Lefebvre, "aspires to be total. [It] expels all peripheral elements with a violence that is inherent in space itself. This centrality—or, perhaps better, this centralization—strives to fulfill its 'totalizing' mission with no philosophy to back it up aside from a strategic one."[4] Unlike what Nietzsche calls the monumental vision of the past that "rules over the other ways of looking at the past," the ancestral memory requires a tangible dialectical opposite in order to rule and in order to demonstrate that it rules.[5] The centrality of genealogical order and enclosure, in the theatrics of the cult of ancestors, rises in opposition to the unbound marginality of unassimilated death. If the broad structure of Vietnamese ancestor worship is a dual organization, and there are categorically no ancestors without ghosts in this organization,[6] it is understandable that the current revival of ancestor worship revitalizes the belief in ghosts at the same time. The act of materializing the existence of ghosts is a way of making tangible the power of ancestors. The empowerment of one side works, in a dual organization, only if it works for both sides.

This movement, which I earlier called "ambidextrous," applies not only to the dual moral symbolism of death but also to the wider historical background of the mass death—the Cold War. What are the implications of the parallel empowerment of ghosts and ancestors for the social history of the forceful geopolitical dualism? A discussion of these implications must focus in part on the fate of the politically troubled dead, who, having sacrificed their lives for the wrong side of the war and been subsequently excluded from public memory, now transform into family ancestors. Then we will turn our view beyond the domain of ancestor worship and will explore how "the decomposition of the Cold War culture" is celebrated on the streets—that is, in the world of the ghosts of tragic death.[7]

PARALLAX VISIONS

In his seminal work *Parallax Visions*, Bruce Cumings raises an important question about Cold War history—how large-scale human tragedies may arise from an optical problem.[8] The historian argues, in line with the so-called revisionist school of international history, that the origin of the Cold War in Asia is found at the geopolitical center, not at the peripheral battlefields.[9] During the decade after the end of the Second World War, the radical political movements in Asia and elsewhere in the Third World became part of the Soviet conspiracy of global communist expansion. Cumings argues that this development did not reflect an actual change in the political reality of the Third World. That anticolonialism came to look identical to pro-communism, according to him, was instead a parallax effect of U.S. foreign politics as the United States shifted from participating in an antifascist alliance to undertaking a crusade against communism. Mary Kaldor writes in a similar light about the geopolitical conditions of Europe in midcentury: "Perceptions about external threats, while real enough as to their effect on action, are shaped as much by the situation of the perceiver as by the situation perceived."[10] The idea of parallax vision entails an apparent change in the look of an object in view that results from a change in the position of the viewer. It is a key concept in astronomy and is employed to explain such situations as that of a star apparently changing in form or disappearing from view because of the earth (hence the observer) changing position in the orbit.[11] Drawing an analogy, Cumings explores the origin of the conflicts in Korea and Vietnam as a product of geopolitical parallax.

Indeed, the postcolonial visions of Vietnamese revolutionaries did not include joining a bloc with the Soviet Union or China, or the contingency of a confrontation with the opposite bloc in the emerging bipolar structure of the international system, particularly with the United States.[12] In 1945, when the nation was liberated from Japan's military occupation, Vietnam's vision of its postcolonial future, as Mark Bradley shows, included the idea that it would "be a market for American manufactured goods." In fact, one Vietnamese spokesperson noted, "We do not see any reason why the Americans should not build a Ford plant in our new country."[13] The Vietnamese anticipated having a fully independent and prosperous nation-state, an idea that was incompatible with the bloc system of the Cold War, which undermined and "outmoded" the sovereignty of the nation-states.[14] Arif Dirlik observes, "To the Vietnamese, viewing the war from the perspective of the struggle for national liberation, France, Japan, and the United States represented successive colonial powers in a history of struggle against outside domination."[15] Given this background, Bradley argues that the Cold War historical framework is insufficient to explain the Vietnam-American conflict. He proposes in its stead a framework that can account for "Vietnamese and American perceptions of each other and their imaginings of Vietnam's postcolonial future." Central to this alternative interpretative framework is the importance of postcolonial transition and the influence of different expectations about the transition upon the formation of bipolar confrontation.

Bradley's persuasive study is "postrevisionist," an orientation that tries to go beyond the earlier trend in international history called "revisionism." In the latter tradition, historians disillusioned with the "orthodox" interpretation of the origin of the Cold War, which put the blame for escalating hostility on the Soviet side, instead turned to the active role played by the United States. The "postrevisionist" approach is currently dominant, in part because of newly accessible archival material held in the eastern bloc countries, which attempts to reassess the East-West relations as a mutually constitutive, reciprocal "joint venture" and also to decenter the Cold War origins.[16] Concerning the revolutionary movements in the peripheral regions, scholars of this tradition have explained the rise of bipolar confrontation within the wider historical context of decolonization. Following Cumings's parallax metaphor, we may say that the revisionist school's key contribution in this sphere of research was its rejection of the positional shift that resulted in the geopolitical parallax. In other words, revisionists sought to tell a different story of the Cold War in the Third World by firmly relating the horizon of the bipolarizing modern world to that of the decolonizing traditional societies.

If the shift from the narrowly defined Cold War paradigm to a wider postcolonial framework has been an important, constructive move by scholars of international history, a shift of perspective in the opposite direction can be equally important for advancing our understanding of the local experience of political conflicts in the past century. The Cold War, as Stephen Whitfield proposes, was a "two-pronged" conflict: it had a geopolitical dimension and a social dimension, each with different temporalities and development cycles.[17] If in one dimension the conflict has ended, it has not necessarily done so in the other dimension. Whitfield coined the term *decomposition* to draw attention to the slow and potentially critical process of the social dimension of this bipolar history coming to an end, partly against the idiom of "the end of the Cold War" dominant in contemporary academic and public discourse, which assumes globally simultaneous, radical temporal rupture. We can extend Whitfield's insights about the Cold War as social and cultural history (as well as geopolitical history) to the conjuncture of postcoloniality and bipolarity expressed by Cumings's parallax visions. The geopolitical parallax affects the social order as well. The idioms of bipolarity may be insufficient or misleading when describing the Vietnam-American War at the level of the international order, as Bradley shows, but they may deepen our knowledge of the war's legacy at the level of the local social order.

The geopolitical parallax that turned ardent believers in national autonomy to subservient followers of the communist bloc may have been an illusion, but it was an illusion that had the power to become a working vision. In the actual, violent battlefields of the Cold War, people who experienced the global conflict experienced it intimately. For them, the conflict was not merely about the doctrine of containment and deterrence, or an aspect of the domino theory or game theory, but it also took root in communal life, cultural communication, and interpersonal relations.[18] The famous Vietnamese poet Pham Duy wrote a song called "A Tale of Two Soldiers" in 1968:

There were two soldiers who lived in the same village
Both loved the fatherland—Vietnam.
There were two soldiers who lived in the same village
Both loved the fields and the earth of Vietnam.

There were two soldiers, both of one family,
Both of one race—Vietnam.
There were two soldiers, both of one family,
Both of one blood—Vietnam.

There were two soldiers who were of one heart,
Neither would let Vietnam be lost.
There were two soldiers, both advancing up a road,
Determined to preserve Vietnam.

There were two soldiers, both were heroes,
Both sought out and captured the enemy troops.
There were two soldiers, both were heroes,
Both went off to "wipe out the gang of common enemies."

There were two soldiers who lay upon a field,
Both clasping rifles and waiting.
There were two soldiers who one rosy dawn
Killed each other for Vietnam
Killed each other for Vietnam.[19]

The song vividly delivers the message that the enemies of the Cold War, who fought it on their feet and with their lives, had the same origin, and that they fought each other because each believed he was defending his home from the menace of the other. One side suffered from a parallax vision of the other's pursuit of national independence as a communist conspiracy; the other mistook the equivalent action on the other side as a sellout to an imperialist ambition. The Cold War, for these foot soldiers of the global conflict, was a field of double parallax visions in which visual distortion was an intersubjective reality. Against this background, it should be made clear that the Cold War's parallax was not merely geopolitical or diplomatic. It created a further parallax between state and society: when a revolutionary movement developed into a revolutionary state, its postcolonial vision turned into a doctrine to be imposed on the society despite the complexity and diversity of actual historical experience.

Marilyn Young notes that Americans remember the conflict in Vietnam mainly as a conflict among the Americans—that is to say, as a kind of civil war between the supporters and opponents of the foreign intervention. She observes that, for the Vietnamese too, the war increasingly appears to have been, in part, a civil war, not merely a clear-cut case of self-defense against foreign aggression.[20] Hue-Tam Ho Tai also observes,

"In Vietnam, . . . the past remains a live presence, impossible to ignore, difficult to assimilate. With its share of winners and losers in what, increasingly, is recognized to have been a civil conflict as much as a war against foreign intervention, postwar Vietnam, at first glance, offers striking parallels with postbellum America [post–Civil War America]; yet the issues involved in grappling with the past are quite different in the two countries."[21] The idea of a conflict between brothers, which these scholars are alluding to, is also being taken up by a growing number of talented Vietnamese writers who are subtly expressing it in novels and poems.[22] This development is related to "the myth of national experience of war" that George Mosse has written about with respect to western Europe during the First and Second World Wars.[23] Mosse considered the homogenization of war memory to be a constitutive element of modern state power and legitimacy, and other historians of the world war conflicts subsequently have highlighted the divergence of war memory within a national community.[24]

The Vietnamese politics of heroic war death is largely based on a prevailing postcolonial vision. Vietnamese commemorative art, including the monument forms found easily in any village or district, clearly renders the sacrifices in the American War in a continuum with earlier struggles against French colonial occupations. As noted earlier, this institution of hero worship made sense, relatively speaking, in the context of northern Vietnam, where the war dead were predominantly the volunteer soldiers who had left their homes to fight in the distant battlefields: communities handed over to the state their precious offspring, and the state brought their bodies back to the community and honored their memory. It is not easy to extend this classical relationship between civil society and national state to the postwar southern regions. The war efforts in these regions did not consist of a clear division between the home front and the distant horizon of actual battlefields but was instead a *xoi dau*, the popular expression for village cold war among southern Vietnamese, which turned secure communal life inside out, into a vicious, confusing battleground. *Xoi dau* is the Vietnamese ceremonial food made of sticky rice and black beans, and people use this black-and-white delicacy as a metaphor for the particularly harsh condition of the people's war. When you eat this sweet, you are obliged to swallow both the white and the black parts; you cannot separate the two. Living in a war zone that, from the perspective of one side, is pacified, and, from the perspective of the other, is liberated, you are forced to acknowledge both realities.

In Cold War historiography, the change of perspective—from the dominant, singular bipolar political framework to the alternative framework of disjunctive parallax effects between decolonization and bipolarization—was an important and constructive paradigm shift. The postcolonial paradigm is superior, in anthropological language, in representing "the native's point of view" compared to the orthodox Cold War paradigm. The relative strength of this postcolonial perspective becomes a weakness, however, when the analyst turns from the sphere of international history to that of local history. Whereas the postcolonial perspective considers the intentions and historical particularities of the peripheral other, it tends to be analytically oblivious to the fact that in Cold War conflicts the peripheral national other has already assimilated the abstract bipolar geopolitical worldview and therefore is not reducible to a homogenous, unifying identity.

The idea of a "global experience" of the Cold War runs up against many obstacles, including the differing experiences of Europe and its former colonies, as well as the equally important difference between northern and southern parts of Europe, not to mention between the eastern and western parts.[25] The same is true with any assumption about "national experience" in the global conflict. In the fields where the conflict took violent form and involved the radical bifurcation of social forces, the assumption can be especially problematic. The postcolonial historical perspective, in my view, has not yet come to terms with the progression of modern political history, in which, ironically, the very "native point of view" the postcolonial discourse tried to represent has turned into a locally hegemonic force, thereby ruling out divergent experience and memories.

The idea that the American War was partly a civil war is, therefore, not a negation of the international dimension of the conflict, which Young herself has written about,[26] but rather a way of going beyond the postcolonial paradigm. More important for our discussion, it also explains the communal initiatives to appropriate the history of the international conflict for local purposes. If the conflicts and struggles were "civil" or "communal," as well as national or international, it is only logical that the community should play a part, as actively as the states, in the process of conflict resolution.

The revival of ancestor worship in Vietnam, then, is not merely a restoration of traditional social ideals but rather an invention of a countermeasure against dominant political convention. In southern and central Vietnam, kinship rarely constitutes a homogeneous political group. The history of their unity is crowded with the history of mutual enmity. When a tomb or temple renovation is under way, those who collaborate in the communal project are both people of a common genealogical origin and people of opposite political origins. Families with a hero title and families stigmatized as "reactionary" *(phan dong)* may come together. The participants may include a village man with a pure family record of three generations of patriotic war martyrs, as well as a man from the town whose record shows a period of employment in the Saigon army.

The contemporary *viec ho* movement (the work of family ancestor worship) encourages the social actors of different political backgrounds to work together for a common objective. When relatives assemble, their specific objective matters a lot. The opening of an ancestral temple triggers the participants' recollection of the times before they started fighting a war in the village. The memory of these times may be partly a fiction, fantasized through songs and poems, but the idea that once their village was a peaceful and prosperous place remains uncontested in family gatherings. In this context, it helps the atmosphere if the place they are collaborating to rebuild was destroyed more than once. The more severe the destruction, ironically, the easier it has been to gather forces to reconstruct it. If the ancestral temple has the history of having succumbed to French explosives and then to a U.S.-made flamethrower, it is better if it also has the opposite history of yielding to the hammers of some excessively revolutionary villagers after the liberation of 1975. If the history of destruction transgressed the frontier of the bipolar conflict, this helped the activity of reconstructing it extend to a wider circle.

If the renovation of temples reunites the living, the renovation of tombs reunites the dead, away from their bipolar histories. The family burials, unlike the state-administered burials, do not separate "the two brothers" of Pham Duy into hero and villain. They incorporate the dead from both sides of the war, both civilians and soldiers, and arrange them mainly according to the principles of kinship and the hierarchy of descent. Hence, in the burial ground of a family in My Lai, the revolutionary war martyr and the former solider of "the puppet army" lie next to each other as brothers. The revolutionary martyr kept his honorable title of *liet si* (revolutionary martyr) even if he was removed from the state war martyr cemetery; the former soldier of the Saigon army was stripped of any indication of his military identity—but everyone who came to visit the graves knew who he was. They offered joss sticks to the Saigon soldier first, according to who he was—the elder brother. On the ancestral altar too, the war dead gathered from across the Cold War's frontier. The My Lai family displayed the state-issued death certificate for the martyr and a faded photograph of the Saigon soldier in civilian clothing side by side, and above them the portrait of their parents—the wife, a victim of the village massacre, and her husband, an old soldier of the French colonial army, made to wear the attire of a mandarin family in the hands of a village portrait artist.

The revived ancestral worship in Vietnam contributes to undoing the legacy of the war by assimilating the historical political duality of "this side" and "that side" to the traditional unity of family *(nha* and *phai)* and lineage *(ho* and *toc)*. As noted earlier, however, the new unity of kinship is not an entirely democratic entity. The soldier of "this side" appears in the ancestral memory with his political identity intact as well as his kinship status, whereas his counterpart on "that side" has to drop his military or political background on his memory's homebound journey. The former blesses the descendents with his historical footing of patriotic service; the latter must have his stigmatic biography concealed so that he can join his descendents. Of the two brotherly soldiers of the Cold War, only one remains a brother as well as a soldier in ancestor worship. The other soldier is demobilized there and becomes only a brother. In this context, kinship works against political history, but only to have the history work within it.

The history of the Cold War is changing in the place of the ancestors. Kinship identity transcends the political bifurcation and—like the nation's drive toward a new socioeconomic form that is also a partial embrace of "the other side" (or incorporation into the other side, depending on how people look at it)—provides an alternative social unity. The philosophy of *doi moi* (Vietnam's socioeconomic "renovation") is open to the principles of market capitalism (although in the official discourse, this is increasingly described as reviving the nation's known heritage of a market economy, as opposed to the relatively recent Chinese-style command economy), and it aims, as Duiker notes, to join the elements of the bifurcated pathways of modernization into a workable whole that some call market socialism.[27] A new constitution was adopted in 1991, guaranteeing economic freedoms, and the thirty-year U.S. trade embargo was removed in 1994. Vietnam's ongoing initiative to accommodate the formerly hostile state actors as partners in economic development led it to the normalization of diplomatic ties with China in 1991 and with South Korea in 1992. The country joined the Association of Southeast Asian Nations in 1995, becoming a full member in 1997, and the Asia-Pacific Economic Cooperation in 1998. In 1997, diplomatic relations with the United States were restored and the size of the standing army was reduced. This rapid development at the national and international level constitutes the wider background of the social transformation at the local level depicted in this book, but it alone does not explain how the local social renovation took on a particular trajectory, bringing the memory of death to the foreground. In order to appreciate the local responses to the global transition, we must first come to terms with the fact that histories of mass death are embedded in the history of the Cold War, and second, we must understand the related importance of creative death remembrance in the transition beyond the bipolar history.

As noted earlier, the place of ancestors in southern and central Vietnam demonstrates a social unity different from the political unity based on a bipolar paradigm. Here, changes in this place are analytically inseparable from changes in its conceptually opposite domain of ghosts. In the ritual world beyond ancestor worship, the bipolar political history is undergoing a different process of decomposition in the milieu of ghosts. Is there also an alternative unity developing in the ritual relationship with displaced ghosts? If there is, is that unity more democratic than the unity of ancestors?

THE POWER OF GHOSTS

Khom, the shrines for wandering ghosts, are usually found in the periphery of a private house or a communal temple. The shrine in a private house typically looks like a birdhouse found in European domestic gardens, a miniature dwelling with a roof, sitting atop a tall vertical column, and the location and orientation varies from house to house. Apart from these places of ghosts within the domestic space, there are also many isolated shrines. These may be found in the hidden corners of a fish-processing factory, on the sand dunes, underneath a communal palm tree, in the midst of a crowded residential compound, or near the ruins of a temple. There is no precise "right" location for "street" shrines for ghosts as a whole, and where they are placed depends on the particular history of apparition. Their forms are also indeterminate: they can be large birdhouses, such as the typical ghost shrine in the domestic garden, or empty Pepsi cans hanging on trees. Each of these street shrines has a unique history involving a unique individual ghost, and the history is normally confined to the immediate circle of trusted neighbors. Among those who share the historical knowledge, the place is known as "powerful" or "auspicious" and receives attentive care from them.

In everyday life in the neighborhood, the shrine's outward appearance says nothing about its significance within the community. The faded Pepsi can on the palm tree could be a much more important place of worship than the richly decorated ancestral temple. Children are aware of this disparity between appearance and power. The buffalo-minding boys in Ha Quang have done naughty things to the village's communal house, such as practicing arithmetic on the temple's fresh black marble with stray bullets. None of these boys, however, has ever allowed a buffalo to rub its back against the palm tree since an incident in which one of them broke his arm while playing football near the tree. The neighborhood elders explained to them that the ghost in the Pepsi can disapproved of chaotic activity and excessive noise in its neighborhood.

The ghosts in these isolated shrines are recognized as powerful not only because they demand specific taboos within the community but also because of their perceived responsiveness to prayers. The parents of the boy with the broken arm prayed to the spirit in the Pepsi can to forgive their son and help the fractured bone heal quickly. Other neighbors related to the ghost shrine in terms of every aspect of their daily life— their grandmother's loss of appetite, the failure of the neighborhood hen to produce eggs, the excessive appetite of the household pigs, the abusive attitudes of the mother-in-law, the prodigalness of the youngest daughter-in-law, and the daughter-in-law's wish for luck with her lottery tickets. When it is recognized that the ghost is no longer responsive to these personal matters and communal affairs, the shrine promptly loses its relevance and is eventually abandoned.

In the independent ghost shrines, the living and the dead build a contractual relationship, independent from predetermined corporeal ties, on the basis of concrete everyday interactions. The relationship, for the ghost, requires the community's recognition of its specific identity and, for the community, the ghost's active participation in the community affairs. In other words, the ghosts in these places, contrary to ancestors, have to labor in order to take part in communal life with the living, and their doing so promotes their unique individuality rather than a transcendental collective identity. The life-making work of ghosts in Vietnam is well illustrated by the particular case history of Ba Ba Linh.

BA BA LINH

There are two strangely empty stretches of land in Tan Khai, a subhamlet of Ha Gia. One of them occupies more than two acres at the heart of the otherwise crowded residential compound. This land borders the newly paved village road on the one side and the renovated modern house of an official of the village People's Committee on the other side. The second, smaller plot is a two minutes' walk from the first and borders a fertile vegetable plantation overlooking an expansive paddy. Both plots looked distinctive to me, being empty but well tended and without weeds, and more so when I heard from the neighbors that both were auspiciously powerful.

These two plots of land have been empty for the last two generations, and a number of people and organizations have attempted to occupy them during the past few years. None of these attempts have been successful, even though the plots nominally have no owner, and instead have resulted in calamity for those who tried to lay claim to them. This is what I was told in a brief introduction to the history of the land by the villagers of Tan Khai, who were anxious to dissuade me from my interest in the two plots, believing that I was interested in owning them. The villagers anticipated that the land would remain unoccupied for the foreseeable future, perhaps for another generation, and the People's Committee official said that he shared this opinion. They told me that it was actually an illusion that the land looked unoccupied. "Ba Ba Linh, she owns the land. This old woman lives on one of the two plots," said a village elder, and he pointed to a small stick inserted at one of its corners.

The alleged owner of the land is called Ba Ba Linh (powerful old woman) or Ba Noi (father's mother) of Du Man by the Tan Khai residents. Before 1948, when she died in tragic circumstances, her family owned a house on one plot and had a vegetable garden on the other. Since then, it is believed, the possessive ghost of this woman has held onto her property and fought against many attempts to take it from her. In the year 1948, the then small, isolated community of Tan Khai had seven households and was a place of *xoi dau*, a Vietnamese expression meaning a cold war within the village. In the wet season of 1948, Ba Ba Linh was alone in her bamboo house. She had lost her husband in 1936, her children shortly after, and her orphaned grandchildren had left the village for an urban ghetto. She survived on the small plot of land where she grew vegetables; the neighbors regularly helped the lonely woman with rice and fish sauce. The villagers who knew her told me that, before she fell into hardship, Ba Ba Linh had been a generous neighbor throughout the difficult colonial years, helping people with food and money.

On the fifth day of the eleventh lunar month of 1948, she spotted a group of French soldiers conducting a house-to-house search. She was ill at the time and waved at the soldiers for help. The soldiers came, pushed her back into the house, closed the shutters, and set fire to the bamboo house. Such atrocities were not uncommon in 1947–1948. A dozen villagers were shot and burned to death in the neighboring Ha Loc commune; 126 villagers of Ha Dong and Giang Dong in June 1948; 23 villagers in Dong Ban in February 1948; 150 women and children in Xuan Diem; 58 villagers in three communes of Dien Hong village; and many more. The villagers recovered Ba Ba Linh's skull from the rubble and buried it in her garden. There was no funeral, and no one commemorated her death day in the ongoing chaos of war. People forgot about her and her death, and the site of her old house turned into a small meadow attracting village buffaloes. Meanwhile the two ancient guava trees flourished on the site and new pine trees took root at the edge of it. Twenty years later, at the height of the American War, however, people of Tan Khai were suddenly forced to rediscover their old neighbor.

In the beginning of 1968, the Tan Khai subhamlet, isolated from the main residential compounds of the village, was relatively peaceful. The residents heard the rumor of the massacres in Ha My and Ha Gia. Although frightened, most were obliged to remain where they were and stay vigilant. They had nowhere else to go, and each family, additionally, was doing exceptionally well economically. Because the entire area had turned into wilderness and most people had left, the number of river lobsters and turtles had grown enormously. Wild river spinach also became abundant along the village stream and the hamlet's lotus flower pond. People made a handsome profit by selling this produce at the marketplace. Fresh vegetables were precious goods in the market; the price of wild spinach was high. Some of the remaining Tan Khai families were hoping to move to Da Nang when they had saved enough money to rent a room in the crowded city. In a few families, the husband was already in Da Nang looking for work in the port or near the army bases, and the wife and children remained in the village, hauling turtles and wild spinach to the Con market at the crossroads.

In one of these divided families, the young wife gave birth in her husband's absence in the first lunar month of 1968. It was the time of the Tet Offensive, and life was chaotic in the city as well as in the village. Her husband did not return to the village for fear of violence (adult men were particularly vulnerable to arbitrary killing in a rural village), and the wife quickly resumed her daily cultivation and food-gathering work. In order to leave the baby safely with her four-year-old daughter, she needed to make a cot. She went to the site of Ba Ba Linh's old residence, cut two branches from the guava tree, and laid them in the shadow to dry them. In a few days, the newborn succumbed to a bout of crying and refused to suck his mother's breast. She assembled a cot using the branches, and that night she had a dream about Ba Ba Linh. She told me about the dream:

> It was Ba Ba Linh. I didn't know who it was. The old lady living in the back of her plot later told me who it was. The woman in my dream was seated underneath the guava tree and scratching her leg. The old lady told me that this was exactly what Ba Ba Linh used to do while she was alive. Ba Ba Linh was angry at me. She said, "Bring the branches back to my home or I will make trouble with your baby." She looked at me with cold eyes and said, "I don't mean to harm your child. I know this is a difficult time for you. I would rather help you than make your life more difficult." Then, she avoided my eyes. Scratching her legs and examining the skin, she said, "Oh, it hurts." And then she said, "Why didn't you ask for my permission before you took advantage of my property? People have forgotten about politeness." Then, she turned to the other side, ignoring me completely. But I could still hear her saying to herself, "Impolite people come and burn my house. They come and take things away without asking permission from the owner of the house. What should we do with these impolite people?"

The next morning, the young mother returned the branches to Ba Ba Linh. She used the two sticks to make a small shrine for her at the edge of the site of her old house, burned a handful of incense sticks, and said the prayer of apology. In the evening, she went back to the site with her newborn baby in her arms, carrying two coconuts from her garden. She offered the coconuts, hoping that this would make the transaction with Ba Ba Linh even, and prayed more. This was the first of many shrines to be built for Ba Ba Linh. After this, the women of the community began to say prayers at Ba Ba Linh's humble shrine each time they faced a dire situation or according to the lunar ritual calendar. During the day, some Saigon soldiers saw the village women kowtowing to the shelf for the ghost, heard the story, and prayed for their own wishes at the site. At night, the peasant militiamen, coming to survey the area, heard the same story. The village women saw that some of these guerilla fighters were praying to Ba Ba Linh before they hurriedly joined their group to move to the next hamlet. When people returned to the village after evacuation during the critical period of the war at the end of the 1960s and beginning of the 1970s, they recall that there was nothing standing in the hamlet, except the small guava tree stick of Ba Ba Linh.

When the villagers began to erect bamboo huts and clear the area for cultivation after the end of the war, Ba Ba Linh's two plots remained untouched and her small shrine continued to attract prayers from the village women. Many encountered her apparition, particularly at dusk. Children on buffaloes saw her carrying water buckets on her shoulder pole. Young women returning from the paddy saw her talking to herself under the guava tree. On the fifteenth day of a lunar month, people spotted a fireball the size of a human head jumping from tree to tree. Flying fireballs were a common phenomenon in villages at this time. People in Ha My recall that an army of fireballs was hopping around the site of the massacre shortly before the annual remembrance day of the massacre. Ba Ba Linh's apparition generated fear among some villagers, while some boys invented the game of staying alone under the guava tree to test each other's audacity. During moonless nights in the rainy season, her phantom presence became particularly apparent and her public appearances more active. Gradually, the community came to accept Ba Ba Linh nearly as a full member. Hence, on the map of the village prepared by the village chief on behalf of the local agricultural cooperative, the two abandoned plots in Tan Khai were marked clearly as "the house and the land of Ba Noi [father's mother] of Du Man." This was in 1977.

At harvesttime in 1982, a village man brought his rice straw and laid it out to dry on the site of Ba Ba Linh's old vegetable plot. He did this against the advice of the villagers. This man had been an elite revolutionary recruited in northern Vietnam during the war and active in the postwar cultural campaigns. He refused to follow the advice that he should seek Ba Ba Linh's consent first by performing coin magic at her shrine. During the days that followed, Ba Ba Linh's neighbors tried to persuade the veteran to remove the hay from the site, and an official from the agricultural cooperative joined this effort. The village chief was also informed of the tension in the community caused by a new intrusion onto Ba Ba Linh's land. He spoke to the family of Du Man, who was the only surviving descendant of Ba Ba Linh and whose son was a member of the Communist Party and an official in the village People's Committee. Du Man's son urged the village chief to talk to the veteran and find a solution. The veteran threatened that he would inform the higher authority about the laxity in the village in moral combat against backward beliefs. He did not say this to the village chief in person, but the rumor about his attitude circulated and this discouraged the village chief from intervening. According to the story told by Du Man's family, the veteran soon began to show symptoms of disorientation and complain about severe headaches. He wandered about the muddy fields, left his flock of ducklings unattended, forced his wife to hand over her shoulder pole to him, and ran about the village footpath carrying empty water buckets. Another villager recalled how the veteran attempted to chew betel nut, which was only for old women. Undergoing what people saw as mental disorientation, the veteran eventually yielded to pressure from his relatives and performed the *xin xam* (bamboo stick magic) in the presence of the village chief. Later he did three consecutive rites of apology at Ba Ba Linh's shrine, as he had learned he must from the bamboo magic, and extended his apology to all the neighbors of the ghost's land, following the specific advice of the village specialist in bamboo magic. Tan Khai oral history has it that, soon afterward, the veteran stopped behaving oddly and abandoned his high-handed attitude toward the small deities of the village, not to mention Ba Ba Linh.

In the 1990s, it appeared to me that Ba Ba Linh's defense of her native place continued to be vigorous. I heard the rumor that the manager of the local brewery was plotting to build a house on her land, and that this man was considering hiring a ritual specialist to clear the ghost's influence from the land. A few members of a local lineage temple association were also interested in the site, and the locals believed that these city dwellers had covertly planted three pine trees there—in their opinion, in preparation for a claim over the land. When one of the guava trees on the land died after having its root severed by the new paved road, the villagers expressed concern about how the old woman would react to the sorrow of losing her favorite object. Nothing happened. It turned out that her grandson had prayed to her on several occasions, explaining the unavoidable circumstances. When a man in an important position took the liberty of carrying home a few fruits from the tree just before it died, however, it was rumored that the ghost chased after him to his town home and punished him dearly for his thoughtlessness. My informants insisted that the pine trees of the family temple association had never taken root in Ba Ba Linh's land, and that their leaves had turned yellow after a season passed. Meanwhile the ghost appeared in their dreams with a threatening message, and the fireball kept reminding the people of Tan Khai of the continued presence of the old villager.

Because of Ba Ba Linh's extraordinary activity, Tan Khai keeps a lucid memory of the fifth and the seventh day of the eleventh lunar month. These are special days—the death anniversaries of the victims of the 1948 French war crime in Tan Khai and Ha Loc. Perhaps more powerfully than any monument or memorial, the history of injustice is kept vigorously alive in the "empty" residue of this small hamlet. The history cries out to be told, and it does so in the historically familiar, culturally intelligible way of *tru bam*—"to defend the native place." The social reality of apparitions in Vietnam, however, tends to be specific to an apparition's subjectivity as much as to the objective circumstances of its occurrence. The village women in the field, loading water spinach into their bamboo baskets, spoke of the ghost's possessiveness as a revelation of her own life memory. After her husband's death in 1936, they told me, Ba Ba Linh had to defend her land and property against the greed of a relative in her husband's family. When all were dead, she held onto the land stubbornly, wishing to hand it over to her surviving grandchildren. "Besides, a poor, common woman like her," one of the village women said, wiping away her sweat and rolling her betel chew, "who is going to be interested in remembering her? She had to work hard herself so that people took her seriously. It's like that before death, for us common women, and it's like that after death. We know that and she knows it. Without a house and land to hand over, who will pay attention to a lone widow?" This middle-aged woman and another woman of her age in the hamlet are apparently the only people of the village who can let their domestic animals graze on the land of Ba Ba Linh without any repercussions.

THE SPIRIT OF A CIVIL SOCIETY

The public lives of ghosts such as Ba Ba Linh create a contradictory spatiality. The places they are associated with and the historical identities they represent have a relationship of mutual ownership. The ghost owns the place; the place possesses the ghost. Their lives demonstrate a particular temporality, too. The enshrined ancestors inherit their identity and entitlement from the preceding generations within a genealogical framework, whereas the ghosts, when they are enshrined, reveal their identity through spontaneous, proactive interactions with human individuals. Social relations between human and ghost come close to sociological imaginations, such as that of Georg Simmel, that see collectivities as networks of interaction rather than as given, substantive entities.[28] Following Simmel, we might even say, first, that the relations are a "symbol of life," in which social life proceeds "not in [the] self-regulating forms but only in the vitality of real individuals, in their sensitivities and attractions, in the fullness of their impulses and convictions."[29] Second, the history of ghosts is also distinguished from the genealogical framework in the scope of this interaction. The door of ancestors is closed to humanity beyond kinship, whereas the place of ghosts invites relationships beyond kinship. Third, and more important for the purpose of this chapter, we may say that the enshrinement of a ghost makes the ghost an individual, whereas the equivalent process for an ancestor means that the ancestor becomes, in a Maussian sense, a moral person—a conception of the individual human being as a member of a significant and ordered collectivity.[30] Of course, both classes of beings have a social life with the living. In the imaginary sphere of the ghosts' own social life, nevertheless, the enshrined ghost, unlike an ancestor, leads a solitary existence, disconnected from the traditional social ties and autonomous from other like beings. The ghost, like the concept of "stranger" in Simmel's work, "is not bound by roots to the particular constituents and partisan dispositions of the group . . . but is a distinct structure composed of remoteness and nearness, indifference and involvement." This state of being, according to Simmel, generates "objective" attitudes to social reality.[31]

The individuality of ghosts relates to the social form of their collective existence. Each enshrined ghost, and its specific historical background, is known to the community, and the ghosts' backgrounds, seen as a whole, demonstrate a great diversity of historical experience and a more *objective* account of the historical reality than is found in ancestor worship.

The ghost of Ba Ba Linh in Tan Khai is traced to a war crime. The area has a number of other ghost shrines that involve histories of civilian killings. The site of "Three Sisters" has a shrine almost invisible to the untrained eye and commemorates three village women who were blown up in their underground shelter in 1967. Their apparition was marked, although it had been known before, when a man attempted to open a shop on the site. Their shrine was built at some point after the three female ghosts allegedly succeeded in deterring the man from possessing their land. The site of "Fishermen Ghosts" remembers the indiscriminate killing of fishing families in 1967 by a convoy of U.S. Marines. The ghosts' apparition included a scene of seventeen adults and boys dragging a boat on the seashore; their shrine holds a miniature boat and fishing net. Although the Three Sister ghosts' identities are known, they have no surviving relatives in the community. Therefore, the villagers would not have remembered them had their ghosts not demonstrated their vitality in the form of an apparition. The Fishermen Ghosts constitute a mixed group of ghosts and ancestors, for some of them have surviving relatives and are remembered in their family ancestral rites. The families ritually associate with their ancestors at the shrine for the fishermen ghosts as well, however, believing that the site has become an important source of power for the protection of fishermen.

At the other corner of the community, there is a small shrine on the back of a family temple where people worship what they believe to be the ghost of a resistance fighter against the French. His shrine is located where the neighbors think the remains of this old patriot are buried. Not far from this place, toward the pine forest, the neighbors regularly burn incense and make small food offerings to what they believe is the ghost of a resistance fighter who served during the American War. The villagers think these two soldiers are from distant places, the soldier of the American War from a more distant place than the other, and that they have quite different moral attitudes. Villagers who know of both ghosts told me stories of some brave village youths who tried to solicit them in order to win the lottery. The old patriot of the anticolonial war gladly participated in the speculation, according to the story, whereas the youths had a bad experience with the communist soldier of the American War. The story said that the wounded communist ghost, swearing and angrily shaking his walking stick, accused the youths of taking part in an immoral economic activity.

In the next seashore community is a ghost shrine built on behalf of the ghosts of three people who died at sea. The residents who built this shrine believe the ghosts are from the same family, originally from Hue, who were boat people. This has been an important place of worship until recently because it was known to have the power to protect boats from the risk of sea storms and pirates. The neighborhood also has a shrine for a child ghost. In the past, this ghost of a small child transformed into a powerful deity to the extent that the community elders decided to enshrine the ghost as one of the tutelary spirits of the community. The child ghost now has the honorable name of Co Tien and a place in the community's whale temple. On the other side of the road dividing the community into two clusters of houses and vegetable gardens, there is a long file of variously shaped ghost shrines along a footpath. These shrines, according to the villagers, are for the errant spirits of village ancestors. The footpath circles the ruins of the communal house, blown to pieces in 1967 in a military action. Following this footpath toward the old village pond, I found a place that I was particularly encouraged to visit. It is frequented by the ghost of a soldier who wears an American-style combat uniform but has the face of a non-Vietnamese Asian. This agile ghost of a foreign soldier is known to be scared of the villagers and to hide himself by diving into the pond each time people spot him. People who knew me were curious to find out whether the ghost would be as timid in front of his compatriot as he was with the Vietnamese villagers.

Not far from the shrine for the Korean GI, "the ghost who walks on his head and with his feet up" has a shrine. The ghost's unusual mode of mobility results from the particular circumstances of its body's interment. This ghost was a fisherman in his previous life, buried alive, head-down feet-up, by a communist hit squad for the charge of treason. The ghost insists, according to the neighbors, that the accusation and the punishment were totally unjust.

In chapter 2, I suggested that ancestral death anniversary rites are a powerful mnemonic instrument. The ancestral rites account for the events of tragic death as part of their general accounting for all genealogically related deaths of the past generations. This genealogical inclusiveness of ancestor worship may work against the political exclusiveness of the state's hero worship.[32] When the war dead are commemorated within the scheme of ancestor worship, they are recalled according to their positions in the genealogical continuity, not according to their positions in political classification. Ancestor worship may work against political exclusiveness, but its genealogical inclusiveness may work against the political history of tragic death. The true ancestor remains a heroic ancestor. Only this ancestor is entitled to exchange his meritorious service to the country for family blessings. The difference between the ancestor of heroic death and the ancestor of tragic death is like that between a man with wealth and a man without any property to hand over to his descendants. The difference can be substantial in the political economy of descent.[33]

The politics of exclusion in hero worship and of neutralization in ancestor worship do not apply to the reality of ghosts in popular Vietnamese culture. Most of the ghosts mentioned above have become part of the community out of a long history of apparition similar to that of Ba Ba Linh and by means of continual interaction with communal affairs. Unlike the process of assimilation in ancestor worship, the enshrinement of ghosts takes place with full recognition of their individual tragic histories. The magical power of these ghosts is in fact inseparable from their specific backgrounds of tragic death, for the power is a manifestation of their will for freedom from the grievous history. Each of their sites has a unique biographical history, but, seen together, they constitute a panoramic representation of the history of violence, the scale of which demonstrates a more objective historical account than in ancestral memory.

The ritual interaction with ghosts does not incorporate the past into a totalizing moral ideal or unifying scheme of history. On the contrary, it unravels the time past to "the heterogeneity of multiple spaces," in which "the intractable otherness of the lost object is preserved and not neutralized through a process of incorporation," in the words of Martin Jay, who reviews Walter Benjamin's militancy against monumental memory.[34] The life-world of ghosts does not acknowledge political frontiers and moral classifications—"this side" and "that side" or the heroic and the tragic—and does not recognize the art of collective memory in which, according to Maurice Halbwachs, the preservation of the past ought to have a specific use value for the present. The memory of the past in this heterogeneous world of tragic death is oblivious to the theory of symbolic conquest and the instrumentality of collective memory in consolidating the parts of a society into a coherent whole.[35] The theatrical, heterogeneous society that is open to all self-making individuals irrespective of their historical backgrounds—this fantastical, and what appears to be advanced, civil society must be a reflection of the aspiration of the living individuals, rather than a material reality in the life of the ghosts. But this was one point I couldn't bring my interlocutors in Vietnam to agree on.

The bipolar political history is coming to an end across the bipolar symbolism of death. How it is coming to an end, however, is not the same for the world of the ancestors and that of ghosts. The transition is different depending on how people place themselves in the structure of worship, and I reiterate that the ritual commemoration in southern and central Vietnam consists of a continual shifting of positions inside the dual structure. Whereas ancestor worship substitutes genealogical order for political order, the ritual interactions with ghosts look as though they depart from conventional notions of social and political order. If the former contributes to reconciling the bifurcated political histories in the name of kinship solidarity, the latter appears to do so by nurturing entirely different norms of relations whose scale goes beyond the community of kinship and the imagined community of the nation.

Conclusion

If we consider the history of the Cold War "from above" and reduce it to the doctrine of deterrence, of imagining war in order to prevent war—which has been a dominant paradigm in international history—it appears that political history and the morality of death have no meaningful relationship. If we consider it "from below" instead and include in it the experience of violent political confrontations within local and national communities, which is what the Cold War actually meant in much of the world in the past century, the political bifurcation of the human community and a moral polarization of death become closely interrelated phenomena.[1] In the history of the global conflict in the latter sense, communities were driven to select politically "good deaths" from the mass of other war deaths and to extract an ideologically coherent genealogy out of the enmeshed history of violence across the ideological border. This book is a story of Ha My and My Lai seen partly in the light of these crisscrossing moral and political bipolarities.

Mass war death is constitutive of modern national memory: this is what we learn from the social history of modern Europe, where the states, facing mass production of death during the First World War, instituted vast memorial projects in the name of the fallen common soldier and transformed the universal experience of bereavement into a positive social force to strengthen national unity.[2] These projects were later replicated in the new postcolonial nation-states of the Third World, providing a crucial theatrical arena—according to Richard Werbner in writing about the experience of Zimbabwe—"for proving the individual's subjection to the state, for asserting the state's encompassment of the personal identities of citizens, and for testing their identification with the nation."[3] The historian John Gillis adds to this established thesis on the relationship between mass war death and national consciousness the important point that collective memory in old Europe, before it was incorporated into national memory, was "highly localized or relatively cosmopolitan."[4] This entails the idea that, through the invention of modern national memory, the local and the cosmopolitan are perceived to be on separate spatial scales. Nation-states, in unifying the locales and differentiating the new unity against the exterior, generate this perception, through which they facilitate their existence as an exclusive mediator between the local and the global. The rise of the modern nation-state as an imagined community, in this perspective, meant not only the invention of a novel unity, as Anderson describes it, but also the invention of disunity between the local and the cosmopolitan.[5]

That localized and cosmopolitan memory can coexist without canceling out each other has also been suggested by other regional contexts and different focuses.[6] Keith Taylor analyzes Vietnamese historiography in this light and supports the notion of the "cosmopolitan vernacular"—the idea that cosmopolitan awareness is embedded in the historical formation of a local traditional Vietnamese culture rather than in a transcendence of parochial local cultures.[7] This way of understanding local political culture was pioneered, in anthropology, by Edmund Leach, who showed how two contrary political formations and conflicting systems of ethics coexist in a single social field. In his monograph published in 1954, which drew upon his work among the hill tribes on the Burmese border with China during the Second World War, Leach painted the Kachin communities as oscillating between two polar ideals of political organization—the feudal, autocratic Shan polity, on the one hand, and the equalitarian, democratic *(gumlao)* principle, on the other—and he described their structural social changes in terms of continual shifts in the focus of political power between the two ideals. In doing so, he went against the then dominant tendency in British social anthropology, which approached social structure from a unilateral perspective and saw it as consisting of a singular organizing principle, such as the rule of descent. For Leach, social structure meant a dynamic interplay between contrasting principles of relationship rather than a unitary system of rules, and he identified ritual action as the principal arena in which the transforming structural patterns of a society are expressed. My own thinking has been guided by an instructive remark from Leach: "Individuals can and do hold contradictory and inconsistent ideas about [social structure]. They are able to do this without embarrassment because of the form in which their ideas are expressed. The form is cultural form; the expression is ritual expression."[8]

Ritual reality in contemporary Vietnamese social life demonstrates a coexistence between, and an animated debate between, two forms of political unity. I have discussed in this light the centralized cult of war heroism and localized ancestor worship—the latter as part of a dialectical unity with the diffused social interactions with ghosts rather than as a closed system of meaning. The key aspect of contemporary Vietnamese memory politics is the fact that the emerging local social forms have redefined the bond between the past generations and the present, thereby challenging the hegemony of the state hierarchy in this crucial domain of political culture. The forceful emergence of ancestors and ghosts into the public arena hitherto dominated by war heroes crystallizes the decisive shift in power relations between the state and the society. Changes in the social life of the dead, in this context, mirror changes in the political life of the living.

National hero worship and communal ancestor worship are both based on a lineage paradigm, the former extending the genealogical ideology of the family to the deep lineage of patriotic heroes in the national history. Their shared paradigm demonstrates a systemic exclusion of alien and ambiguous identities. Despite their similarities, ancestor worship is esthetically distinctive from its extended, politicized counterpart, and the revived ancestor worship in southern and central Vietnam has magnified this distinctiveness. The place of ancestor worship demonstrates the relation of exclusion explicitly through concrete symbols, unlike modern hero worship, which conquers bad death and obliterates its traces. Its uniqueness lies in the dual structural representation of death and the structural propensity to materialize the peripheral background in order to signify the central object. In other words, the real difference between national memory and local memory is the structure of differences internal to the latter.

Concerning the three classes of the dead in Vietnamese social reality, the ritual ties with ghosts best illustrate the magical unity between the local and the cosmopolitan. Nowhere is this unity of conflicting formations more explicit than in the practice of the ritual actor, who shifts between the structural opposites of death by moving across the house of worship and the open space of tragic death. The "negative space" of death is where, in Robert Hertz's words, "death will be eternal, because society will always maintain towards these accursed individuals the attitude of exclusion."[9] But it also, as Michael Taussig writes, "is preeminently a space of transformation."[10] This is where the enemies of the Cold War can coexist, Vietnamese villagers and foreign soldiers may interact in the identical ritual gesture, and the individuals who suffered tragic death may transform into powerful public figures irrespective of their historically determined identities of kinship or nationality.

The ghosts of tragic death in the Vietnamese worldview are at once excessively bound and radically unbound in time and space, and the Vietnamese ritual interaction with ghosts consists of a constellation of parallax visions. From one angle, these beings are fixed to the place of violent death and incarcerated within the very drama of unjust violence. Their incarceration in both a spatial and a temporal sense characterizes the fate of these subaltern beings. From another angle, however, ghosts take on a completely different identity. They are believed to be free and mobile beings able to cross territorial boundaries and ritually relate to communities and individuals in the living world irrespective of kinship ties. Racial identity, nationality, political ideology, genealogical identity, and social status—these classifications, which are central to ancestor and hero worship, are irrelevant in the relational field of human and ghost. The meaning of war death in what Taussig calls the "anarchical and rebellious" space of death is independent of the secular hierarchy of values and of the political esthetics of sublimation.[11] This is the home of tragic death, where tragedy is a universal human condition and its meaning works to embrace the entirety of humanity rather than to divide and classify it.

Art theory contains the idea of "positive negative space," a radical departure from the traditional view that representing the landscape consists of dividing the space into positive space and negative space. Positive space is made up of the objects that come to the painter's view, whereas negative space is the background with which the painter locates the central object in his or her representation. A new art movement at the turn of the last century changed the status of negative space.[12] In Cubism and its "pictorial language" in particular, the background in painting became a positive element, equally important as the foreground objects, thereby bringing to an end a long Western artistic tradition that had begun as early as the fifteenth century.[13] Stephen Kern describes this esthetical revolution:

One common effect of this transvaluation was a leveling of former distinctions between what was thought to be primary and secondary in the experience of space. It can be seen as a breakdown of absolute distinctions between the plenum of matter and the void of space in physics, between
subject and background in painting, between figure and ground in perception, between the sacred and the profane space of religion. Although the
nature of these changes differed in each case, this striking thematic similarity
among them suggests that they add up to a transformation of the metaphysi-
cal foundations of life and thought.[14]

Kern suggests that the esthetics of transvaluation was intimately related
to the reality of the war of mass violence and mass death. He quotes
Gertrude Stein, who believed that the war from 1914 to 1918 and the art
of Cubism both had the same composition, "of which one corner was as
important as another corner." The war departed from the composition of
previous wars, in which "there was one man in the center surrounded by
a lot of other men," and, likewise, the composition of modern art broke
down the traditional rule that rendered the negative space an inert void,
devoid of esthetic relevance.[15]

These insights from European cultural history are instructive for
understanding the relations between ancestors and ghosts in the esthetics
of revived Vietnamese domestic ritual. Vietnamese ritual practices do not
situate the space of ghosts merely as a background to make the ancestral
cult stand out; they approach it as attentively and as intimately as they do
the latter. The "negative space" of ghosts is an element as important as
the "positive space" of ancestors in the composition of the ritual landscape. Transvaluation of the figure and the ground in ancestor worship is
the most prominent aspect of the contemporary ritual revival, and it is a
structural condition generated by the ambidextrous social practice.

In Kern's account of the cultural history of Europe at the turn of the
last century, the development of the Cubist perspective in art was inseparable from the rise of perspectivism in moral and political philosophy
and the social relativity of space that it advocated. The Cubists no longer
depended on "the convention of illusionistic, one point perspective."[16]
They painted objects "not from one point of view at a time, but from several points of view to give us simultaneous views of the object."[17] Kern
writes, with reference to the work of the formidable Spanish philosopher
Ortega y Gasset: "Ortega's philosophy of perspectivism in its social and
political implications lined up clearly on the side of pluralism and democracy against monism and monarchy. It implied that the voices of many,
however untrained or chaotic, are a desirable check on the judgment of a

single class, a single culture, or a single individual."[18] For Leach, too, esthetics was inseparable from ethical and political questions. One of his main intellectual concerns, expressed through the relativity of Kachin social structure, was the implication of the theoretical preoccupation with the rule of descent.[19] He believed that a social order is a constant struggle between hierarchical and democratic social forms, and that this is manifested in rituals, which in many indigenous cultures are the principal means of esthetic expression. Against this background, he insisted, "esthetics and ethics are identical," and he suggested that it is through the study of esthetics that we come to an understanding of the ethical rules of a society.[20]

The esthetics of Vietnamese domestic ritual consists of a constellation of contrary visions. Shifting between the side of the gods or ancestors and the opposite side, of the ghosts, the ritual action associates with different modes of life and manifests different worldviews. The actor's moving body demonstrates the esthetics of relativity, but, in a crucial way, it is also a powerful ethical statement.

The space of wandering ghosts, for those who engage with it, is not merely an imaginary habitat of the tragic dead but also a stimulus that invokes the memory of their own life during the war: that is, how they were forced into a life of displacement after their homes and villages were annihilated. As evident in Nguyen Du's poetic world, the narrative or ritual engagement with ghosts is a way of expressing (and preserving) self-identity in painful exile or coerced displacement. Therefore, when people face the shrine for ghosts and pray that the ghosts will experience a less grievous afterlife, what they have in front of them is not only the ecology of the wandering ghosts but also the historical memory of a life like that of the wandering ghosts. When they face the interior shrine for ancestors, likewise, the act signifies not only that the dead kinsmen are back in their proper place but also that they themselves are finally moving away from the memory of displacement. This self-and-other awareness embedded in the ritual act is expressed, in the village social renovation, by the parallel, correlative form it takes, encompassing the place of the dead and that of the living. If the worship of ancestors and the ritual ties with ghosts are both expressions of historical self-consciousness, we may say that the wider structure within which these take place encompasses the memory of the violent past and the hope for a peaceful, secure future, and that it does not privilege one against the other in doing so. Both are equally important elements for the constitution of the historical self.

I have tried to situate the memory of mass village death within this relative spaciality of death and the moral practice of death remembrance that nurtures it. Death in the Ha My and My Lai massacres was too tragic to permit the victims to enter the place of heroes, and too violent for them to be admitted to the "positive space" of ancestors, but it was nevertheless too real to the village to be relegated to the invisible margins of hero worship or to the negative background of ancestor worship. An ideal place for remembering the victims of the mass death, if there is such a place, might be home, where they can be remembered as ancestors. Yet it ought to be a home where their identities are accepted, not measured on the scale of heroic virtues and genealogical merit, for the simple reason that the victims exist in the horizon of history. It should be a place where kinship, free from traditional ideologies and political control, reconciles with the universal ethic that all human beings have the right to be remembered. The revitalized memory of the mass death relies on this universal norm as well as on the morality of local kinship unity—that is, the restoration of the unity of the local and the cosmopolitan.

Conceptualizing the space of tragic death as "anarchical," as Taussig does, therefore, is problematic. The other side of the moral order will appear chaotic only when one imagines it at a distance and from the standpoint of the ordered polity, whereas the imagined absence of order may actually mean the presence of an entirely different normative order for those who engage with it.[21] If the uncultivated space of death indeed has a "rebellious" potential, I believe that it must do so on a certain, distinct, normative basis. Otherwise we risk compromising the political actions in the periphery, be they real or imaginary, turning them into a mere rejoinder, critical or otherwise, to the actions of the social center. James Scott argues that there is an idea of justice, consisting of "the norm of reciprocity and the right to subsistence," in the economic practice of Vietnamese peasants, and in a similar light Taussig himself writes of "a use value orientation" of the Cauca Valley peasants in Columbia.[22] The peasants undertook an act of organized resistance, according to Scott, only when the intensity of economic exploitation reached the level at which their basic rights to subsistence were violated.[23] By the same token, and looking at the notion of a subsistence ethic within a wider scope, I believe there is a specific idea of justice in the Vietnamese practice of commemoration. If the chaotic space of death is in fact a region of moral memory where every individual death and every category of death has a fundamental right to social recognition, the movement from this outer world to the inner ritual realm does not mean a unilateral transition from anarchy to polity.

When the victims of the tragic mass killings of 1968 are brought into the place of ancestors, or the place of heroes, this does not merely indicate that the ghosts of village women and children have transformed into honorable family ancestors or meritorious heroes of a people's war. Rather, their *mobili animi* signifies a fundamental change within the political order.[24] On their homebound journey, these ghosts may remember their experience of displacement—as did some of the ghosts introduced in this book, and as do most Vietnamese when they undertake renovating their dwelling places—rather than annihilate this memory from their consciousness. If they do so, they may bring home from the street an idea of justice and may awaken people at home, living or dead, to the idea that all human death—"good death" or "bad death" and from "this side" or "that side"—has the inalienable right to be grieved and consoled.

Then, the transformation of the ghosts of 1968, a generation after the end of the war, will mean an end to the geopolitical vision that created their deaths in the first place—the Cold War. And it will mean the end of the illusion that made them ghosts: the illusion that "society, its peace recovered, can triumph over death."[25] Liberation from grievance, for the victims of mass death in the Year of the Monkey, is a way of transcending the bipolar politics and the politics of symbolic conquest, but in the sense of recovering the unity of humankind denied in the former and a universal norm concealed in the symbolic forms of communal unity.

Notes

PREFACE AND ACKNOWLEDGMENTS

1. Heonik Kwon, "The Saddle and the Sledge: Hunting as Comparative Narrative in Siberia and Beyond," *Journal of the Royal Anthropological Institute* 4 (1998): 115–27.

2. Marshall Sahlins, *Culture in Practice* (New York: Zed Books, 2000).

INTRODUCTION

1. Ministry of Defense Institute of Military History, *The Vietnam War and the Korean Army*, vol. 3 (Seoul: Ministry of Defense Institute of Military History, Republic of Korea, 2003), p. 412.

2. Quoted from Quang Ngai General Museum, *A Look Back upon Son My* (Quang Ngai: Quang Ngai General Museum, 1998), p. 12.

3. Robert M. Blackburn, *Mercenaries and Lyndon Johnson's "More Flags": The Hiring of Korean, Filipino, and Thai Soldiers in the Vietnam War* (Jefferson, NC: McFarland, 1994).

4. Shaun K. Malarney, *Culture, Ritual, and Revolution in Vietnam* (New York: RoutledgeCurzon, 2002), pp. 56–72.

5. "The commemorative fever" is quoted from Hue-Tam Ho Tai, ed., *The Country of Memory: Remaking the Past in Late Socialist Vietnam* (Berkeley: University of California Press, 2001), p. 1; about the idea of *viec ho,* see Pham Con Son, *Tinh Than Gia Toc* (The spirit of the family) (Hanoi: Nha xuat ban van hoa dan toc, 1998), pp. 189–97; for the international background of the reform, see Nayan Chanda, "Indochina beyond the Cold War: The Chill from Eastern Europe," in Börye Liunggren, ed., *The Challenge of Reform in Indochina* (Cambridge: Harvard Institute of International Development, 1993), pp. 19–38.

6. Malarney, *Culture, Ritual, and Revolution in Vietnam,* pp. 9, 199–206.

7. For the domestic background of the reform, see Gabriel Kolko, *Vietnam: Anatomy of a Peace* (New York: Routledge, 1977), ch. 2; Börye Liunggren, ed., *The Challenge of Reform in Indochina* (Cambridge: Harvard Institute of International Development, 1993); Gareth Porter, *Vietnam: The Politics of Bureaucratic Socialism* (Ithaca: Cornell University Press, 1993); William S. Turley and Mark Selden, eds., *Reinventing Vietnamese Socialism: Doi Moi in Comparative Perspective* (Boulder, CO: Westview, 1993).

8. Hy Van Luong, "Economic Reform and the Intensification of Rituals in Two North Vietnamese Villages, 1980–90," in Börye Liunggren, ed., *The Challenge of Reform in Indochina* (Cambridge: Harvard Institute of International Development, 1993), pp. 259–92. Also Robert Templer, *Shadows and Wind: A View of Modern Vietnam* (London: Abacus, 1999), p. 72.

9. Luong, "Economic Reform and the Intensification of Rituals," pp. 270–82.

10. Tai, *The Country of Memory,* pp. 3, 7.

11. Hue-Tam Ho Tai, "Monumental Ambiguity: The State Commemoration of Ho Chi Minh," in K. W. Taylor and J. K. Whitmore, eds., *Essays into Vietnamese Pasts* (Ithaca: Cornell Southeast Asia Program, 1995), p. 273; Malarney, *Culture, Ritual, and Revolution in Vietnam,* pp. 108–47.

12. Patricia M. Pelley, *Postcolonial Vietnam: New Histories of the National Past* (Durham, NC: Duke University Press, 2002), p. 168; David Marr, *Vietnamese Tradition on Trial, 1920–1945* (Berkeley: University of California Press, 1981), p. 285.

13. Le Van Dinh, *Le culte des ancêtres en droit annamite: Essai historique et critique sur le Huong-Hoa* (Paris: Editions Domat-Montchrestien, 1934), p. 15. All translations in this book are my own unless otherwise noted.

14. Ibid., pp. 18–19.

15. See Caroline Humphrey, *Karl Marx Collective: Economy, Society, and Religion in a Siberian Collective Farm* (Cambridge: Cambridge University Press, 1983), pp. 402–17; also Roger Bastide, "Mémoire collective et sociologie de bricolage," *Année sociologique* 21 (1970): 65–108.

16. Hannah Arendt, *The Human Condition,* 2nd ed. (1958; reprint, Chicago: University of Chicago Press, 1998), pp. 71–73.

17. See Richard A. Wilson, "Representing Human Rights Violations," in Richard Wilson, ed., *Human Rights, Culture, and Context: Anthropological Perspectives* (London: Pluto Press, 1997), p. 155.

18. Paul Giran, *Magie et religion annamites* (Paris: Librairie Maritime et Coloniale, 1912), p. 46; Gerald Hickey, *Village in Vietnam* (New Haven: Yale University Press, 1964), pp. 121.

19. Caroline Humphrey, "No Place Like Home in Anthropology: The Neglect of Architecture," *Anthropology Today* 4, no. 1 (1988): 17.

20. Edward Casey, *Getting Back into Place: Toward a Renewed Understanding of the Place-World* (Bloomington: Indiana University Press, 1993), pp. 132, 140–41.

21. E. P. Thompson, *Customs in Common* (New York: The New Press, 1993).

22. Immanuel Wallerstein, "1968, Revolution in the World-System: Theses

and Queries," in *The Essential Wallerstein* (New York: The New Press, 2000), pp. 355–74. See also Tariq Ali and Susan Watkins, *1968: Marching in the Streets* (New York: Free Press, 1998); Dominick Cavallo, *A Fiction of the Past: The Sixties in American History* (New York: Palgrave, 1999).

23. Marilyn Strathern writes in her stimulating book: "To switch from one perspective to another is to switch whole domains of explanation" (see chapter 3 of the present volume). *Reproducing the Future: Anthropology, Kinship, and the New Reproductive Technologies* (Manchester: Manchester University Press, 1992), p. 107.

1. THE BIPOLARITY OF DEATH

1. Le Van Dinh, *Le culte des ancêtres en droit annamite: Essai historique et critique sur le Huong-Hoa* (Paris: Editions Domat-Montchrestien, 1934), p. 14.

2. Léopold Cadière, *Croyances et pratiques religieuses des viêtnamiens*, bk. 1 (Paris: Ecole Française d'Extrême-Orient, 1957), pp. 6–24.

3. Nguyen Van Huyen, *The Ancient Civilization of Vietnam* (Hanoi: The Gioi, 1995), pp. 60–63.

4. Neil L. Jamieson, *Understanding Vietnam* (Berkeley: University of California Press, 1993), pp. 11–12.

5. Arnold van Gennep, *The Rites of Passage* (Chicago: University of Chicago Press, 1960), pp. 164–65; also Stephen F. Teiser, *The Ghost Festival in Medieval China* (Princeton: Princeton University Press, 1988), pp. 217–21.

6. For an in-depth discussion of this system of interpersonal reference, see Hy Van Luong, *Discursive Practices and Linguistic Meanings: The Vietnamese System of Person Reference* (Amsterdam: John Benjamins, 1990), pp. 132–36.

7. James J. Fox, "On Bad Death and the Left Hand: A Study of Rotinese Symbolic Inversions," in R. Needham, ed., *Right and Left: Essays on Dual Symbolic Classification* (Chicago: University of Chicago Press, 1973), p. 351; John Middleton, "Lugbara Death," in M. Bloch and J. Parry, eds., *Death and the Regeneration of Life* (Cambridge: Cambridge University Press, 1982), p. 142.

8. See Gustave Dumoutier, *Rituel funéraire des Annamites: Etude d'ethnographie religieuse* (Hanoi: Schneider, 1904), pp. 150–51.

9. Janet Carsten and Stephen Hugh-Jones, eds., *About the House: Lévi-Strauss and Beyond* (Cambridge: Cambridge University Press, 1995), pp. 2–3.

10. Shaun K. Malarney, *Culture, Ritual, and Revolution in Vietnam* (New York: RoutledgeCurzon, 2002), p. 179.

11. Tan Viet, *Tap Van Cung Gia Tien* (Prayer book for ancestor worship) (Hanoi: Nha xuat ban van hoa dan toc, 1994), pp. 105–12.

12. See also the idea of *ngrieng* among the highland minorities of Vietnam and the related Malay notion of *hanlotu:* K. M. Endicott, *An Analysis of Malay Magic* (Singapore: Oxford University Press, 1970); Georges Condominas, *We Have Eaten the Forest: The Story of a Montagnard Village in the Central Highlands of Vietnam* (New York: Kondansha International, 1994).

13. Debbora Battaglia, *On the Bones of the Serpent: Person, Memory, and Mortality in Sabarl Island Society* (Chicago: University of Chicago Press, 1990), pp. 67–70. Her accounts also demonstrate a certain paradox in mortuary mem-

ory: whereas the *piwapiwa* are by definition unremembered spirits of the dead, the *baloma* become as such through appropriate ritual separation of their memory from the living, which Battaglia presents as a process of "forgetting."

14. Maurice Bloch and Jonathan Parry, eds., *Death and the Regeneration of Life* (Cambridge: Cambridge University Press, 1982), pp. 15–16. See also Maurice Bloch, *Placing the Dead* (New York: Seminar Press, 1971), pp. 164–65.

15. Godfrey Lienhardt, *Divinity and Experience: The Religion of the Dinka* (Oxford: Oxford University Press, 1961), pp. 298–319; Jack Goody, *Death, Property, and the Ancestors* (Stanford: Stanford University Press, 1962), pp. 235–69.

16. Untimely death is not always a counterfertility symbol. For instance, among the Kuna Indians of Panama, Carlo Severi writes, "whereas the proximity of the corpse of an adult to the living is strongly proscribed, the proximity of the corpse of a child is regarded as positive, since it inseminates the barren (usually sterile) land inhabited by the living." "Cosmology, Crisis, and Paradox: On the White Spirit in the Kuna Shmanic Tradition," in M. S. Roth and C. G. Salas, eds., *Disturbing Remains: Memory, History, and Crisis in the Twentieth Century* (Los Angeles: Getty Research Institute, 2001), p. 195.

17. Bloch and Parry, *Death and the Regeneration of Life,* p. 16.

18. Middleton, "Lugbara Death," p. 145.

19. Robert Hertz, *Death and the Right Hand* (London: Cohen and West, 1960), p. 86.

20. The quote is from Lienhardt, *Divinity and Experience,* p. 317.

21. See Edith Wyschogrod, *Spirit in Ashes: Hegel, Heidegger, and Man-Made Mass Death* (New Haven: Yale University Press, 1985). Also, David N. Power and Kabasele F. Lumbala, eds., *The Spectre of Mass Death*, special issue, *Concilium* (London), no. 3 (1993): ix, 116.

22. Jonathan Parry, "Sacrificial Death and the Necrophagous Ascetic," in M. Bloch and J. Parry, eds., *Death and the Regeneration of Life* (Cambridge: Cambridge University Press, 1982), p. 83.

23. Derek Summerfield, "The Social Experience of War and Some Issues for the Humanitarian Field," in P. J. Bracken and C. Petty, eds., *Rethinking the Trauma of War* (New York: Free Association Books, 1998), p. 26.

24. Malarney, *Culture, Ritual, and Revolution in Vietnam,* p. 180.

25. Lady Borton, *After Sorrow: An American among the Vietnamese* (New York: Kodansha International, 1995), p. 16. The fifteenth day of the seventh lunar month is the traditional Day of Wandering Ghosts.

26. Bloch and Parry, *Death and the Regeneration of Life,* p. 18.

27. Louis Dumont, *Essays on Individualism: Modern Ideology in Anthropological Perspective* (Chicago: University of Chicago Press, 1986), p. 233.

28. Bloch and Parry, *Death and the Regeneration of Life,* pp. 15–18. In his interpretation of ancient Chinese Taoist text, Roger Ames writes, "As long as a person is remembered, he or she has a place and a life. . . . The problem is not death, but our fear of death, a fear that is unwarranted." "Death as Transformation in Classical Daoism," in J. Malpas and R. C. Solomon, eds., *Death and Philosophy* (New York: Routledge, 1998), pp. 63–64.

29. Maurice Bloch, *Prey into Hunter: The Politics of Religious Experience* (Cambridge: Cambridge University Press, 1992), pp. 4–7, 20–22.

30. Richard Huntington and Peter Metcalf, *Celebrations of Death: The Anthropology of Mortuary Ritual,* 2nd ed. (Cambridge: Cambridge University Press, 1991), p. 6.

31. Robert Parkin, introduction to Robert Hertz, *Sin and Expiation in Primitive Society,* trans. and ed. Robert Parkin, Occasional Paper no. 2 (Oxford: British Centre for Durkheimian Studies, 1994), p. 18.

32. Fox, "On Bad Death and the Left Hand," pp. 342–68.

33. Dumont, *Essays on Individualism,* pp. 228–33.

34. In Dumont's words, the symbolic opposition is a universal fact, whereas the added asymmetry is cultural value. Ibid., p. 228. Also, Robert Hertz, "The Pre-eminence of the Right Hand: A Study in Religious Polarity," in R. Needham, *Right and Left: Essays on Dual Symbolic Classification* (Chicago: University of Chicago Press, 1973), p. 8.

35. Hertz, "The Pre-eminence of the Right Hand," p. 8; also Hertz, *Death and the Right Hand,* p. 113.

36. Bruce Kapferer, *Legends of People, Myths of State: Violence, Intolerance, and Political Culture in Sri Lanka and Australia* (Washington, DC: Smithsonian Institution Press, 1988), pp. 119–208; Joe Lunn, *Memoirs of the Maelstrom: A Senegalese Oral History of the First World War* (Portsmouth, NH: Neinemann, 1999).

37. George Mosse, *Fallen Soldiers: Reshaping the Memory of the World Wars* (Oxford: Oxford University Press, 1990), p. 7.

38. Jay Winter, *Sites of Memory, Sites of Mourning: The Great War in European Cultural History* (Cambridge: Cambridge University Press, 1995).

39. Martin Jay, "Against Consolation: Walter Benjamin and the Refusal to Mourn," in J. Winter and E. Sivan, eds., *War and Remembrance in the Twentieth Century* (Cambridge: Cambridge University Press, 1999), pp. 225–30; see also Tzvetan Todorov, *Les abus de la mémoire* (Paris: Arléa, 1995), pp. 51–61.

40. The quote is from Stephen Kern, *The Culture of Time and Space, 1880–1918* (Cambridge: Harvard University Press, 1983), pp. 287–312.

41. Cited in Wyschogrod, *Spirit in Ashes,* p. 12. See also Alex King, "Remembering and Forgetting in the Public Memorials of the Great War," in Adrian Forty and Susan Küchler, eds., *The Art of Forgetting* (New York: Berg, 1999), pp. 147–69.

42. André Glucksmann, *Dostoievski à Manhattan* (Paris: Robert Laffont, 2002), pp. 18–19.

43. Vo Nguyen Giap, *People's War, People's Army* (New York: Pracger, 1962), p. 43.

44. See Jonathan Schell, *The Real War* (New York: Pantheon, 1988), pp. 193–204. On the idea and reality of the so-called thinking machine of destruction, see Manuel de Landa, *War in the Age of Intelligent Machines* (New York: Zed Books, 1991).

45. James S. Olson and Randy Roberts, *My Lai: A Brief History with Documents* (Boston: Bedford, 1998), p. 16.

46. James W. Trullinger, *Village at War: An Account of Conflict in Vietnam* (Stanford: Stanford University Press, 1994), pp. 116–25.

47. Better than any other evidence, this proves that the "inhabitant-soldier"

of wartime Vietnamese villages was not a soldier but fundamentally an ordinary civilian; it is a crime of war to violate the civilian noncombatant's inalienable rights for survival under any circumstances of armed conflicts. See Judith G. Gardam, *Non-Combatant Immunity as a Norm of International Humanitarian Law* (London: Brill, 1993).

48. John R. Gillis, ed., *Commemorations: The Politics of National Identity* (Princeton: Princeton University Press, 1994), pp. 3–24.

49. Jean Baudrillard, *Symbolic Exchange and Death* (London: Sage, 1993), p. 144.

50. Mark P. Bradley, "Contests of Memory," in Hue-Tam Ho Tai, ed., *The Country of Memory: Remaking the Past in Late Socialist Vietnam* (Berkeley: University of California Press, 2001), pp. 199–216.

51. On regional variation in the memory of war, see Jay Winter and Jean-Louis Robert, *Capital Cities at War: Paris, London, Berlin, 1914–1919* (New York: Cambridge University Press, 1997), pp. 20–24; See Hue-Tam Ho Tai, "Faces of Remembrance and Forgetting," in her *The Country of Memory: Remaking the Past in Late Socialist Vietnam* (Berkeley: University of California Press, 2001), p. 172.

52. Pham Van Bich, *The Vietnamese Family in Change: The Case of the Red River Delta* (Richmond, Surrey: Curzon, 1999), p. 240.

53. Patricia M. Pelley, *Postcolonial Vietnam: New Histories of the National Past* (Durham: Duke University Press, 2002), pp. 168–92; Shaun K. Malarney, "'The Fatherland Remembers Your Sacrifice': Commemorating War Dead in North Vietnam," in Hue-Tam Ho Tai, ed., *The Country of Memory: Remaking the Past in Late Socialist Vietnam* (Berkeley: University of California Press, 2001), pp. 46–76.

54. About the *phan huynh* ceremony, in which the descendents honor the dead parents by ritually burning a copy of the royal warrant of mandarin nomination, see Nguyen Van Huyen, *The Ancient Civilization of Vietnam*, pp. 56–58.

55. On the "invented tradition" of war commemoration, see Eric Hobsbawm, "Mass-Producing Traditions," in E. Hobsbawm and T. Ranger, eds., *The Invention of Tradition* (Cambridge: Cambridge University Press, 1983).

56. Thomas W. Laqueur, "Memory and Naming in the Great War," in John R. Gillis, ed., *Commemorations: The Politics of National Identity* (Princeton: Princeton University Press, 1994), p. 151.

57. Hue-Tam Ho Tai, "Commemoration and Community," in *The Country of Memory: Remaking the Past in Late Socialist Vietnam* (Berkeley: University of California Press, 2001), p. 228.

58. For a graphical demonstration of "the tree of genealogy," see Pham Con Son, *Tinh Than Gia Toc* (The spirit of the family) (Hanoi: Nha xuat ban van hoa dan toc, 1998), p. 7.

59. Tim Ingold, *The Perception of the Environment: Essays in Livelihood, Dwelling, and Skill* (New York: Routledge, 2000), p. 142.

60. Ibid.

61. Hy Van Luong, "Vietnamese Kinship: Structural Principles and the Socialist Transformations in Northern Vietnam," *Journal of Asian Studies* 48, no. 4 (1989): 742.

62. Ibid., pp. 745, 754.

63. Other specialists who raise the idea include Janet Carsten, *The Heat of the Hearth: The Process of Kinship in a Malay Fishing Community* (Oxford: Clarendon, 1997), pp. 23–26; Shelly Errington, *Meaning and Power in a Southeast Asian Realm* (Princeton: Princeton University Press, 1989), and her "Recasting Sex, Gender, and Power: A Theoretical and Regional Overview," in J. M. Atkinson and S. Errington, eds., *Power and Difference: Gender in Island Southeast Asia* (Stanford: Stanford University Press, 1990), pp. 54–55.

64. Hy Van Luong develops these ideas to what he calls "gerontocratic structure" versus "meritocratic structure" in his *Discursive Practices and Linguistic Meanings,* pp. 128–45.

65. Maurice Halbwachs, *On Collective Memory,* trans. and ed. L. A. Coser (Chicago: University of Chicago Press, 1992), pp. 193–235.

66. The quote "an arena of contradictory and contestable perspectives" comes from David Parkin, "Ritual as Spatial Direction and Bodily Division," in D. de Coppet, ed., *Understanding Rituals* (New York: Routledge, 1992), p. 13. Caroline Humphrey correctly points out that the study of ritual structure is not undertaken for its own sake but to understand the specific "instrumental use of the structures by the people of the culture concerned." "On Some Ritual Techniques in the Bull-Cult of the Buryat-Mongols," *Proceedings of the Royal Anthropological Institute of Great Britain and Ireland* (1973): 15.

67. Paul Connerton, *How Societies Remember* (Cambridge: Cambridge University Press, 1989), p. 71.

68. Gerald Hickey, *Village in Vietnam* (New Haven: Yale University Press, 1964), p. 121.

69. Victor Turner, *Dramas, Fields, and Metaphors: Symbolic Action in Human Society* (Ithaca: Cornell University Press, 1974), p. 50.

70. Hertz, "The Pre-eminence of the Right Hand," p. 21.

71. Henri Lefebvre, *The Production of Space* (Oxford: Blackwell, 1991), p. 332.

72. See Shaun Malarney, "The Limits of 'State Functionalism' and the Reconstruction of Funerary Ritual in Contemporary Northern Viet Nam," *American Ethnologist* 23, no. 3 (1996): 540–60. For a similar interpretation of ritual revival in China, see D. E. MacInnis, *Religion in China Today: Policy and Practice* (Maryknoll, NY: Orbis, 1989); Jun Jing, *The Temple of Memories: History, Power, and Morality in a Chinese Village* (Stanford: Stanford University Press, 1996).

73. Errington, "Recasting Sex, Gender, and Power," p. 44.

74. Clifford Geertz, *The Interpretation of Cultures* (New York: Basic Books, 1973), p. 170.

75. Quoted from Smadar Lavie, Kirin Narayan, and Renato Rosaldo, eds., *Creativity/Anthropology* (Ithaca: Cornell University Press, 1993), p. 2. Anna L. Tsing argues that the margins are the places from which the assumptions of the dominant values can be seen more clearly. *In the Realm of the Diamond Queen* (Princeton: Princeton University Press, 1993), pp. 13–17.

76. Edward Casey, *Getting Back into Place: Toward a Renewed Understanding of the Place-World* (Bloomington: Indiana University Press, 1993), pp. 131, 280.

77. On the expression of memory, see Paul Antze and Michael Lambek, eds., *Tense Past: Cultural Essays in Trauma and Memory* (New York: Routledge, 1996), p. xvii.

2. MASSACRES IN THE YEAR OF THE MONKEY, 1968

1. In Vietnamese, this phrase is "Tinh quan dan nhu ca voi nuoc," meaning literally, "The affectionate relationship between the army and the people is like what fish feel for water." In popular revolutionary slogans, the doctrine took on a more vivid image: "Without water, fish die. Without fish, the water is spoiled."

2. Truong Chinh, *Primer for Revolt* (New York: Praeger, 1963), pp. 102–17.

3. On the idea of just war, see Robert W. Tucker, *The Just War: A Study in Contemporary American Doctrine* (Baltimore: Johns Hopkins University Press, 1960). Also J. B. Elshtain, ed., *Just War Theory* (Oxford: Blackwell, 1992); B. Paskins and M. Dockrill, *The Ethics of War* (London: Duckworth, 1979). On the doctrine of total war and its derivative true war, see W. B. Gallie, *Philosophers of Peace and War* (Oxford: Oxford University Press, 1978), chs. 2 and 3. Also compare Raymond Aron, *Clausewitz: Philosopher of War* (London: Routledge and Kegan Paul, 1976); and John Keegan, *War and Our World* (London: Hutchinson, 1998).

For the historical background of the rise of the total war paradigm and its cultural implications, see B. R. Posen, "Nationalism, the Mass Army, and Military Power," in J. Comaroff and P. Stern, eds., *Perspectives on Nationalism and War* (Luxembourg: Gordon and Breach, 1995). On the historical relationship between premodern peasant unrests and modern mass mobilization, see Georges Condominas, "La guérilla viet: Trait culturel majeur et pérenne de l'espace social vietnamien," *L'Homme* 164 (2000): 17 – 36. For the explanation of the latter in terms of expansion of colonial capitalism, see Eric Wolf, *Peasant Wars of the Twentieth Century* (New York: Harper and Row, 1969), chs. 4 and 5; Jeffery Paige, *Agrarian Revolution: Social Movements and Export Agriculture in the Underdeveloped World* (New York: Free Press, 1975). For a "moral economy" approach to the political mobilization of Vietnamese peasants, see Hy Van Luong, *Revolution in the Village: Tradition and Transformation in North Vietnam, 1925 – 1988* (Honolulu: University of Hawaii Press, 1992); James C. Scott, *The Moral Economy of the Peasant: Rebellion and Subsistence in Southeast Asia* (New Haven: Yale University Press, 1976).

4. Vo Nguyen Giap, *People's War, People's Army* (New York: Praeger, 1962), p. 33. See also J. Girling, *People's War: The Conditions and Consequences in China and South East Asia* (London: Allen and Unwin, 1969); F. E. Wakeman, *History and Will: Philosophical Perspectives of Mao Tse-tung's Thought* (Berkeley: University of California Press, 1973).

5. Truong Chinh, *Primer for Revolt*, p. 107.

6. Ibid., p. 116.

7. Vo Nguyen Giap, *People's War*, p. 43; Francis Fitzgerald, *Fire in the Lake: The Vietnamese and the Americans in Vietnam* (Boston: Little, Brown, 1972), pp. 157–64; Douglas Pike, *Viet Cong: The Organization and Techniques of the National Liberation Front of South Vietnam* (Cambridge: MIT Press, 1966), pp.

166–93, 224–25. See also Paul Mus, "The Role of the Village in Vietnamese Politics," *Pacific Affairs* 22 (1949): 265–71.

8. Bernard B. Fall, "Viet Cong—the Unseen Enemy in Viet-Nam," in M. G. Raskin and B. B. Fall, eds., *The Viet-Nam Reader* (New York: Random House, 1965), pp. 252–61; Townsend Hoopes, *The Limits of Intervention* (New York: David McKay, 1969), p. 64; Jonathan Schell, *The Real War* (New York: Pantheon, 1988), pp. 193–204.

9. James W. Trullinger, *Village at War: An Account of Conflict in Vietnam* (Stanford: Stanford University Press, 1994), pp. 116–29; Huynh Kim Khanh, *Vietnamese Communism, 1925–1945* (Ithaca: Cornell University Press, 1982); Lam Truong Buu, *Colonialism Experienced: Vietnamese Writings on Colonialism, 1900–1931* (Ann Arbor: University of Michigan Press, 2000).

10. Jonathan Neale claims: If "you could not find the guerrillas, and usually you couldn't, you killed the people until they told the Communists to stop. The body count was not a trick or a bureaucratic obsession—it was the strategy. The pressure from Washington reached all the way down. Every general and colonel who passed the pressure down, who made the men kill, was making his career." *The American War in Vietnam, 1960–1975* (Chicago: Bookmarks, 2001), p. 77. See also David L. Anderson, "What Really Happened?" in David L. Anderson, ed., *Facing My Lai: Moving beyond the Massacre* (Lawrence: University Press of Kansas, 1998), p. 7; Sam Adams, *War of Numbers: An Intelligence Memoir* (South Royalton, VT: Steerforth, 1994).

11. A former U.S. Marine recalled, "In order to save the village, we had to destroy it."

12. Noam Chomsky, preface to John Duffett, ed., *Against the Crime of Silence* (New York: Clarion, 1970), pp. xiv–xv.

13. Frank Baldwin, Diane Jones, and Michael Jones, *America's Rented Troops: South Koreans in Vietnam* (Philadelphia: American Friends Service Committee, 1975).

14. *Toi Ac Xam Luoc Thuc Dan Moi Cua De Quoc My o Viet Nam* (Crimes committed by America during her neocolonial invasion of Vietnam) (Hanoi: Nha xuat ban chinh tri quoc gia, 1975), pp. 30–52, 58–113.

15. *Vietcong*, or *VC*, is the term by which Americans referred to the National Front for the Liberation of South Vietnam, a communist-led alliance of a dozen political and religious groups, formed in 1960.

16. Ho Khang, *The Tet Mau Than 1968 Event in South Vietnam* (Hanoi: The Gioi, 2001), p. 31.

17. Marvin E. Gettleman, Jane Franklin, Marilyn B. Young, and H. Bruce Franklin, eds., *Vietnam and America: The Most Comprehensive Documented History of the Vietnam War* (New York: Grove, 1995), pp. 390–91.

18. For the modern history of Ha My, I relied extensively on *Dau Tranh Cach Mang Cua Dang Bo Va Nhan Dan Xa Dien Duong, 1930–1975* (The revolutionary struggle of the Communist Party and the people of Dien Duong Commune, 1930–1975). I read this document as a typewritten and handwritten manuscript during my visit to Ha My in 2001. The edited, substantially modified version was subsequently published in 2003 by Nha xuat ban Tam Ky in Tam Ky under the same title.

19. *Di Tich Thang Canh Quang Ngai* (Relics of Quang Ngai's places to visit) (Quang Ngai: So van hoa thong tin Quang Ngai, 2001), pp. 180–82; Le Khong Khanh, "Tinh Khe—Son My, Dat Va Nguoi" (Tinh Khe—Son My [My Lai], land and people), a private collection of a local journalist; *Lich Su Dang Bo Thi Xa Hoi An, 1930–1975* (History of the Communist Party in Hoi An, 1930–1975) (Da Nang: Nha xuat ban tong hop Da Nang, 1996), pp. 29–47.

20. In both areas, the U.S. First Marine Division and the Korean Second "Blue Dragon" Marine Brigade were major ground fighting forces in 1966–69. See Shelby L. Stanton, *The Rise and Fall of an American Army: U.S. Ground Forces in Vietnam, 1965–1973* (New York: Dell, 1985), pp. 63–65; and Ministry of Defense Institute of Military History, *The Vietnam War and the Korean Army*, vol. 3 (Seoul: Ministry of Defense Institute of Military History, Republic of Korea, 2003), pp. 3–8.

21. *Lich Su Dang Bo Quang Nam Da Nang, Tap III, 1954–1975* (History of the Communist Party in Quang Nam and Da Nang, vol. 3, 1954–1975) (Da Nang: Nha xuat ban Da Nang, 1996), pp. 191–99.

22. "Xom Tay, Dat Va Nguoi" (Xom Tay, land and people), a handwritten manuscript of village history kept by a village elder. This document also emphasizes that the village's early ancestors were powerful healers as well as excellent scholars: "Cu Thay Than and others excelled in scholarship and medical knowledge.... There was a huge willow tree at the temple, and there was a powerful scholar and spiritual person in this place."

23. "Tinh Khe—Son My, Dat Va Nguoi"; also *Quang Ngai: Dat Nuoc, Con Nguoi, Van Hoa* (Quang Ngai: Land, people, and culture) (Quang Ngai: So van hoa thong tin Quang Ngai, 2001), pp. 46–120.

24. Hue-Tam Ho Tai, *Radicalism and the Origins of the Vietnamese Revolution* (Cambridge: Harvard University Press, 1992), pp. 10–56; Huynh Kim Khanh, *Vietnamese Communism*, pp. 52–53.

25. "Hop Mat Xom Tay Ha My" (Meetings among the people of Xom Tay, Ha My), a private collection of poems and public speeches by the village poet and calligrapher Nguyen Minh Dat.

26. *Dau Tranh Cach Mang Cua Dang Bo Va Nhan Dan Xa Dien Duong*, pp. 28–30.

27. *Lich Su Luc Luong Vu Trang Nhan Dan Tinh Quang Nam, Tap I: Khang Chien Chong Thuc Dan Phap, 1945–1954* (History of the people's army in Quang Nam province, vol. 1: Resistance against the French, 1945–1954) (Hanoi: Nha xuat ban quan doi nhan dan, 2001), pp. 19–21.

28. *Dau Tranh Cach Mang Cua Dang Bo Va Nhan Dan Xa Dien Duong*, p. 29.

29. Tai, *Radicalism and the Origins of the Vietnamese Revolution*, pp. 10–31; Phan Xuyen, "Nhung Ngay Cuoi Doi Cua Phan Boi Chau" (The last days of Phan Boi Chau), *Xua Nay*, no. 78B (August 2000): 20–21; Nguyen Khac Vien, *Vietnam: A Long History* (Hanoi: The Gioi, 1993), pp. 170–75.

30. See Charles Fourniau, *Vietnam, domination coloniale et résistance nationale, 1858–1914* (Paris: Les Indes Savantes, 2002), pp. 698–704.

31. For the general situation of this period, see Pierre Brocheux, *The Mekong Delta: Ecology, Economy, and Revolution, 1860–1960* (Madison: University of

Wisconsin Press, 1995), pp. 151–54; Fitzgerald, *Fire in the Lake,* p. 178. For an eyewitness report of the situation, see Ngo Vinh Long, *Before the Revolution: The Vietnamese Peasants under the French* (New York: Columbia University Press, 1991), pp. 129–30.

32. On the corruption of the corvée system to a forced labor system, see J. Goudal, *Probleme du travail en Indochine* (Geneva: Bureau International du Travail, 1937), p. 34.

33. Scott, *The Moral Economy of the Peasant,* p. 91.

34. *Dau Tranh Cach Mang Cua Dang Bo Va Nhan Dan Xa Dien Duong,* pp. 34–35. See also Scott, *The Moral Economy of the Peasant,* p. 236.

35. *Lich Su Luc Luong Vu Trang Nhan Dan Tinh Quang Nam,* pp. 28–31; *Lich Su Dang Bo Thi Xa Hoi An,* pp. 36–47.

36. *Dau Tranh Cach Mang Cua Dang Bo Va Nhan Dan Xa Dien Duong,* pp. 39–40.

37. See Pike, *Viet Cong,* pp. 47–48.

38. On November 29, 1946, the Communist Party issued the following appeal: "Compatriots all over the country[:] The French actions infringing on Vietnam's sovereignty are very likely to spread. The situation is extremely serious. Stand ready to fight in self-defence at any place. Every Vietnamese citizen must eagerly take up the sacred task of defending the sovereignty of the Motherland. Through united efforts we will win." Cited from *The 30-Year War, 1945–1975* (Hanoi: The Gioi, 2002), p. 87. The Soldier-Villager Committee was a task-specific organization rather than an institution. It played a formative role when situations were critical, and became less visible and deceptively dormant in peaceful conditions. See Jacques Dalloz, *La guerre d'Indochine, 1945–1954* (Paris: Seuil, 1987), p. 139.

39. *Dau Tranh Cach Mang Cua Dang Bo Va Nhan Dan Xa Dien Duong,* pp. 53–54.

40. Ibid., pp. 12–14.

41. See Seymour M. Hersh, *My Lai 4: A Report on the Massacre and Its Aftermath* (New York: Random House, 1970), pp. 48–49.

42. Dalloz, *La guerre d'Indochine,* pp. 115–202.

43. Jonathan Schell, *The Real War* (New York: Pantheon, 1987), p. 114.

44. *Dau Tranh Cach Mang Cua Dang Bo Va Nhan Dan Xa Dien Duong,* pp. 123–24.

45. Ibid., pp. 135–39.

46. To Lan, "Special Relationships between Traditional Viet Villages," *The Traditional Village in Vietnam* (Hanoi: The Gioi, 1993), pp. 295–96, 301–4.

47. From the written text of the speech delivered in February 1999, copied in my field notes.

48. See Pike, *Viet Cong,* pp. 224–25.

49. *Dau Tranh Cach Mang Cua Dang Bo Va Nhan Dan Xa Dien Duong,* pp. 106–7.

50. The Buddhist crisis originated on May 8, 1964, in the central Vietnamese city of Hue, when government troops fired into the crowd that gathered to protest the government order that banned the display of banners on the Buddha's anniversary. See Robert Scigliano, "Vietnam: Politics and Religion," *Asian Sur-*

vey 1, no. 1 (1964): 666–73; Charles A. Joiner, "South Vietnam's Buddhist Crisis: Organization for Charity, Dissidence, and Unity," *Asian Survey* 4, no. 7 (1964): 915–28; Fitzgerald, *Fire in the Lake,* pp. 276–302.

51. *Dau Tranh Cach Mang Cua Dang Bo Va Nhan Dan Xa Dien Duong,* p. 106. The Geneva Peace Accords, signed by France and Vietnam in 1954, ended the first Indochinese War (French War) and ordered the temporary partition of the country at the seventeenth parallel. The agreement included an agenda according to which national elections would be held in 1956 to unify the country, which did not happen.

52. *Giai Phong,* June 1, 1967.

53. By 1969, about fifty thousand South Korean troops were engaged in combat in Vietnam. There were an additional fifteen thousand civilian laborers and technicians. Their participation in the war contributed significantly to the economic takeoff of South Korea as an Asian industrial force. See Se Jin Kim, "South Korea's Involvement in Vietnam and Its Economic and Political Impact," *Asian Survey* 10, no. 6 (1970): 519–32; Carl E. Meacham, "Money for Men," *New Republic* (October 9, 1971): 7–9. For the U.S. administration, their participation was crucial not only for justifying the war by internationalizing it but also for easing the burden on the U.S. ground forces. See Yu-Mi Moon, "The Participation of Korean Troops in the Vietnam War" (Ph.D. diss., Seoul National University, 1994), pp. 68–83; Robert M. Blackburn, *Mercenaries and Lyndon Johnson's "More Flags": The Hiring of Korean, Filipino, and Thai Soldiers in the Vietnam War* (Jefferson, NC: McFarland, 1994), pp. 31–66; Stanley Larson and James Collins, *Allied Participation in Vietnam* (Washington, DC: Department of the Army, 1985).

54. See Jonathan Schell, *The Military Half: An Account of Destruction in Quang Ngai and Quang Tin* (New York: Alfred A. Knopf, 1968).

55. For brief accounts of massacres in the province of Quang Ngai, see *Di Tich Thang Canh Quang Ngai,* pp. 206–8, 211–14; Dai Cuong, *Lich Su Viet Nam Tap III* (History of Vietnam, vol. 3) (Hanoi: Nha xuat ban giao duc, 2001), pp. 207–8.

56. *Dau Tranh Cach Mang Cua Dang Bo Va Nhan Dan Xa Dien Duong,* pp. 138–39.

57. *Lich Su Dang Bo Quang Nam Da Nang,* pp. 182–85, 240–47; Chu Cam Phong, *Nhat Ky Chien Tranh* (Diary of a war) (Hanoi: Nha xuat ban van hoc, 2000), pp. 18–26, 125–39; *Dang Bo Huyen Duy Xuyen Xuat Ban* (The Communist Party of Duy Xuyen District) (Da Nang: Nha xuat ban Da Nang, 1964), pp. 85–87.

58. *Ho So Toi Ac Cua Linh Pac Chung Hy* (The crimes of the soldiers of Pac Chung Hy [the president of South Korea, 1962–1979]), report from BK25 to VK25, A85 on March 25, 1968, Quang Nam Province, Archive Da Nang; *Ve Cuoc Dau Tranh Chong Bon Nam Trieu Tien Cua Dong Bac Dien An Thu Thang Loi* (Victory in the struggle against the Korean mercenaries by the people of Dien An), report from PK25, So 5 TB/VP on March 1, 1968, Quang Nam Province, Archive Da Nang. A government newspaper of North Vietnam reported the incidents in April of that year: "To Cao Toi Ac Da Man Cua My Va Tay Sai o Quang Ngai, Quang Nam (We denounce the savage crimes of the

Americans and their henchmen in Quang Ngai and Quang Nam)," *Nhan Dan,* April 17, 1968.

59. *Di Tich Thang Canh Quang Ngai,* pp. 206–14; *Bao An Dat Va Nguoi* (Defending the land and the people) (Da Nang: Nha xuat ban Da Nang, 1999), pp. 162–63.

60. The U.S. special forces trained thousands of recruits from ethnic minority groups at Hoa Cam, south of Da Nang, in the early 1960s. See John Prados, *The Hidden History of the Vietnam War* (Chicago: Ivan R. Dee, 1995), pp. 74–76.

61. See Michael Bilton and Kevin Sim, *Four Hours in My Lai* (New York: Penguin, 1992), chs. 4 and 5.

62. Hersh, *My Lai 4,* p. 75.

63. As recorded by a village elder in "Xom Tay, Dat Va Nguoi," "The blood [of the victims] covered our land, and their bodies were not properly buried. There was no funeral for them. . . . The enemy burned down the entire village and flattened the graveyards. The tombs of our ancestors were desecrated, and the enemy assaulted the dead bodies [of the victims] and mass-buried them in the hope of concealing their crime. Such criminal acts are unheard-of in human history." For the traditional Vietnamese laws against the desecration of tombs, see Gustave Dumoutier, *Rituel funéraire des Annamites* (Hanoi: Schneider, 1904), pp. 254–60.

64. Another common form of political protest was to block the roads with ancestor altars and perform ceremonies to hold up troop movements. This tactic was used mainly against the government troops. See Trullinger, *Village at War,* p. 125.

65. The official accounts by the ROK Army claim 4,687 ROK casualties in Vietnam and 41,400 enemy casualties.

66. This extract is cited from his original draft manuscript written for inclusion in *Dau Tranh Cach Mang Cua Dang Bo Va Nhan Dan Xa Dien Duong;* part of the essay was edited out of the printed version (Tam Ky: Nha xuat ban Tam Ky, 2003). The list of heroic entitlements, however, is included in the book (pp. 175–76).

67. W. R. Peers, *The My Lai Inquiry* (New York: W. W. Norton, 1979), pp. 229–45; United States Department of the Army, "Report of the Department of the Army Review of the Preliminary Investigations into the My Lai Incident," in Joseph Goldstein, Burke Marshall, and Jack Schwartz, eds., *The My Lai Massacre and Its Cover-up: Beyond the Reach of Law?* (New York: Free Press, 1976), pp. 20–372; James S. Olson and Randy Roberts, *My Lai: A Brief History with Documents* (Boston: Bedford Books, 1998), p. 24; Telford Taylor, "War Crimes: Son My," in Jay W. Baird, ed., *From Nuremberg to My Lai* (Lexington, MA: D. C. Heath and Company, 1972), p. 265.

68. Seymour M. Hersh, *Cover-Up: The Army's Secret Investigation of the Massacre at My Lai 4* (New York: Random House, 1972), p. 268. Also Bilton and Sim, *Four Hours in My Lai,* p. 14.

69. Marilyn Young, *The Vietnam Wars, 1945–1990* (New York: Harper-Perennial, 1991), p. 244; Olson and Roberts, *My Lai,* p. 25; Tim O'Brien, "The Mystery of My Lai," in David L. Anderson, ed., *Facing My Lai: Moving beyond the Massacre* (Lawrence: University Press of Kansas, 1998), pp. 171–78.

70. Olson and Roberts, *My Lai,* p. 10.

71. Ibid., p. 16. Townsend Hoopes, the undersecretary of the U.S. Air Force from 1967 to 1969, blames the cultural gap for this error of mistaking civilians for combatants: "Americans could not get to the heart of local politics in Vietnam, because the Vietnamese would not permit the necessary intimacy, and because it was beyond U.S. capability to provide enough operatives with the knowledge and skill to break through the formidable barriers of language and cultural difference." *The Limits of Intervention,* pp. 70–71.

72. Olson and Roberts, *My Lai,* p. 16. On the dynamics of depersonalization in atrocious mass violence, see Tzvetan Todorov, *Facing the Extreme: Moral Life in the Concentration Camps* (London: Phoenix, 2000), pp. 158–78.

73. See Neale, *The American War in Vietnam,* p. 130.

74. On the general situation after the Tet Mau Than event of 1968, compare Ronald H. Spector, *After Tet: The Bloodiest Year in Vietnam* (New York: Free Press, 1993), and Ho Khang, *The Tet Mau Than 1968 Event in South Vietnam* (Hanoi: The Gioi, 2001).

75. See the intriguing analysis of posttraumatic stress disorder symptoms by Allan Young, "Bodily Memory and Traumatic Memory," in Paul Antze and Michael Lambek, eds., *Tense Past: Cultural Essays in Trauma and Memory* (New York: Routledge, 1996), pp. 99. I thank Michael Lambek for bringing this important work to my attention. Also Allen Young, *The Harmony of Illusions: Inventing Post-Traumatic Stress Disorder* (Princeton: Princeton University Press, 1995), pp. 124–28.

76. On the state of denial, see Stanley Cohen's *States of Denial: Knowing about Atrocities and Suffering* (Cambridge: Polity Press, 2001).

77. Trullinger, *Village at War,* p. 129.

78. Personal communication with Ha Phuc Mai, the director of the Da Nang War Museum, who advised the project.

79. On the role of Cao Dai in the politics of war, see Jayne Werner, *Peasant Politics and Religious Sectarianism: Peasant and Priest in the Cao Dai in Vietnam* (New Haven: Yale University Southeast Asian Studies, 1981).

80. Interviews with the family of the wartime village chief in An Bang, in December 1997.

81. Henri Lefebvre, *The Production of Space* (Cambridge: Blackwell, 1991), pp. 292–96.

3. A GENERATION AFTERWARD

1. Maurice Halbwachs, *On Collective Memory,* trans. and ed. L. A. Coser (Chicago: University of Chicago Press, 1992), pp. 38–40.

2. Pierre Nora, "Between Memory and History: *Les lieux de memoire,*" *Representations* 26 (1989): 13.

3. Paul Fussell, *The Great War and Modern Memory* (Oxford: Oxford University Press, 1975).

4. Stephen Kern, *The Culture of Time and Space, 1880–1918* (Cambridge: Harvard University Press, 1983), p. 293.

5. Paul Connerton, *How Societies Remember* (Cambridge: Cambridge University Press, 1989), p. 65.

6. Le Van Dinh, *Le culte des ancêtres en droit annamite: Essai historique et critique sur le Huong-Hoa* (Paris: Editions Domat-Montchrestien, 1934), p. 14.

7. John R. Gillis, ed., *Commemorations: The Politics of National Identity* (Princeton: Princeton University Press, 1994), p. 5.

8. Nguyen Van Huyen, *The Ancient Civilization of Vietnam* (Hanoi: The Gioi, 1995), p. 61.

9. Quang Ngai General Museum, *A Look Back upon Son My* (Quang Ngai: Quang Ngai General Museum, 1998); Minh Tue, "Di Tich Danh Thang Son My," *Xua Nay*, no. 75B (2000): 26.

10. For this reason, the villagers have recently removed the remains of their relatives from the museum site. The museum still demonstrates a few graves, all of which became dummy graves by the end of the 1990s.

11. The term *tomb group* comes from Maurice Bloch. See his *Placing the Dead* (New York: Seminar Press, 1971), pp. 108–22.

12. Paul Ricoeur, *Oneself as Another* (Chicago: University of Chicago Press, 1992), p. 3.

13. Jürgen Habermas, *The Philosophical Discourse of Modernity* (Cambridge: Polity Press, 1987), p. 297.

14. The quote is from Joseph Dunne, "The Storied Self," in R. Kearney, ed., *Paul Ricoeur: The Hermeneutics of Action* (London: Sage, 1996), p. 114.

15. Léopold Cadière, *Croyances et pratiques religieuses des viêtnamiens*, bk. 3 (Paris: Ecole Française d'Extrême-Orient, 1957), pp. 41–42. Philip Taylor objects to Cadière's tendency to consider "animism" as a timeless, privileged, authentic religiosity of Vietnam, and I have my own doubts about the validity of the nature versus supernature scheme, which basically reiterates the arbitrary division between the profane and the sacred in Durkheimian sociology of religion. Taylor, *Goddess on the Rise: Pilgrimage and Popular Religion in Vietnam* (Honolulu: University of Hawaii Press, 2004), p. 8. However, I find Cadière's other parallel notion of "visible" and "invisible" relevant for understanding ritual revival as a social process of elicitation (making the invisible available to vision). For an exemplary work in this light, see Jane Monning Atkinson, *The Art and Politics of Wana Shamanship* (Berkeley: University of California Press, 1989), chs. 2 and 3.

16. On the metaphors of *am duong*, see Paul Giran, *Magie et religion annamites* (Paris: Librairie Maritime et Coloniale, 1912), pp. 30–31.

17. Hue-Tam Ho Tai writes, "[Memory] works forward as well as backward; the past is shaped by the future as much as the future is shaped by the past. Memory creates meaning for particular events or experiences by inscribing them in a larger framing narrative, be it personal or collective. Whether implicitly or explicitly, in this larger narrative is embedded a sense of progression and the vision of the future for which the past acts as prologue." *The Country of Memory: Remaking the Past in Late Socialist Vietnam* (Berkeley: University of California Press, 2001), p. 2.

18. Patricia M. Pelley, *Postcolonial Vietnam: New Histories of the National Past* (Durham, NC: Duke University Press, 2002), p. 117.

19. See Shaun K. Malarney, "'The Fatherland Remembers Your Sacrifice': Commemorating War Dead in North Vietnam," in Hue-Tam Ho Tai, ed., *The*

Country of Memory: Remaking the Past in Late Socialist Vietnam (Berkeley: University of California Press, 2001), pp. 46–76.

20. During my field research, I had an opportunity to explore the activities of the Vietnamese and the U.S. MIA (Missing in Action) missions in the central region, whose results are not published yet. For the controversy of the U.S. MIA/POW politics, see Bruce H. Franklin, *M.I.A. or Mythmaking in America* (New Brunswick, NJ: Rutgers University Press, 1993).

21. Shaun K. Malarney, *Culture, Ritual, and Revolution in Vietnam* (New York: RoutledgeCurzon, 2002), p. 176.

22. Katherine Verdery, *The Political Lives of Dead Bodies: Reburial and Postsocialist Change* (New York: Columbia University Press, 1999), p. 22.

23. Philip Taylor, *Fragments of the Present: Searching for Modernity in Vietnam's South* (Honolulu: University of Hawaii Press, 2001).

24. Cited from Robert Stern, *Hegel and the Phenomenology of Spirit* (New York: Routledge, 2002), p. 140.

25. Hy Van Luong, "Economic Reform and the Intensification of Rituals in Two North Vietnamese Villages, 1980–90," in Börye Liunggren, ed., *The Challenge of Reform in Indochina* (Cambridge: Harvard Institute of International Development, 1993), pp. 259–92.

26. Emily Ahern, *The Cult of the Dead in a Chinese Village* (Stanford: Stanford University Press, 1973), p. 247; Hugh Baker, *Chinese Family and Kinship* (New York: Columbia University Press, 1979), p. 88.

27. Ha Van Tan and Nguyen Van Ku, *Dinh Viet Nam* (Community hall in Vietnam) (Ho Chi Minh: Nha xuat ban Thanh Pho Ho Chi Minh, 1998), p. 108.

28. Roger T. Ames, "Death as Transformation in Classical Daoism," in J. Malpas and R. C. Solomon, eds., *Death and Philosophy* (New York: Routledge, 1998), p. 60.

29. I employ the word *feudal* when presented without quotation marks, in a purely epochal sense and with no such negative qualitative connotations as in the official Vietnamese political discourse of feudalism *(chu nghia phong kien)*.

30. See Jean Chesneaux and Georges Boudarel, "Le Kim Van Kieu et l'esprit public vietnamien aux xix et xx siècles," in M. Durand, ed., *Mélanges sur Nguyen Du* (Paris: Ecole Française d'Extrême-Orient, 1966), pp. 153–92.

31. On Nguyen Du, see Nguyen Thach and Truong Chinh, *Nguyen Du: Tac Pham Va Lich Su Van Ban* (Nguyen Du: His works and their history) (Ho Chi Minh: Nha xuat ban Thanh Pho Ho Chi Minh, 2000).

32. For a text of Nguyen Du's poem "Van te co hon thap loa chung sinh," which deals with the spectrum of tragic death, see Tan Viet, *Tap Van Cung Gia Tien* (Prayer book for ancestral worship) (Hanoi: Nha xuat ban van hoa dan toc, 1994), pp. 105–14.

33. About the syncretism of Buddhism and spirit beliefs, see Minh Chi, Ha Van Tan, and Nguyen Tai Thu, *Le Bouddhism au Vietnam* (Hanoi: The Gioi, 1993), pp. 124–36. Also Stanley J. Tambiah, *Buddhism and the Spirit Cults in Northeast Thailand* (New York: Cambridge University Press, 1970).

34. The quote is from Mary Kaldor, *The Imaginary War* (Oxford: Blackwell, 1990).

35. The quote "a powerful, intrusive and atheist Vietnamese state" comes from Robert Templer, *Shadows and Wind: A View of Modern Vietnam* (London: Abacus, 1999), p. 265. The quote "vestiges of feudal, colonialist, and bourgeois cultures" comes from William Duiker, *Vietnam: Revolution in Transition* (Boulder, CO: Westview, 1995), p. 189.

36. Pelley, *Postcolonial Vietnam*, pp. 116–17.

37. Malarney, *Culture, Ritual, and Revolution in Vietnam*, pp. 44–50.

38. Tran Bach Dang, *Bui Thi Me, Ke Chuyen Doi Minh* (Bui Thi Me, a story of her life) (Ho Chi Minh: Nha xuat ban tre, 2001); Karen G. Turner and Phan Thanh Hao, *Even the Women Must Fight: Memories of War from North Vietnam* (New York: John Wiley and Sons, 1998), pp. 171–73; Hue-Tam Ho Tai, "Faces of Remembrance and Forgetting," in *The Country of Memory: Remaking the Past in Late Socialist Vietnam* (Berkeley: University of California Press, 2001), pp. 173, 179.

39. Nguyen Van Huyen, *The Ancient Civilization of Vietnam*, pp. 62–63.

40. Cited in David Marr, *Vietnamese Tradition on Trial, 1920–1945* (Berkeley: University of California Press, 1981), p. 91.

41. In Vietnamese: "Doi cha an man doi con khat nuoc."

42. Son Nam, *Nghi Thuc Va Le Bai Cua Nguoi Viet Nam* (Vietnamese ceremonies and worship) (Ho Chi Minh: Nha xuat ban tre, 1997), pp. 12–19.

43. Luong, "Economic Reform and the Intensification of Rituals in Two North Vietnamese Villages, 1980–90," pp. 285–90.

44. Nguyen Van Huy et al., "The Village God's Journey," in Nguyen Van Huy and Laurel Kendall, eds., *Vietnam: Journeys of Body, Mind, and Spirit* (Berkeley: University of California Press, 2003), p. 222.

45. Luong, "Economic Reform and the Intensification of Rituals in Two North Vietnamese Villages, 1980–90," p. 289.

46. James Scott, *The Moral Economy of Peasants* (New Haven: Yale University Press, 1976).

47. Carles Salazar, *A Sentimental Economy* (Oxford: Berghan, 1996), p. 5.

48. Scott, *The Moral Economy of Peasants*, p. 11.

49. Sherry Ortner raises a similar point that the idea of moral economy, although it works against simplistic rendering of economic rationality in the discourse of liberal political economy, is as generalizing as the latter and not grounded in the concrete cultural forms through which moral principles are expressed. "Resistance and the Problem of Ethnographic Refusal," *Comparative Studies in Society and History* 37 (1995): 173–93.

50. Adam Smith, endorsing the puritanical attitude toward money, wrote that the principle of parsimony that prompts us to save is "the desire of bettering our condition, a desire which, though generally calm and dispassionate, comes with us from the womb, and never leaves us till we go into the grave." *The Wealth of Nations* (Harmondsworth: Penguin, 1970), p. 305.

51. Marilyn Strathern, *The Gender of the Gift* (Cambridge: Cambridge University Press, 1988), p. 271.

52. Ibid., p. 272.

53. Nguyen Van Huyen, *The Ancient Civilization of Vietnam*, p. 60.

4. ANCESTORS IN THE STREET

1. According to James C. Scott, rumors and gossip are "a kind of democratic voice" in a politically controlled rural environment. And gossip is never "disinterested" but "a partisan effort." *Weapons of the Weak: Everyday Forms of Peasant Resistance* (New Haven: Yale University Press, 1985), p. 282.

2. Pierre Bourdieu, *The Logic of Practice* (Cambridge: Polity Press, 1990), p. 276.

3. See Stevan Harrell, "When a Ghost Becomes a God," in A. Wolf, ed., *Religion and Ritual in Chinese Society* (Stanford: Stanford University Press, 1974).

4. Franz Boas, *Race, Language, and Culture* (New York: Macmillan, 1940), p. 603.

5. Tzvetan Todorov, *Facing the Extreme: Moral Life in the Concentration Camps* (London: Phoenix, 2000), pp. 158–78.

6. Paul Giran, *Magie et religion annamites* (Paris: Librairie Maritime et Coloniale, 1912), pp. 101–2.

7. See Gustave Dumoutier, *Rituel funéraire des annamites: Etude d'ethnographie religieuse* (Hanoi: Schneider, 1904), pp. 17–20.

8. Nguyen Van Huyen, *The Ancient Civilization of Vietnam* (Hanoi: The Gioi, 1995), pp. 53–57.

9. Jennifer Cole, "The Work of Memory in Madagascar," *American Ethnologist* 25, no. 4 (1998): 614.

10. Shaun K. Malarney, *Culture, Ritual, and Revolution in Vietnam* (New York: RoutledgeCurzon, 2002), p. 42.

11. Emile Durkheim, *The Elementary Forms of Religious Life,* trans. K. E. Fields (1915; reprint, New York: Free Press, 1995), p. 280.

12. Ibid., p. 277.

13. Léopold Cadière, *Croyances et pratiques religieuses des viêtnamiens* (Paris: Ecole Française d'Extrême-Orient, 1957), p. 59.

14. Nguyen Du's "Remembering Ten [Twelve] Forms of Death" goes:

Those who died beheaded
Those who had many friends and relatives but died lonely
Mandarins (in exile)
Those who died in the battlefield
Those whose death nobody knew about
Students who died on the way back from exam
Those who were buried hurriedly with no coffin and no clothing
Those who died at sea under thunderstorm
Merchants
Those who died with a shoulder hardened by too many bamboo poles carried on it
Prostitutes
Innocent souls who died in prison
    Tan Viet, *Tap Van Cung Gia Tien* (Prayer book for ancestor worship)
    (Hanoi: Nha xuat ban van hoa dan toc, 2001), pp. 71–75

15. Edward S. Casey, *Spirit and Soul: Essays in Philosophical Psychology,* 2nd ed. (Putnam, CT: Spring Publications, 2004), p. 324.

16. Liisa H. Malkki, *Purity and Exile: Violence, Memory, and National Cos-*

mology among Hutu Refugees in Tanzania (Chicago: University of Chicago Press, 1995).

17. Stanley Karnow, *Vietnam: A History* (London: Pimlico, 1994), pp. 113–16; Nguyen Van Huyen, *The Ancient Civilization of Vietnam*, pp. 156–57.

18. See Pierre Gourou, *Esquisse d'une étude de l'habitation annamite* (Paris: Ecole Française d'Extrême-Orient, 1936).

19. Arthur P. Wolf, in his study of popular religions in a Taiwanese village, examined the villagers' interest in ghosts. He suggested that ghosts and ancestors can have a fixed status or can be assigned to interchangeable categories, depending on how we look at them. He noted that the status of an ancestor depends on the particular milieu of the genealogical relationship that defines it, beyond which the given status no longer applies. Wolf suggested that the moral hierarchy between ancestors and ghosts is a relative, place-specific phenomenon rather than a general order applicable across places. In order to illustrate this point, Wolf introduced an episode in which a village man claimed to have seen "a white object floating across the fields" and identified the object as a ghost on its way to join the ancestral ceremony prepared by a village family. What is a ghost to the man, therefore, must be an ancestor to the family, and on the basis of this experience, Wolf wrote his famous observation: "Whether a particular spirit is viewed as a ghost or as an ancestor depends on the point of view of a particular person. *One man's ancestor is another man's ghost.*" "Gods, Ghosts, and Ancestors," in Arthur Wolf, ed., *Religion and Ritual in Chinese Society* (Stanford: Stanford University Press, 1974), p. 146, emphasis in the original.

20. Zygmund Bauman, *Modernity and Ambivalence* (Ithaca: Cornell University Press, 1991), pp. 55–56.

21. Michael M. Fischer's essay "Ethnicity and the Arts of Memory" elaborates on the idea of bifocal identity as a condition of ethnographic project. In James Clifford and George E. Marcus, eds., *Writing Culture: The Poetics and Politics of Ethnography* (Berkeley: University of California Press, 1986), pp. 199, 213–23.

22. Tim Ingold strives to reconcile place with mobility by uncovering how human movement is intrinsic to the constitution of place. In doing so, he advances a critique of the Cartesian tradition that has reduced, according to him, place to a mere location in space, meaningful only in terms of abstract indicators empty of social meanings. Later, I return to a related issue and explore how we may conceive of the ritual arena between "house" and "street" as a *locus animus* (see the conclusion to this volume). Ingold, *The Perception of the Environment*, chs. 10 and 13. See also Edward S. Casey, *The Fate of Place: A Philosophical History* (Berkeley: University of California Press, 1997), ch. 9.

23. Shelly Errington, "Recasting Sex, Gender, and Power: A Theoretical and Regional Overview," in J. M. Atkinson and S. Errington, eds., *Power and Difference: Gender in Island Southeast Asia* (Stanford: Stanford University Press, 1990), p. 54.

24. The names introduced in this story are pseudonyms. I visited the family on numerous occasions beginning in 1996.

25. About the *zar* spirit possession cult in northern Sudan, Janice Boddy

writes, "To observe possession trance in another is to witness a paradox. . . . During trance the two [the identities of the possessed and her intrusive *zar*] are brought into intimate and often perplexing association, and those describing the episode often refer to the woman and her spirit interchangeably. Yet this risk of confusion, this ambiguity, is, I think, key to the aesthetics and therapeutics of *zar* in Hofriyat." The same can be said about the *xac* practices in Vietnam. However, the paradox of identities in spirit possession entails not only the relationship between the living body and the possessing spirit but also the spirit's two oscillating identities—that is, between an embodied historical subject and disembodied memory. See Boddy, "Spirits and Selves in Northern Sudan: The Cultural Therapeutics of Possession and Trance," *American Ethnologist* 15, no. 1 (1988): 26–27.

26. Don Lam, "A Brief Account of the Cult of Female Deities in Vietnam," *Vietnamese Studies,* no. 1 (1999): 7.

27. Nelson Goodman, *Ways of Worldmaking* (Indianapolis: Hackett, 1978), p. 5.

5. HEROES AND ANCESTORS

1. John R. Gillis, ed., *Commemorations: The Politics of National Identity* (Princeton: Princeton University Press, 1994), pp. 3–24.

2. On mass death in the First World War, see George Mosse, *Fallen Soldiers: Reshaping the Memory of the World Wars* (Oxford: Oxford University Press, 1990), p. 7. On memorials as forceful emblems of national unity, see Thomas W. Laqueur, "Memory and Naming in the Great War," in John R. Gillis, ed., *Commemorations: The Politics of National Identity* (Princeton: Princeton University Press, 1994), pp. 150–67.

3. Eric Hobsbawm and Terence Ranger, eds., *The Invention of Tradition* (Cambridge: Cambridge University Press, 1983).

4. Benedict Anderson, *Imagined Communities: Reflections on the Origin and the Spread of Nationalism* (New York: Verso, 1983), pp. 37–46.

5. Ibid., pp. 197–98; Clifford Geertz, *The Interpretation of Cultures* (New York: Basic Books, 1973), p. 240.

6. Shaun K. Malarney, *Culture, Ritual, and Revolution in Vietnam* (New York: RoutledgeCurzon, 2002), pp. 43–50.

7. In his recent, widely circulated manual *Viec Ho,* which discusses the ritual and practical actions entailed in networking the multiple sites of ancestor worship, the popular writer Tan Viet asserts, "The family temple and the family graveyard are two places where the family's vitality is concentrated." *Viec Ho* (Hanoi: Nha xuat ban van hoa dan toc, 2000), p. 5.

8. Le Anh Dung, "Xay Dung Toc Ho Van Hoa o Dien Ban (Rebuilding family culture in Dien Ban District)," *Van Hoa Quang Nam* (January 1999): 9.

9. James Trullinger mentions the importance of appropriating the ancestral cult for revolutionary mobilization. *Village at War: An Account of Conflict in Vietnam* (Stanford: Stanford University Press, 1994), pp. 44–45.

10. Ha Van Tan and Nguyen Van Ku, *Dinh Viet Nam* (Community hall in Vietnam) (Ho Chi Minh: Nha xuat ban thanh pho Ho Chi Minh, 1998), pp. 75–

76. Some communal houses in northern Vietnam were used as medical stations for wounded soldiers during the resistance war. See Nguyen Van Huy et al., "The Village God's Journey," in Nguyen Van Huy and Laurel Kendall, eds., *Vietnam: Journeys of Body, Mind, and Spirit* (Berkeley: University of California Press, 2003), p. 222.

11. William Duiker, *Vietnam: Revolution in Transition* (Boulder, CO: Westview, 1995), p. 189, and his "Ideology and Nation-Building in the Democratic Republic of Vietnam," *Asian Survey* 17, no. 5 (1977): 416.

12. With reference to the collectivization of agriculture in the 1950s in northern Vietnam, Benedict J. Tria Kerkvliet writes, "A prominent theme in the recent history of rural Vietnam is debate, bargaining, and interaction between the state and villages." "Village-State Relations in Vietnam: The Effect of Everyday Politics on Decollectivization," *Journal of Asian Studies* 54, no. 2 (1995): 415.

13. Nguyen Van Huyen, *The Ancient Civilization of Vietnam* (Hanoi: The Gioi, 1995), p. 83.

14. "Hop Mat Xom Tay Ha My" (Meetings among the people of Xom Tay, Ha My), a private collection of poems and public speeches by the village poet and calligrapher Nguyen Minh Dat.

15. See Nguyen Van Huy et al., "The Village God's Journey," pp. 227–33; Thanh Chiem, "Mieu Ong Cop o Hoi An" (The Tiger Temple in Hoi An), *Du Lich* (Spring 1998): 37.

16. The *tu dan dien* and *tu dan tho* were part of the general category of communal land—*cong dien* (communal rice land) or *cong tho* (communal horticultural land)—and served to provide resources for village ritual activities. The communal land of a lineage that provided income for a family-based ancestral cult is usually called *huong hoa,* meaning literally "fire and incense." See Nancy Wiegersma, *Vietnam: Peasant Land, Peasant Revolution* (London: Macmillan, 1988), pp. 53–56. Also To Lan, "On Communal Land in the Traditional Viet Village," *The Traditional Village in Vietnam* (Hanoi: The Gioi, 1993), pp. 156–94.

17. The Vietnamese peasants have a strong tendency to disapprove of the ownership of village land by an outsider. See Pierre Gourou, *La terre et l'homme en Extreme-Orient* (Paris: Armand Colin, 1952), pp. 49–50.

18. Cited from the copy of the five-page petition letter kept by the chairman of the Funeral Organizing Committee.

19. Tan Viet, *Viec Ho,* pp. 4–5.

20. Ibid.

21. John Bodnar employs these quoted expressions in his analysis of the controversies on the Vietnam Veterans Memorial in Arlington, Virginia. "Public Memory in an American City," in John R. Gillis, ed., *Commemorations: The Politics of National Identity* (Princeton: Princeton University Press, 1994), p. 87.

22. Kerkvliet, "Village-State Relations in Vietnam," p. 412.

23. See Duiker, *Vietnam: Revolution in Transition,* pp. 190–91.

24. Huu Ngoc, "Springtime Breaks Out," *Sunday Viet Nam News* (November 2, 2001).

25. *Hoi An Thi Xa Anh Hung* (The heroes of Hoi An) (Da Nang: Nha xuat ban Da Nang, 1999), pp. 17–23.

26. Le Nhu Thuy, "Nha Tho Toc Le Viet: Doi Dieu Ghi Nhan" (From the

temple of the founders of Le Viet family), *Van Hoa Quang Nam,* no. 20 (2000): 20–21.

27. Hue-Tam Ho Tai, "Faces of Remembrance and Forgetting," in *The Country of Memory: Remaking the Past in Late Socialist Vietnam* (Berkeley: University of California Press, 2001), pp. 180–81.

28. On the maternal icon as a gendered or kinship-ideological symbol, see Iris Jean-Klein, "Mothercraft, Statecraft, and Subjectivity in the Palestinian Intifada," *American Ethnologist* 27, no. 1 (2000): 100–127; Julie Peteet, "Icons and Militants: Mothering in the Danger Zone," *Signs: Journal of Women in Culture and Society* 23, no. 1 (2000): 103–29.

29. Nguyen Quynh, "Tra Kieu: Di Tich Lich Su, Van Hoa, Du Lich-Can Duoc Danh Thuc" (Tra Kieu: The need to revive its historic and cultural heritage for tourist development), *Van Hoa Quang Nam,* no. 26 (2001): 24–25.

30. James Scott, *Weapons of the Weak: Everyday Forms of Peasant Resistance* (New Haven: Yale University Press, 1985), p. 282.

31. David Lan writes about the peasant guerrillas in Zimbabwe: "All the evidence suggests that guerrillas and peasants held two contrasting ideas in their heads at the same time and, by referring to both, arrived at effective courses of action. Ancestral protection and rigorous military discipline were both essential. . . . The one train of thought does not preclude the other." *Guns and Rains: Guerrillas and Spirit Mediums in Zimbabwe* (London: James Currey, 1985), p. 209.

32. Cited from a copy of the four-page, first application letter.

33. Cited from a copy of the second application letter.

34. *Noi chon nhau cat ron,* meaning where the placenta and umbilical cord are buried: that is, the native place.

35. Paul Giran, *Magie et religion annamites* (Paris: Librairie Maritime et Coloniale, 1912), pp. 427–33.

36. Sherry B. Ortner, "Patterns of History: Cultural Schemas in the Foundings of Sherpa Religious Institutions," in E. Ohnuki-Tierney, ed., *Culture through Time: Anthropological Approaches* (Stanford: Stanford University Press, 1990), pp. 57–93.

37. See Bruce Kapferer, *Legends of People, Myths of State: Violence, Intolerance, and Political Culture in Sri Lanka and Australia* (Washington, DC: Smithsonian Institution Press, 1988), pp. 136–39.

6. GRIEVOUS DEATH

1. Maurice Bloch, *Placing the Dead* (New York: Seminar Press, 1971), ch. 2; and his "Tombs and States," in S. C. Humphreys and H. King, eds., *Mortality and Immortality: The Anthropology and Archaeology of Death* (London: Academic Press, 1981).

2. Edmund Leach, *Political Systems of Highland Burma: A Study of Kachin Social Structure* (London: Bell, 1954), p. 12.

3. Maurice Bloch, *Prey into Hunter: The Politics of Religious Experience* (Cambridge: Cambridge University Press, 1992).

4. Paul Antze and Michael Lambek, eds., *Tense Past: Cultural Essays in Trauma and Memory* (New York: Routledge, 1996), p. xvi.

5. See Hou Ching-lang, *Monnaies d'offrande et la notion de Trésorerie dans la religion chinoise* (Paris: Collège de France, 1975).

6. Jean-Claude Schmitt, *Ghosts in the Middle Ages: The Living and the Dead in Medieval Society* (Chicago: University of Chicago Press, 1998), pp. 23–24.

7. Léopold Cadière, *Croyances et pratiques religieuses des viêtnamiens*, bk. 3 (Paris: Ecole Française d'Extrême-Orient, 1957), pp. 182–83; Nguyen Van Huyen, *The Ancient Civilization of Vietnam* (Hanoi: The Gioi, 1995), pp. 236–39. Each soul is believed to have multiple manifestations. In all, humans have three *hon* and seven (for men) or nine (for women) *via*.

8. The material soul of one who died a good death can be reawakened when the entombed body faces a crisis caused by, for instance, the intrusion of tree roots.

9. The traditional Vietnamese classification of seventy-two different tragic deaths presents a particular category of grievous death for "people who died in prison, accused falsely." This death, collapsing the boundary between prison and the symbolic prison of afterlife, is considered to be a category of death that is most challenging to the rituals of soul liberation.

10. See Richard Norman, *Ethics, Killing, and War* (Cambridge: Cambridge University Press, 1995), ch. 5.

11. From his collection of speeches and essays, "Xom Tay, Dat Va Nguoi" (Xom Tay, land and people), a handwritten manuscript of village history kept by a village elder.

12. Michael Rowlands investigates the notion of self-sacrifice demonstrated in modern war memorials in terms of a theory of religious sacrifice and purification. He writes, "The dead as the sacrificed play their role . . . as an idealized icon, cleansed of transitory weaknesses and moral stains." "Remembering to Forget," in Adrian Forty and Susan Küchler, eds., *The Art of Forgetting* (New York: Berg, 1999), p. 136.

13. One particularly conservative village official believes, even today, that the mass grave held the bodies of *phan dong*—the frightening label meaning "counterrevolutionary." He had in mind the victims of the massacre whose purpose of remaining in the village at the time of the killing, in his opinion, had been to make money rather than to protect the village. He heard that the Ha Gia area in 1968 had been abundant with wild vegetables and turtles, which were sold for a high price in urban markets (see chapter 8). To this official, it was a disgrace to corrupt the purity of the place of war martyrs with the bodies of these dubious political elements.

14. Henri Lefebvre, *The Production of Space* (Cambridge: Blackwell, 1991), pp. 332–33.

15. Quoted from my transcript of the conversation, recorded on January 2002.

16. The materials include red clay for flesh, mulberry branches for the bones, *sinh tue* leaves for the ribs and spine, colored threads for veins, an egg for the stomach, a mirror for the heart, black beans for the eyes, rice for teeth, and a small papaya for the skull. Water-fern roots are used for hair for those who died

at sea, and maize fibers for the hair of those who died on land. The dummy body is wrapped in a long white-and-red cloth and put into a small coffin of precise depth and width. For a terrestrial death, the formal application for repatriation of the soul *(bai cung)* is made to a terrestrial deity called To Su, rather than to its maritime equivalent, Ha Ba.

17. Georg Simmel, *On Individuality and Social Forms*, ed. D. Levine (Chicago: University of Chicago Press, 1971), p. 356.

7. THE STONE OF FURY

1. Because of this mark, visitors unaware of village history have the impression that Thuy Bo is a site of American war crimes. Visitors who know the history wonder why the foreign soldiers wear the mark of the U.S. army rather than that of the ROK army.

2. Michael Rowlands observes, "For the sense of personal sacrifice to be validated, war memorials have to be to some extent a special category where resolution is achieved by the extent to which visual forms unproblematically affirm 'that they did not die in vain.' Such cannot be said of Holocaust memorials, for example, where nobody can claim that the deaths served any purpose whatsoever." "Remembering to Forget," in Adrian Forty and Susan Küchler, eds., *The Art of Forgetting* (New York: Berg, 1999), p. 142.

3. Brian S. Willson, "Bob Kerrey's Atrocity, the Crime of Vietnam, and the Historic Pattern of US Imperialism," in Adam Jones, ed., *Genocide, War Crimes, and the West* (London: Zed Books, 2004), p. 178. See also Andrew E. Hunt, *The Turning: A History of Vietnam Veterans against the War* (New York: New York University Press, 1999).

4. "South Korea's Vietnam," *Newsweek* (April 10, 2000): 32–40. See also James Sterngold, "South Korea's Vietnam Veterans Begin to Be Heard," *New York Times,* May 10, 1992.

5. Eunji Kang and Soo Sun Chae, *Dream for Peace and Reconciliation: Korean Soldiers in Vietnam and the Scar of War,* Korea Report 21 (Seoul: Korean House for International Solidarity, 2000), pp. 24–25. The woman's initiative may turn out to be an important episode for historians of East Asia in the future, for the political development of this region will heavily depend on the emergence of nations' awareness that their turbulent national pasts are in fact intimately connected internationally.

6. *Tuoi Tre Chu Nhat,* July 30, 2000, p. 11.

7. Personal communication with Gu Su Jeong, July 2002.

8. Jacques Derrida, *Cosmopolitanism and Forgiveness* (New York: Routledge, 2001), p. 30.

9. Personal communication with the consulate of Republic of Korea in Ho Chi Minh City, July 2002.

10. Edward Relph, "Modernity and the Reclamation of Place," in David Seamon, ed., *Dwelling, Seeing, and Designing: Toward a Phenomenological Ecology* (Albany: SUNY Press, 1993), p. 34.

11. James C. Scott, *Seeing Like a State* (New Haven: Yale University Press, 1998), pp. 309–41.

12. James Young, *The Texture of Memory: Holocaust Memorials and Meaning* (New Haven: Yale University Press, 1993), pp. 31–32. See also Susanne Küchler's depiction of "the consequences of abandoning *memoria* for a new understanding of the place of memory not in objects, but in the space created by rendering absent the products of memory work—a place that is evoked and rather substituted by objects." "The Place of Memory," in Adrian Forty and Susan Küchler, eds., *The Art of Forgetting* (New York: Berg, 1999), p. 54.

13. Hue-Tam Ho Tai, "Monumental Ambiguity: The State Commemoration of Ho Chi Minh," in K. W. Taylor and J. K. Whitmore, eds., *Essays into Vietnamese Pasts* (Ithaca: Cornell Southeast Asia Program, 1995), p. 273.

14. John Bodnar, "Public Memory in an American City," in John R. Gillis, ed., *Commemorations: The Politics of National Identity* (Princeton: Princeton University Press, 1994), p. 87.

15. Ervin Staub notes, "Support and affirmation by the world can contribute to processes within the group that help members grieve and feel empathy with themselves." "Preventing Genocide," in Levon Chorbajian and George Shirinian, eds., *Studies in Comparative Genocide* (New York: St. Martin's Press, 1999), p. 256.

16. Interview with the *thay boi* in Ha My, February 2001; and telephone conversation with the victim's former wife, February 2001.

8. THE DECOMPOSITION OF THE COLD WAR

1. Quoted from Stephen Kern, *The Culture of Time and Space, 1880–1918* (Cambridge: Harvard University Press, 1983), p. 151.

2. Katherine Verdery, *The Political Lives of Dead Bodies: Reburial and Post-socialist Change* (New York: Columbia University Press, 1999), p. 108.

3. Peter van der Veer, "The Victim's Tale: Memory and Forgetting in the Story of Violence," in Hent de Vries and Samuel Weber, eds., *Violence, Identity, and Self-Determination* (Stanford: Stanford University Press, 1997), p. 196.

4. Henri Lefebvre, *The Production of Space* (Cambridge: Blackwell, 1991), p. 332.

5. Friedrich Nietzsche, *On the Advantage and Disadvantage of History for Life*, trans. Peter Preuss (Indianapolis: Hackett Publishing, 1980), p. 17.

6. See Arthur P. Wolf, "Gods, Ghosts, and Ancestors," in Arthur Wolf, ed., *Religion and Ritual in Chinese Society* (Stanford: Stanford University Press, 1974), p. 146.

7. I borrow this expression from Stephen Whitfield's *The Culture of the Cold War* (Baltimore: Johns Hopkins University Press, 1991), p. 205.

8. Bruce Cumings, *Parallax Visions* (Durham, NC: Duke University Press, 1999).

9. On the background of revisionist and postrevisionist schools of international history, see Allen Hunter, ed., *Rethinking the Cold War* (Philadelphia: Temple University Press, 1998), pp. 8–11.

10. Mary Kaldor, *The Disintegrating West* (New York: Pelican Books, 1979), p. 9.

11. Alan Hirshfeld, *Parallax: The Race to Measure the Cosmos* (New York: W. H. Freeman, 2001), p. xii.

12. Mark P. Bradley, *Imagining Vietnam and America: The Making of Post-colonial Vietnam, 1919–1950* (Chapel Hill: University of North Carolina Press, 2000), p. 6.

13. Ibid., p. 189.

14. Mary Kaldor, *The Imaginary War* (Oxford: Blackwell, 1990).

15. Arif Dirlik, " 'Trapped in History' on the Way to Utopia: East Asia's 'Great War' Fifty Years Later," in T. Fujitani, G. M. White, and L. Yoneyama, eds., *Perilous Memories: The Asia-Pacific War(s)* (Durham, NC: Duke University Press, 2001), p. 302.

16. Hunter, ed., *Rethinking the Cold War*, pp. 8–16.

17. Whitfield, *The Culture of the Cold War*.

18. See John Borneman, *Belonging in the Two Berlins: Kin, State, Nation* (Cambridge: Cambridge University Press, 1992).

19. Cited in Neil L. Jamieson, *Understanding Vietnam* (Berkeley: University of California Press, 1993), pp. 321–22.

20. Marilyn Young, "The Vietnam War in American Memory," in Marvin E. Gettleman et al., eds., *Vietnam and America* (New York: Grove, 1995), pp. 516–17. See also Hue-Tam Ho Tai, *The Country of Memory: Remaking the Past in Late Socialist Vietnam* (Berkeley: University of California Press, 2001), p. 5.

21. Tai, *The Country of Memory*, p. 5.

22. William Duiker, *Vietnam: Revolution in Transition* (Boulder, CO: Westview, 1995), pp. 191; Tai, *The Country of Memory*, pp. 5–8. Some of the most notable works of fiction in this regard are Nguyen Huy Thiep's *The General Retires and Other Stories* (1992), Bao Ninh's *The Sorrow of War* (1993), and Duong Thu Huong's *Novel without a Name* (1996).

23. George Mosse, *Fallen Soldiers: Reshaping the Memory of the World Wars* (Oxford: Oxford University Press, 1990), p. 7.

24. See, for instance, Jay Winter and Jean-Louis Robert, *Capital Cities at War: Paris, London, Berlin, 1914–1919* (Cambridge: Cambridge University Press, 1997), pp. 20–24.

25. See John Borneman, *Subversions of International Order: Studies in the Political Anthropology of Culture* (Albany: State University of New York Press, 1998), pp. 2–5.

26. Marilyn B. Young, *The Vietnam Wars, 1945–1990* (New York: Harper-Perennial, 1991).

27. Duiker, *Vietnam*, pp. 154–62; Gabriel Kolko, *Vietnam: Anatomy of a Peace* (New York: Routledge, 1977), ch. 1.

28. Georg Simmel, *On Individuality and Social Forms*, ed. D. Levine (Chicago: University of Chicago Press, 1971), p. 139.

29. Ibid.

30. Michael Carrithers, "An Alternative Social History of the Self," in Michael Carrithers, Steven Collins, and Steven Lukes, eds., *The Category of the Person* (Cambridge: Cambridge University Press, 1985), p. 235.

31. Simmel, *On Individuality and Social Forms*, p. 145.

32. It is telling that Jacques Derrida conceptualizes this process of exclusion or effacement as a production of "ghosts" in modern archival institutions.

Archive Fever: A Freudian Impression, trans. Eric Prenowitz (Chicago: University of Chicago Press, 1995).

33. Jack Goody argues, for instance, "In the main, it is those from whose death one benefits [in terms of inheritance] that one fears as ancestors." *Death, Property, and the Ancestors* (Stanford: Stanford University Press, 1962), p. 410.

34. Martin Jay, "Against Consolation: Walter Benjamin and the Refusal to Mourn," in Jay Winter and Emmanuel Sivan, eds., *War and Remembrance in the Twentieth Century* (Cambridge: Cambridge University Press, 1999), p. 238.

35. Maurice Halbwachs, *On Collective Memory,* trans. and ed. L. A. Coser (Chicago: University of Chicago Press, 1992), pp. 25–26, 51.

CONCLUSION

1. E. P. Thompson is remembered not only for his monumental popular history of the English working class and their "moral economy" but also for his political writings and activism "from below" against the Cold War in Europe. I discuss his works in a separate monograph now in preparation. See "Ends and Histories," in M. Kaldor, ed., *Europe from Below* (London: Verso, 1991), pp. 7–25.

2. On memorial projects for the fallen common soldier, see Thomas W. Laqueur, "Memory and Naming in the Great War," in John R. Gillis, ed., *Commemorations: The Politics of National Identity* (Princeton: Princeton University Press, 1994), p. 155. On turning bereavement into a positive social force, see Benedict Anderson, *Imagined Communities: Reflections on the Origin and the Spread of Nationalism* (New York: Verso, 1983), pp. 181–206.

3. Richard Werbner, "Smoke from the Barrel of a Gun: Postwars of the Dead, Memory, and Reinscription in Zimbabwe," in *Memory and Postcoloniality,* ed. Richard Werbner (London: Zed, 1998), p. 72.

4. Gillis, ed., *Commemorations,* p. 5.

5. Anderson, *Imagined Communities,* ch. 2.

6. See Jane Schneider, "Spirits and the Spirit of Capitalism," in E. R. Wolf, ed., *Religious Regimes and State Formation* (New York: SUNY Press, 1991), pp. 181–219. Also Marilyn Strathern, "Parts and Wholes: Refiguring Relationships in a Post-Plural World," in Adam Kuper, ed., *Conceptualizing Society* (New York: Routledge, 1992), p. 99; Janice Boddy, *Wombs and Alien Spirits: Women, Men, and the Zar Cult in Northern Sudan* (Madison: University of Wisconsin Press, 1989), p. 165; Heike Behrend, "Power to Heal, Power to Kill," in Heike Behrend and Ute Luig, eds., *Spirit Possession: Modernity and Power in Africa* (Oxford: James Currey, 1999), pp. 25–26.

7. K. W. Taylor, "Surface Orientations in Vietnam: Beyond Histories of Nation and Religion," *Journal of Asian Studies* 53, no. 4 (1998): 974.

8. Edmund Leach, *Political Systems of Highland Burma* (London: Bell, 1954), p. 4. Similarly, Victor Turner writes, "Georg Simmel, Lewis Coser, Max Gluckman, and others have pointed out how conflict, if brought under gradual control, stopping short of massacre and war, may actually enhance a group's 'consciousness of kind.' Conflict forces the antagonists to diagnose its source,

and in so doing to become fully aware of the principles that bond them beyond and above the issues that have temporarily divided them." Victor Turner, "Dewey, Dilthey, and Drama: An Essay in the Anthropology of Experience," in Victor Turner and Edward M. Bruner, eds., *The Anthropology of Experience* (Urbana: University of Illinois Press, 1986), p. 40.

9. Robert Hertz, *Death and the Right Hand* (London: Cohen and West, 1960), p. 86.

10. Michael Taussig, *Shamanism, Colonialism, and the Wild Man: A Study in Terror and Healing* (Chicago: University of Chicago Press, 1987), p. 7.

11. Ibid., p. 368; Martin Jay, "Against Consolation: Walter Benjamin and the Refusal to Mourn," in J. Winter and E. Sivan, eds., *War and Remembrance in the Twentieth Century* (Cambridge: Cambridge University Press, 1999), pp. 225–26.

12. Stephen Kern, *The Culture of Time and Space, 1880–1918* (Cambridge: Harvard University Press, 1983), pp. 152–53.

13. Edward F. Fry, *Cubism* (London: Thames and Hudson, 1966), p. 9; John Golding, *Cubism: A History and an Analysis* (London: Faber and Faber, 1959), p. 17.

14. Kern, *The Culture of Time and Space*, p. 153.

15. Ibid., p. 288.

16. Fry, *Cubism*, p. 14.

17. Hans Hess, *Pictures as Arguments* (London: Sussex University Press, 1975), p. 36.

18. Kern, *The Culture of Time and Space*, p. 152.

19. Edmund Leach, "Social Anthropology: A Natural Science of Society? (1976)," in *The Essential Edmund Leach,* vol. 1, ed. Stephen Hugh-Jones and James Laidlaw (New Haven: Yale University Press, 2000), pp. 80–97. For background information, see Jack Goody, *The Expansive Moment: Anthropology in Britain and Africa, 1918–1970* (Cambridge: Cambridge University Press, 1995), pp. 88–94.

20. Leach, *Political Systems of Highland Burma*, p. 12.

21. See Renato Rosaldo, *Culture and Truth: The Remaking of Social Analysis* (London: Routledge, 1989), pp. 102–5.

22. James C. Scott, *The Moral Economy of the Peasant: Rebellion and Subsistence in Southeast Asia* (New Haven: Yale University Press, 1976), pp. 13–14; Michael Taussig, "The Genesis of Capitalism amongst a South American Peasantry: Devil's Labor and the Baptism of Money," *Comparative Studies of Society and History* 19, no. 2 (1977): 132.

23. James Scott, *The Moral Economy of the Peasant*, pp. 10–12.

24. *Mobili animi*, for Machiavelli, denotes "the mobile spirit of the mass" that may make "men with power tremble incessantly." Cited from Waldemar Voisé, "La Renaissance et les sources des sciences politiques," *Diogène*, no. 23 (1958): 61.

25. Hertz, *Death and the Right Hand*, p. 86.

Index

Text: 10/13 Sabon
Display: Sabon
Cartographer: Bill Nelson
Indexer: Andrew Christenson
Compositor: BookMatters, Berkeley
Printer and binder: Maple-Vail Manufacturing Group